Earth Heritage

CONSERVATION

DEDICATION

This book is dedicated to the memory of Chris Stevens, who died in September 1993.

His enthusiasm and insight was crucial to the preparation of *Earth Science Conservation in Great Britain – A Strategy* which was published by the former Nature Conservancy Council in 1990. This book is one of the outcomes of that strategy. Chris helped to ensure its production, both by his continued enthusiastic support and comments on early drafts, and by providing the first significant funding from English Nature for its development.

The Geological Society in association with The Open University

The Course Team

Chair and general editor

Chris Wilson, Open University

Authors

Peter Doyle, University of Greenwich

Glynda Easterbrook, Open University

Elspeth Reid, Inverness College

Eric Skipsey, Open University

Chris Wilson, Open University

Contributors and critical readers

Sheila Dellow, Geologists' Association

Mike Harley, English Nature

Rod Jones, Countryside Council for Wales

Alan McKirdy, Scottish Natural Heritage

Chris Stevens, English Nature/Joint National Nature Conservation Committee

External assessor

Christopher Green, Royal Holloway and Bedford New College

Course production

Clare Butler, Editor

John Taylor, Graphic Artist

Sian Lewis, Graphic Designer

Rita Quill, Secretary

Kathryn Stewart, Research Assistant

Connie Tyler, Indexer

The Open University gratefully acknowledges the financial support of English Nature, Scottish Natural Heritage, Countryside Council for Wales, the Dennis Curry's Charitable Trust, The Geologists' Association Curry Fund and Chevron (UK), which made the production of *Earth Heritage Conservation* possible.

The Course Team wish to thank many colleagues in the country conservation agencies and the Geologists' Association for their help in providing information, comments and illustrations. We are grateful to members of The Open University Course Teams for allowing us to modify or use verbatim teaching text from Open University courses, most notably S102 *Science: a foundation course* and S236 *Geology*.

Designed, edited and typeset by The Open University

Printed in the UK by City Print (Milton Keynes) Ltd

ISBN 1 897799 03 9

1.1

For further information on Open University packs and courses, write to the Central Enquiry Service, PO Box 200, The Open University, Walton Hall, Milton Keynes MK7 6YZ.

CONTENTS

WHAT IS EARTH HERITAGE CONSERVATION?

Earth heritage conservation (EHC) is concerned with the maintenance of landforms, natural and artificial exposures of rocks, and sites where geological processes can be seen in action today. Conservation of this heritage ensures that future generations can continue to learn about the geological history of the planet and their immediate environment through education and research, and that the public can enjoy the beauty of natural physical features.

HOW TO USE THIS BOOK

This book is designed to be read by three types of reader. They are defined on the basis of their prior knowledge and experience of the subject matter of geology, and their familiarity with biological conservation. The three categories are:

◆ amateur and professional geologists who are not familiar with the rationale and methods of Earth heritage conservation;

◆ voluntary and professional conservationists familiar with the rationale and methods of biological conservation, but with little or no knowledge of the geological sciences and the rationale and methods of Earth heritage conservation;

◆ individuals with a general interest in the countryside who have no geological knowledge or experience of practical conservation.

From the table opposite, you can judge how to use this book to suit your needs.

Throughout parts of the text there are questions and activities designed to encourage you to pause and consolidate your understanding and to apply newly acquired knowledge and skills to interpret geological information or suggest conservation strategies.

Chapter 2 of this book, 'Minerals, rocks and Earth processes', makes extensive use of a kit collection of minerals and rocks. If you want to buy this collection, or find out where you can have access to or borrow a kit, write to the Department of Earth Sciences, The Open University, Milton Keynes, MK7 6AA, marking the envelope 'EHC' and enclosing a stamped addressed envelope.

The specimens in the kit are illustrated in the colour plate booklet which accompanies this book, so if you are not able to borrow a kit you can refer to the colour plates at the appropriate points instead.

Part of this book	Category of reader		
	Geologically knowledgeable but unfamiliar with conservation	**Experience of biological conservation, but no geological knowledge**	**No expertise in geology or conservation**
1 Introducing Earth heritage conservation Ten site descriptions introducing some basic geological vocabulary and showing why and how they are conserved	Read through quickly, concentrating on site use and methods of conservation	Study carefully to learn some basic geological vocabulary and to gain insights into the rationale and methods of Earth heritage conservation	
2 Introducing geology for Earth heritage conservation A basic introduction to minerals, rocks, fieldwork, Earth processes and Earth history	No need to read	Study carefully in order to understand how sites contribute to our understanding of the history of the Earth	
3 Conservation in action The need for Earth heritage conservation; types of site and how they can be conserved; increasing public awareness	Study carefully and consider how to contribute to conservation activities	Study carefully and contrast the rationale and methods of Earth heritage conservation with those of biological conservation Consider how to integrate biological and Earth heritage conservation	Study carefully and consider how to contribute to conservation activities

◆ PART 1 ◆
INTRODUCING EARTH HERITAGE CONSERVATION

Study comment

The purpose of the single chapter in Part 1 of this book is to give you a 'feel' for the need for Earth heritage conservation, and to introduce some of the geological and conservation terminology that will be used in Parts 2 and 3. As you will see, understanding Earth heritage conservation requires a familiarity with some basic geology. By examining a number of Earth heritage conservation sites, we will introduce some of the concepts and terminology discussed in detail in Parts 2 and 3. Do not worry at this stage if you do not fully understand them all – this will come later. But when you have finished studying this chapter, you will have a clearer picture of the scope of the book. You will be aware of the need for Earth heritage conservation, the variety of people and professions that are involved in this activity, and some of the ways in which commercial and other interests can be reconciled with conservation objectives.

Allow 2–3 hours to study Chapter 1.

INTRODUCING EARTH HERITAGE CONSERVATION

1.1 Introduction

Great Britain is the cradle of the science of geology. It was here that many of the periods of geological time were first defined and named. Countless eminent geologists, professional and amateur, have sharpened their eyes and scientific minds on Britain's Earth science sites. Yet these sites, which display the visible evidence of the Earth's formation and transformation through rocks, fossils and landforms, have been disappearing at an accelerating rate in the face of the many pressures imposed by our modern way of life. Increasingly, quarries, gravel pits, old mines and caves are pressed into service as waste disposal sites! Eroding cliffs, with their extensive exposures of rock sections, the source of sand and shingle beaches elsewhere, are rendered invisible and geomorphologically impotent behind concrete. Rocky mountain crags are shrouded by conifers. Even the shape of the land itself is changing as features are levelled and whittled away to feed the insatiable demand for development land and construction materials.

It is fortunate indeed that at such a time as this there should be a flowering of interest in the Earth sciences and in conservation in general. Throughout the land, people are growing more and more aware of the inextricable links between the health of the planet and the welfare of humans, between knowledge of the past and foresight for the future, between care for the environment and the continuance of a world fit to live in. And now, with the existence of so many national and local groups dedicated to the conservation of our national heritage, we have the will and the means to take effective steps to safeguard the legacy of the past for the generations to come.

(Extract from Sir David Attenborough's foreword to *Earth Science Conservation in Great Britain – A Strategy*, Nature Conservancy Council, 1990.)

The bulk of Chapter 1 consists of a brief description of ten sites under the headings of:

◆ The geological/geomorphological features of the site;

◆ Why is it conserved?

◆ How is it conserved?

◆ Who uses it?

◆ How are conservation and other interests reconciled?

All but one of the sites have been identified as being of national importance, and are designated as Sites of Special Scientific Interest (SSSIs). These sites have statutory protection, which is described in Chapter 8. Until 1991, they were designated by the Nature Conservancy Council (NCC) but now they are overseen by the new country agencies (NCAs): English Nature, Scottish Natural Heritage and the Countryside Council for Wales. One site (Tedbury Camp Quarry in Somerset) is recognized as a Regionally Important Geological/geomorphological Site (RIGS) and is conserved on a voluntary basis, involving collaboration between local interests and the quarry owner. RIGS are discussed in Chapters 8 and 9.

The sites are introduced in order of their age, starting with the youngest. The first two show geological processes in action today. The sediments and rocks exposed in the remaining sites were formed during various periods in the past.

As stated in the opening quotation, Great Britain is the cradle of the science of geology, and many of the intervals of geological time were named here. Table 1.1 shows the names given to the periods of geological time over the past 570 million years. Note that in this table, the oldest periods are at the bottom and the youngest at the top; this arrangement is always used when tabulating data concerned with Earth history.

You can see that many of the names in Table 1.1 are based on British localities. They were named by pioneering geologists, who discovered that rocks of particular periods of time are characterized by distinctive assemblages of fossils which enable rock successions of the same relative age to be identified in many parts of the world. Sir Charles Lyell recognized in the 1830s that in the Cainozoic (sometimes spelt Cenozoic) Era modern species appear as fossils, becoming progressively more abundant in younger sediments. For example, 3% of Eocene species are alive today, and as many as 30–50% of Pliocene species exist today. Lyell chose to use Greek prefixes to subdivide the Cainozoic according to this observation.

Box 1.1 Geology and Earth science

What is geology?

'Geology is the science which investigates the successive changes that have taken place in the organic and inorganic kingdoms of nature; it enquires into the cause of these changes, and the influence they have exerted in modifying the surface and external structure of our planet.' (Sir Charles Lyell, *Principles of Geology*, 1830.)

What is Earth science?

Earth science is the application of principles, methods and approaches of mathematics and the basic sciences, and those special to the Earth sciences (geology, geochemistry, geophysics, geomorphology, oceanography, climatology, etc.) to the elucidation of the history of the Earth and the use of this knowledge to recognize and solve resource and environmental problems for the benefit of humanity.

Table 1.1 Origin of the names of the time periods in the stratigraphic column for the past 570 million years

Eras	Periods in bold type, epochs in normal type	Age of base in millions of years	Country where defined	Derivation of name
CAINOZOIC (recent life)	**Quaternary**			
	Holocene	0.01	England	Holos: whole
	Pleistocene	1.6	England	Pleiston: most
	Tertiary			
	Pliocene	5.3	England	Pleios: more
	Miocene	23	England	Meion: less
	Oligocene	36.5	Germany	Oligos: few
	Eocene	53	England	Eos: dawn
	Palaeocene	65	Germany	Palaeos: old
MESOZOIC (middle life)	**Cretaceous**	135	France	Creta: chalk
	Jurassic	205	Switzerland	Jura Mountains
	Triassic	250	Germany	Threefold division recognized in Germany
UPPER PALAEOZOIC (ancient life)	**Permian**	290	Russia	The town of Perm in Russia
	Carboniferous	355	England	Carbon: coal
	Devonian	410	England	Devon
LOWER PALAEOZOIC (ancient life)	**Silurian**	438	Wales	Silures: Celts of the Welsh borders
	Ordovician	510	Wales	Ordovices: Celts of north Wales
	Cambrian	570	Wales	Cambria: Latin for Wales

The stratigraphic column is the array of geological time units that results from stacking them vertically with the oldest at the base, overlain by successively younger units.

Five hundred and seventy million years is such an immense period of time that it is difficult to comprehend, but the history of the Earth stretches much much further back in time (through the Precambrian, not shown in Table 1.1), for it originated 4.6 billion (4 600 000 000) years ago. In order to appreciate the immensity of such a period of time, the analogy shown in Figure 1.1 should help.

The ten sites reviewed in this chapter provide a means of introducing the different subdisciplines of the Earth sciences. The descriptions of the sites given in the next three sections are arranged in order of increasing age, ending with a site containing fossils of some of the oldest known land plants.

Figure 1.1
The geological timescale compressed into one year.

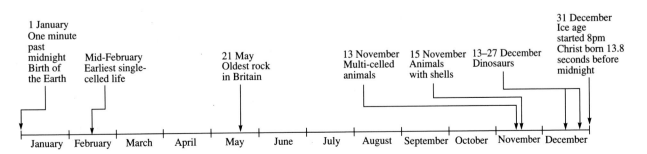

1 January
One minute past midnight
Birth of the Earth

Mid-February
Earliest single-celled life

21 May
Oldest rock in Britain

13 November
Multi-celled animals

15 November
Animals with shells

13–27 December
Dinosaurs

31 December
Ice age started 8pm
Christ born 13.8 seconds before midnight

January February March April May June July August September October November December

1.2 Landscapes in the making

The two sites described in this section are recognized as conservation sites because they show how rock debris or sediments in the form of boulders, cobbles, gravel, sand and mud are transported and deposited by sea and river currents to produce distinctive landforms. If these sediments are then buried, they will eventually be converted to *sedimentary* rock as their constituent grains are cemented together. These sites are therefore of particular interest to geomorphologists and sedimentologists.

Box 1.2 Some subdisciplines of Earth science

Geomorphology is the study of landforms and the processes that sculpture them.

Sedimentology is the study of modern and ancient sediments and sedimentary rocks and the processes that produce these materials.

Using their knowledge of the processes that form modern sediments, sedimentologists are able to interpret their observations of sedimentary rocks in terms of their depositional environments. For example, the sandy beach at Morfa Harlech is a present-day field laboratory that can help illuminate how ancient reservoirs for water, oil and gas formed.

Morfa Harlech, Gwynedd

Geomorphology of the site

Morfa Harlech is a large active sand dune system at the mouth of the Glaslyn/ Dwyrydd estuary in west Wales. The beach and dune system widens northwards from a line of former cliffs (Figure 1.2). In the wider part there occur several sub-parallel ridges which mark successive stages in the seaward growth of the system. This growth has been fed by sand eroded from Morfa Dyffryn (another dune system) and by river-borne sediments from the sea bed in Cardigan Bay. Between the ridges occur damp hollows or 'slacks' in which a wide variety of plants and invertebrates live. Morfa Harlech is protected to a degree from wave attack by Sarn Badrig, a ridge of glacial material that extends some 20 km into Cardigan Bay.

Why is it conserved?

Most of the dune system at Morfa Harlech is relatively free from direct human impact, and so it is a natural laboratory where the processes that build the dunes can be studied. However, the growth of the dune system was due partly to human agency, through land reclamation within the estuary and on nearby coastlines.

The dunes are of great importance as a geomorphological and biological system.

Who uses the site?

The site is used to demonstrate the processes of sand dune formation to students, and by biologists cataloguing the plant and invertebrate life of the dunes and the damp slacks between them.

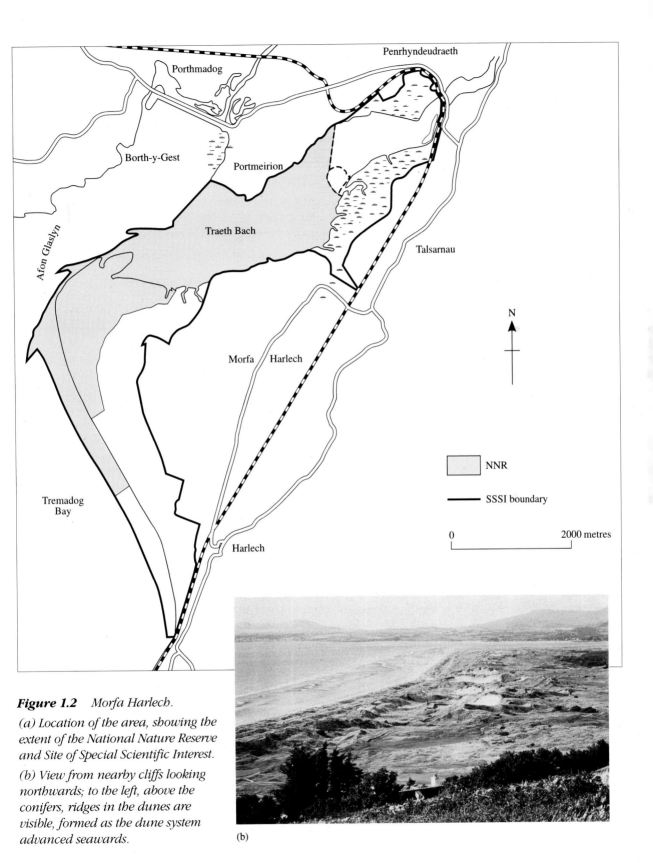

Figure 1.2 *Morfa Harlech.*

(a) Location of the area, showing the extent of the National Nature Reserve and Site of Special Scientific Interest.

(b) View from nearby cliffs looking northwards; to the left, above the conifers, ridges in the dunes are visible, formed as the dune system advanced seawards.

(b)

13

The beach is an important recreational area, and part of the site is occupied by a car park. In addition, the Royal St Davids golf course is situated in the southern part. A small amount of grazing occurs on the site.

How is it conserved?

Part of the site forms part of a National Nature Reserve (NNR); this area is leased from the landowner by the Countryside Council for Wales which therefore has direct control over it. The area that lies outside the NNR is conserved through a series of management agreements with landowners. The NNR area is managed by a warden and ancillary staff who carry out site management work as required. This includes controlling the grazing of the site, which serves to maintain the mobility of the dune system by preventing scrub from developing and the sands from stabilizing.

How are conservation and other interests reconciled?

The site is located in an area of low population density, so that there is no pressure to develop it. Outside the NNR boundaries, erosion triggered by visitors sometimes necessitates dune restoration work, involving fencing off areas and planting grass.

River Feshie, Highland Region

Geomorphology of the site

The River Feshie drains the northern side of the Cairngorm Mountains near Aviemore in Scotland. It transports large amounts of gravel during floods; these gravels are building out to produce a fan-shaped deposit in the River Spey (Figure 1.3). It has developed on a landscape significantly affected by glaciation, the last period of which ended only 13 000 years ago.

Why is it conserved?

The River Feshie site is conserved because it is significant for geomorphological research for two reasons:

◆ it provides a unique opportunity to study present-day river processes transporting and depositing gravel and how these processes change landforms;

◆ it contains a record of changes in river processes since the disappearance of ice from the region.

Who uses the site?

The site is used by research geomorphologists and student parties.

How is it conserved?

As with any site in which active processes occur, conservation requires that human activities be kept to a minimum. However, as described below, flooding problems mean that there is pressure from other interests to interfere with the site.

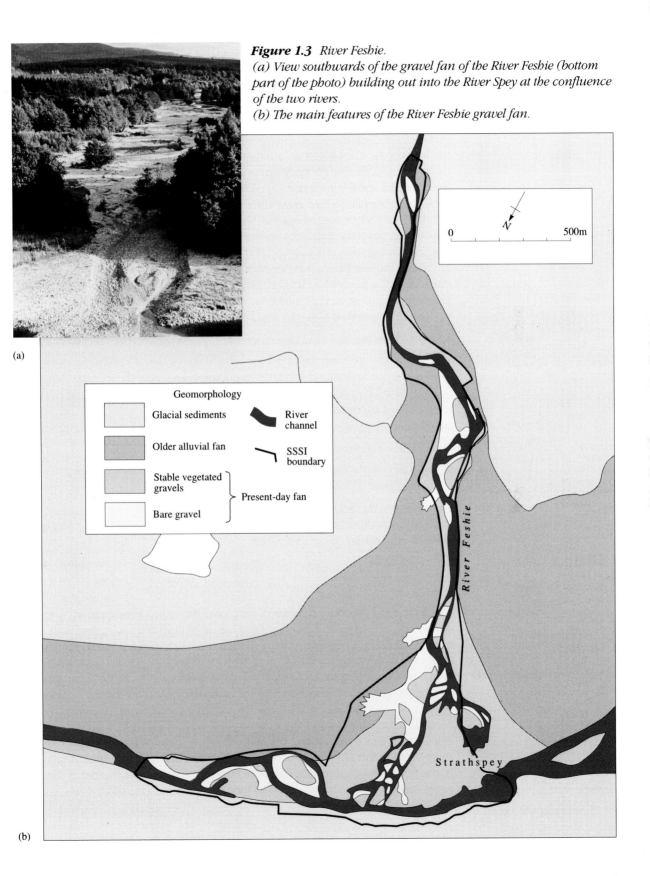

Figure 1.3 *River Feshie.*
(a) View southwards of the gravel fan of the River Feshie (bottom part of the photo) building out into the River Spey at the confluence of the two rivers.
(b) The main features of the River Feshie gravel fan.

(a)

Geomorphology

Glacial sediments

Older alluvial fan

Stable vegetated gravels

Bare gravel

Present-day fan

River channel

SSSI boundary

River Feshie

Strathspey

0   500m

N

(b)

Major floods in the River Feshie during recent winters have caused significant damage in the lower reaches of the valley. Extensive areas of agricultural land have been flooded and bank erosion has eaten into agricultural land, a gliding airstrip and the public road on the east side of the valley. A critical element of the problem concerns the gravel fan formed by the River Feshie at its confluence with the River Spey. It appears that build-up of the fan causes the Spey floodwaters to back up, exacerbating flooding up-valley. With heightened awareness of this flood hazard, there is now considerable pressure from landowners to alleviate the problem, particularly since grant aid is available. Measures proposed include bulldozing flood protection banks from the river-bed gravels, realigning and deepening channels, and diverting flow from particular pressure points. However, not only would such measures conflict severely with the geomorphological interest of the site, but past experience of such works indicates that their effectiveness is likely to be limited, given the power of the Feshie in flood. Continued maintenance would be inevitable and, in effect, the river would cease to operate as a natural system.

A research project has now been commissioned to look at these problems and produce:

◆ detailed documentation and geomorphological maps of the four reaches of the river which comprise the recognized conservation site, to identify the most important and sensitive areas;

◆ an assessment of the impact of particular threats to different parts of the site;

◆ management recommendations for the site;

◆ possible alternative flood-protection measures compatible with effective conservation of the geomorphological interest of the site.

The results of this work will also be of wider value in dealing with similar problems on other active river sites, and should mark a significant step forward in conservation management expertise.

1.3 Ice age sites

The realization that the landforms of the Lake District had been created by ice dates back to 1813, with observations made by William Buckland, Professor of Geology at Oxford University. He noted features such as steep-sided and flat-bottomed valleys (Figure 1.4(a)), and deep scratches on exposed rock surfaces, which could not be accounted for by erosion by water. As a devout Christian, he was reluctant to accept the possibility of such a radical occurrence as a period of erosion by ice. However, in 1840 he brought the pioneer Swiss geologist Louis Agassiz to the Lake District. Agassiz soon demonstrated that the landforms in Britain were exactly consistent with the existence of valley glaciers similar to those still present in the Alps. Subsequent study has confirmed that much of Britain has been affected by a succession of glacial periods over the last two million years, separated by interglacial periods with temperatures similar to those of the last 10 000 years (Figure 1.4(b)).

Humid mountain landscape

Glaciation

cirque glacier

ice cap

ice fall

main valley glacier joined by tributaries

Post-glacial humid

horn

arête

tarn

waterfall

lake

(a)

Figure 1.4 *The extent and some of the effects of ice ages in Britain.*

(a) The development of glacial features (before, during and after glaciation) in highland areas, such as north Wales, the Lake District and Scotland. As ice fills pre-existing river valleys, it modifies their shapes through glacial erosion. Rock debris incorporated into the ice makes it extremely abrasive, like the sand on sandpaper. As the ice 'flows' down the valleys, it changes their former V-shaped cross-sectional profiles to U-shapes, and produces the characteristic landforms shown in the middle stretch. When the ice melts a new landscape emerges, carrying the unmistakable features of glacial erosion such as U-shaped glacial valleys, cirques and hanging valleys.

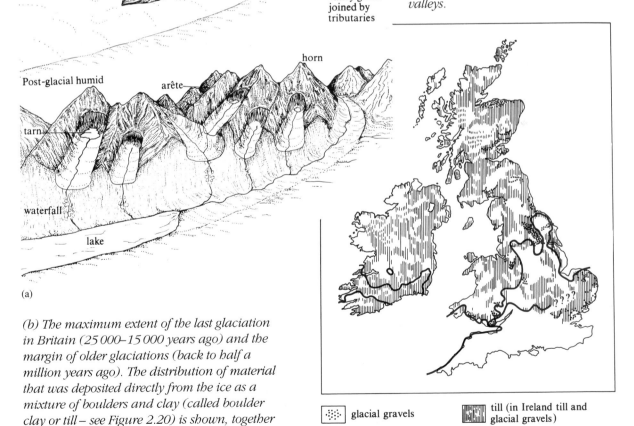

(b) The maximum extent of the last glaciation in Britain (25 000–15 000 years ago) and the margin of older glaciations (back to half a million years ago). The distribution of material that was deposited directly from the ice as a mixture of boulders and clay (called boulder clay or till – see Figure 2.20) is shown, together with gravels that were deposited by streams running off the ice.

(b)

| | glacial gravels | | till (in Ireland till and glacial gravels) |

⌇ maximum extent of last glaciation

⌇ margins of older glaciations

17

Achnasheen Terraces, Ross and Cromarty

Geology and geomorphology of the site

This site consists of a series of terraces of sediments that were deposited during the final stages of ice retreat in Scotland. The terraces were deposited as deltas building into a lake from streams originating from two stagnant glaciers: one originally flowed eastwards towards Achnasheen, and the other north-eastwards (Figure 1.5).

Why is it conserved?

The Achnasheen Terraces are one of the best examples in Scotland of a suite of glacial outwash terraces that mark the final episode in the retreat of the Scottish ice sheet.

Figure 1.5

The Achnasheen Terraces.
(a) The south-eastern terrace.
(b) The location of the terraces and the SSSI.
(c) The possible past distribution of stagnant ice, deltas deposited by meltwater, and a former lake.

(a)

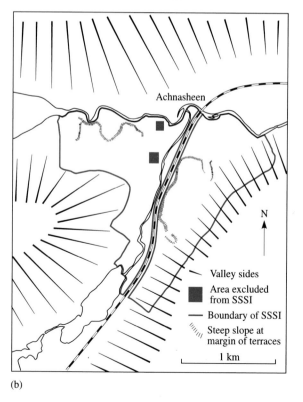

Valley sides

▪ Area excluded from SSSI

— Boundary of SSSI

⁖ Steep slope at margin of terraces

1 km

(b)

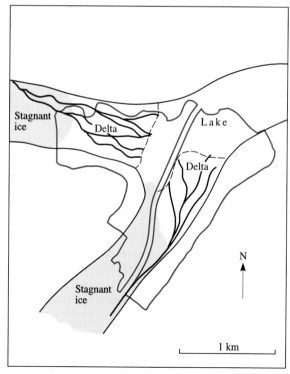

(c)

How is it conserved?

No specific action is needed other than to resist sand and gravel extraction in the area, in order to prevent destruction of the landforms.

Who uses the site?

The site is an important one for geomorphologists and geologists studying the recent climatic history of Scotland, and is valuable for teaching purposes.

How are conservation and other interests reconciled?

Conservation and extraction of the sands and gravels of the terraces cannot be reconciled. In 1975, a planning application was made to extract 7.5 million tonnes of sand and gravel. The former Nature Conservancy Council objected to these plans, and they were subsequently rejected by the Scottish Development Council. An appeal against this decision to the Secretary of State for Scotland was withdrawn shortly before the public inquiry.

Moor Mill Quarry, Hertfordshire

Geology of the site

Moor Mill Quarry is in the Colne Valley, near St Albans. When worked for sand and gravel, the quarry exposed sediments that were deposited in a period when the northern part of the Thames Valley was glaciated, about 140 000 years ago. The sequence of sediments exposed in the quarry is as follows (the oldest unit at the base; see also Figure 1.6 (c), page 20):

4   Smug Oak Gravel: sands and gravels (5 m)

3   East End Green Till: chalky till (chalk fragments 'floating' in bluish clay) (6 m)

2   Moor Mill Laminated Clay: very finely layered clays and silts (2.6 m)

1   West Mill Gravel: sands and gravels (6.5 m), overlying an irregular surface of Chalk of Cretaceous age

Various features of the lowest sand and gravel unit (1) indicate that it was deposited in extremely cold conditions not far from an ice sheet. Streams that deposited the sediments flowed from the north-east. Within the second unit, 246 pairs of laminations (fine layers) of clay followed by silt occur. These are interpreted as having been deposited in a lake dammed by an ice sheet to the north. Each lamina represents one year of deposition, with the coarser silt laminae being deposited by spring and summer meltwaters, and the finer clay forming in still water conditions during the autumn and winter. The third unit, the chalky till, was deposited beneath an ice sheet, and the fourth unit (sands and gravels) formed as the ice melted and meltwater streams flowed westwards (the opposite direction to the currents that deposited the sands and gravels of the first unit).

It is thought that the advance of the ice sheet recorded in the succession of sediments at Moor Mill Quarry resulted in the diversion of the River Thames from its original northerly course to its present-day location (Figure 1.7, page 21).

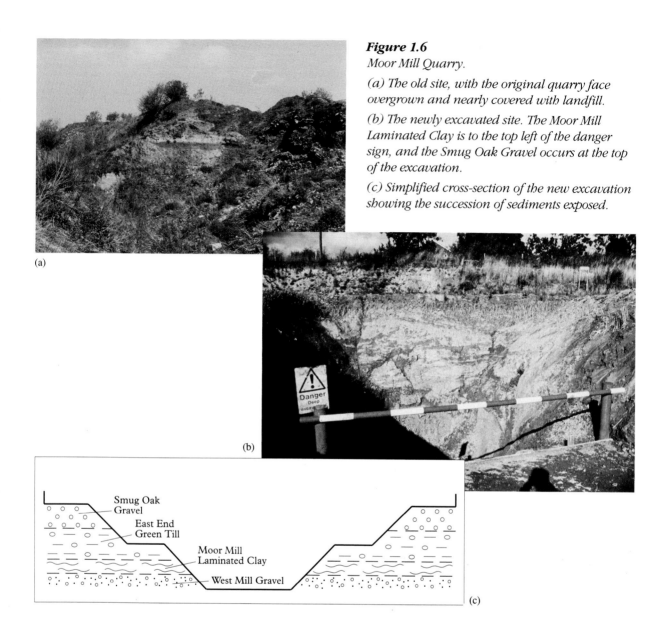

Figure 1.6
Moor Mill Quarry.

(a) The old site, with the original quarry face overgrown and nearly covered with landfill.

(b) The newly excavated site. The Moor Mill Laminated Clay is to the top left of the danger sign, and the Smug Oak Gravel occurs at the top of the excavation.

(c) Simplified cross-section of the new excavation showing the succession of sediments exposed.

(a)

(b)

Smug Oak Gravel
East End Green Till
Moor Mill Laminated Clay
West Mill Gravel

(c)

Why is it conserved?

The site shows a record of past climatic change that resulted in the diversion of the course of the River Thames, and so needs to be preserved for the continued study of a succession of sediments laid down in association with a major advance of an ice sheet across southern England.

How is it conserved?

See below.

Who uses the site?

The site is used only for scientific research, as it needs to be pumped dry to make the entire succession of sediments accessible.

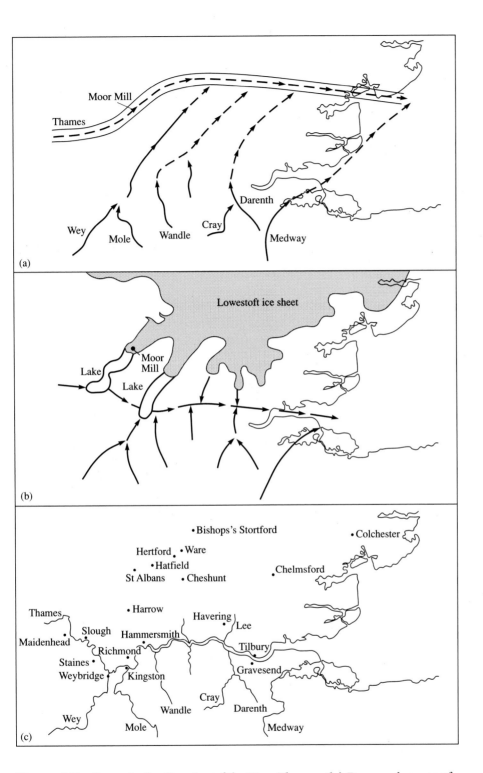

Figure 1.7 *Stages in the diversion of the River Thames. (a) Presumed course of the river before glaciation 0.5 million years ago. (b) The probable configuration of ice, ice-dammed lakes and rivers 400 000 years ago. (c) The present course of the river.*

How are conservation and other interests reconciled?

When the site was originally notified as a Site of Special Scientific Interest (SSSI), it already had permission for infilling by waste material, and so unsightly landfill material was situated close to the exposed face (Figure 1.6(a)). When the owners of the quarry applied to modify the existing planning permission to improve the landfill design, negotiations took place between them, English Nature and Hertfordshire County Council to preserve the site. To do so would have resulted in the loss of a considerable volume of space available for tipping. Fortunately, old borehole data indicated that an unworked area of gravel existed away from the landfill area. The landowner agreed to excavate a new exposure to replace the old quarry face (Figure 1.6(b)). Once this was done, a new SSSI was notified, and the old site denotified. The new exposure continues to be available for scientific study, although it is partly filled with water and so needs pumping out before visits can be made. Moor Mill is an excellent example of conservation interest (English Nature), industry (Redland Aggregates) and a local authority working together in a constructive and imaginative way.

1.4 Rock sites

This section examines sites in which rocks (and sometimes fossils and minerals) are exposed in coastal cliffs, quarries and mines. The final example is a case where conservation requires that the rocks of interest remain buried beneath fields!

In common parlance, the term 'rock' is taken to mean something hard. But to the geologist, a rock is any aggregate of mineral material that was formed in the geological past – that is, more than a few thousand years ago. So a geologist's rock can be a loose sand, a soft clay, or a hard granite.

Barton Cliffs, Hampshire

Geology of the site

The cliffs at this coastal site (near Christchurch) expose the Barton Clay and Becton Sand formations. Both these rock units consist of sedimentary rocks, formed by the chemical and physical breakdown of older rocks and the subsequent transport and deposition of the rock debris (sand and mud in this case) to form new rocks. Rock 'formations' are defined objectively on the basis of their grain size and other features such as colour, fossil content and structures produced by water currents. The site is the global standard reference section for part of the Eocene Epoch, which is a division of the Tertiary Period (see Table 1.1 on page 11). This part of the Eocene Epoch is termed the Bartonian Stage, which spans the period from 46 to 50 million years ago.

Barton Cliffs are internationally known for the rich and diverse fossil assemblage which they have yielded (Figure 1.8(b)). These fossils provide evidence for palaeontologists to interpret the nature of palaeoenvironments (past environments) during the Tertiary Period. The fossil fauna is the best preserved and most varied of the British Tertiary and is particularly well known for molluscs, reptiles, mammals and birds. Fossil plant remains are also abundant and include

(a)

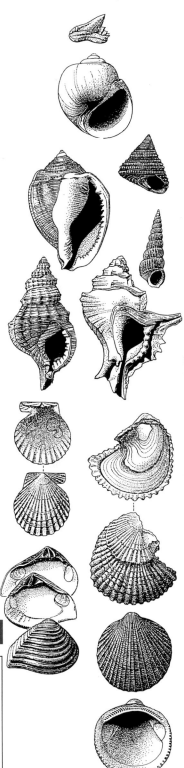

Figure 1.8 *Barton Cliffs. (a) General view looking east, showing the cliff and the extent of the existing coastal defences in front of the cliff. Cliff erosion is caused by marine erosion undermining the base, which leads to landslipping above. (b) A selection of fossils from Barton Cliffs: a shark's tooth (enlarged × 2), gastropods (sea snails) and bivalves (both about half actual size).*

conifers, fern pinnules, fruits and seeds, making this stretch of cliffs a critical site for the study of Tertiary palaeobotany.

The cliff exposures are constantly renewed by marine erosion at the foot of the cliffs (Figure 1.8(a)). Removal of material from the base undermines the cliffs, causing material to slip from the upper parts. Without this constant renewal of the faces, new fossil material would not be available for collection.

Box 1.3 Some subdisciplines of Earth science (continued)

Stratigraphy is the study of rock strata (their physical composition and structure, and any fossils they contain) from place to place. Such studies are the essential basis on which Earth history is determined and economic resources – particularly oil, gas and coal – are found.

Palaeontology is the study of fossils, both animals and plants. It contributes to the correlation of rock units, by identifying their relative age on the basis of their fossil content, and to the interpretation of past depositional environments (see Section 2.6).

(b)

Why is it conserved?

The reason is simple: the site is an international reference section for the Bartonian Stage and so is of global importance to researchers working in the fields of stratigraphy and palaeontology.

In addition to their research value, Barton Cliffs are also a key educational site with plenty of scope for fossil collecting (the erosional effect of which is insignificant compared with wave erosion).

How is it conserved?

Ideally, the site should be left unprotected against marine erosion so that it is constantly renewed. As there is such a large volume of the rock formations behind the cliff, removal of material by erosion is not a problem from a conservation point of view.

Who uses the site?

The site is used by stratigraphers and palaeontologists from academia and industry (particularly oil companies), school and university students and amateur collectors.

How are conservation and other interests reconciled?

Stretches of the cliffs within the site have been progressively lost over the last 20 years through the construction of coastal protection works to guard against land loss. Despite this, a complete stratigraphic succession through the Bartonian has always been maintained. However, in 1988 Christchurch Borough Council submitted plans to extend the sea defences eastwards from Chewton Bunny (Figure 1.9). This extension threatened to break the stratigraphic continuity of the exposed Bartonian rocks. The Council's initial plans included installing rock armour (piles of large blocks of rock) against the cliff foot and cutting drains into the cliff itself (Figure 1.9(a)). Subsequent negotiations resulted in an alternative scheme in which the rock armour was replaced by an offshore bastion designed to reduce wave energy and prevent further cliff erosion without obscuring the cliff exposures (Figure 1.9(b)). This modification was acceptable to both English Nature and Christchurch Borough Council. Unfortunately, the council insisted on retaining the drains within the proposed scheme, despite English Nature's belief that such drains were unnecessary. As a consequence of this continued conflict, English Nature had no choice but to call in the application for determination at a public inquiry.

The resulting inquiry, held in May 1991, was primarily concerned about whether or not the proposed drainage work was necessary. At the inquiry, Christchurch Borough Council did not dispute the scientific value of the site, but argued that without the drains the cliff would slump, allowing the sea to break through into an area of landfill immediately behind the coast at Chewton Bunny. It was also argued that if the coast were breached at this point, it could destabilize the ground beneath nearby property. English Nature gave evidence at the inquiry, and also called a palaeontologist from the Natural History Museum, who emphasized the

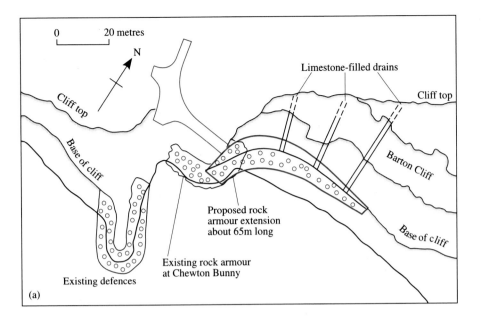

(a)

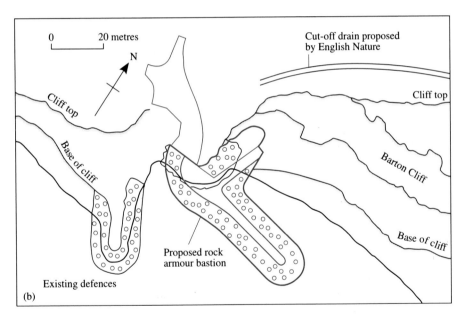

(b)

Figure 1.9 *Alternative coastal protection schemes for Barton Cliffs.*

(a) Original scheme proposed by Christchurch District Council to place rock armour over the cliff comparable to that already installed on nearby cliffs.

(b) Modified scheme after consultation with English Nature.

scientific value of the site and the importance of stratigraphic continuity. An expert on cliff stability also gave evidence on behalf of English Nature and outlined an alternative method of draining the cliffs which did not involve any damage to the site.

The outcome of the inquiry was a typical British compromise: one drain instead of three.

Southerham Grey Pit, East Sussex

Geology of the site

The site, near Lewes, is a large disused quarry in the lower part of the Chalk, which was deposited during the later part of the Cretaceous Period (see Table 1.1 on page 11). The Chalk is a very fine-grained limestone (see Specimen E in the mineral and rock collection or Plate 1E in the colour plate booklet), formed from the calcareous remains of tiny organisms that floated in abundance in the surface waters of late Cretaceous seas all over north-west Europe. The lower part of the Chalk is significantly thicker here than in other locations, and is relatively fossiliferous compared with other intervals, which contain very few fossils. This site is the last remaining Lower Chalk pit in the Lewes area in which fossil fish can be found.

Why is it conserved?

The site is one of the most important Chalk sites in western Europe, and contains the only exposures in Britain of the rock unit called the Chalk Marl, and so has significant research value. It also has educational value for school and higher education fieldwork activities.

How is it conserved?

Retention of a significant length of quarry face is essential in order to retain the research and educational value of the site.

Figure 1.10
Southerham Grey Pit.

(a) The existing quarry.

(b) Plan of the site, showing the existing quarry with the proposed conservation sections to the north and east of the present faces.

Who uses the site?

The site is visited by palaeontologists and stratigraphers working in academia and industry, and by local schools for educational purposes.

How are conservation and other interests reconciled?

Waste Management Ltd and English Nature have been involved for some time in negotiations over a proposed landfill scheme at this site. Waste Management Ltd wish to infill the site and this conflicts with English Nature's obligation to maintain an exposure in the quarry. Recently a compromise scheme was reached which involved filling only part of the site with waste, retaining the eastern pit face and cutting a new trench just behind the existing northern face to provide a new exposure (Figure 1.10).

However, East Sussex County Council opposed the scheme because the quarry was scheduled as on a possible route for a new road. Consequently, a public inquiry was held during May and June of 1991. English Nature gave evidence to the effect that whilst they would like to see the quarry left undisturbed, it would be possible to partially fill the site without destroying its scientific value. It was made absolutely clear, however, that complete infill would destroy an extremely valuable site for both research and education. The inquiry ruled that the landfill plans were premature on the grounds that the site is on a possible route for a new road. This means that the valuable Chalk sequence will remain exposed.

Tynebottom Mine and Dump, Cumbria

Geology of the site

This is a disused lead mine (abandoned in 1873) situated beside the River South Tyne just outside the village of Gangill in Cumbria. The mine workings are reached via adits (inclined tunnels) driven from the river bank through boulder clay deposited during the last ice age, and then into the Carboniferous Limestone. Spoil from the mine was dumped at the surface near to the river.

Tynebottom Mine is one of the numerous lead mines in the Alston District of the northern Pennines. Two vertical veins containing lead–zinc minerals cut one another here, and around their intersection, horizontal 'flats' of minerals were deposited by hot mineral-rich waters rising through joints in the limestone, and dissolving and replacing it. In the mine dump, samples of rare cobalt–nickel and silver minerals have been found.

Why is it conserved?

The value of the mine and the dump is in the presence of the unusual minerals mentioned above, and the insights these give mineralogists into the origin of mineral deposits in the Pennine area.

How is it conserved?

As this is a research site in which the amount of minerals of interest is small, the mine and the dump need to be preserved as they are, with collecting only permitted to research mineralogists. In addition, work is needed to keep the entrance to the mine open to allow continued access.

(a)

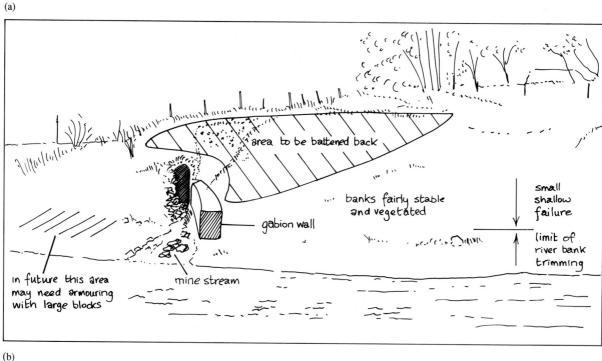

(b)

Figure 1.11 *Tynebottom Mine SSSI. (a) Part of a photomontage showing the mine adit and water draining from it into the River South Tyne. (b) Sketch of the above, showing the nature of the proposed work to be done to stabilize the site (for a photograph of a gabion, see Figure 6.4(c)). The former mine workings extended to the opposite bank of the river where most of the dumped mine waste material is situated.*

28

Box 1.4 Some subdisciplines of Earth science (continued)

Mineralogy is the study of minerals, including their economic uses. Minerals are naturally occurring substances with definable chemical compositions and characteristic physical properties (colour, hardness, crystal shape, etc.).

Who uses the site?

As stated above, only research mineralogists, with permission from English Nature, use the site.

How are conservation and other interests reconciled?

Recently, Northumbrian Water wished to construct a sewage pipeline across the line of the mine adit. English Nature negotiated with Northumbrian Water to ensure that the work would not affect the integrity of the mine and the adit in any way. They also wished to ensure that the mine dump was not interfered with during construction work, either by temporary or permanent buildings being sited near it, or by using it for hardcore. In addition, it was hoped that the two organizations would contribute financially to a cheap engineering solution to reduce erosion by the River South Tyne in the vicinity of the mine entrance.

Northumbrian Water agreed to undertake the strengthening and stabilization works within the main entrance to the site. The contractors for the work are now aware of the site's significance and have undertaken not to use the mine spoil for hardcore or any other reason.

Successful negotiations between English Nature and the relevant bodies resulted in the rerouting of the planned Pennine Way bridlepath so as not to disturb or move any of the old spoil tip material. English Nature have now placed a simple sign at the site which informs users of the long-distance pathway of the significance of the SSSI and requests that they only collect mineral specimens from the site in a responsible manner.

Tedbury Camp Quarry, Somerset

Geology of the site

The site is a disused limestone quarry near Frome. Limestones of two different ages are exposed in the quarry.

The older limestones are Early Carboniferous in age, and were deposited between 360 and 325 million years ago in shallow tropical seas that covered much of England and Wales (see Figure 2.11 for a reconstruction of what the sea bottom might have looked like at this time). Parts of the Carboniferous Limestone are composed almost entirely of the hard parts of organisms (see Specimen D in the kit, or Plate 1D in the colour plate booklet).

The Carboniferous Limestone forms characteristic limestone scenery, including limestone pavements, swallowholes (funnel-shaped depressions or holes usually

Figure 1.12 *Tedbury Camp Quarry.*

(a) View showing the virtually planar surface of Carboniferous Limestone on which the younger Jurassic limestones were deposited; the latter are visible at the back of the quarry. Some of the inclined beds in the Carboniferous Limestone form slightly upstanding ridges running across the planar surface. (These dip at about 60° to the right – the top surface of one bed is in shadow at the bottom right of the photograph.) The planar surface is an unconformity *which represents a time gap of 145 million years. The surface was formed by wave erosion in just the same way as similar flat surfaces are formed around present-day coasts.*

(a)

(b) A modern example of erosion by the sea producing an almost planar surface (a wave-cut platform) in dipping beds of Carboniferous Limestone on the coast of the Gower peninsula in south Wales.

(b)

linked to cave systems) and caves in many areas, the best known being in the Pennines.

The younger limestones exposed at Tedbury are Middle Jurassic in age. They too were deposited in tropical seas, but are much younger, at 180–165 million years old. Limestones of the same age and character underlie the Cotswolds.

As can be seen in Figure 1.12(a), the beds of rock in the younger Jurassic limestones are flat, just as they were when they were deposited on the sea bottom. But the beds in the older Carboniferous Limestone are inclined quite steeply, at an angle of about 60°. Thus there is what is called an *angular discordance* between the two limestone formations; this is termed an *unconformity*. The sequence of events that produced this unconformity between the two limestones at Tedbury is shown in Figure 3.7.

You will examine the rocks and unconformity surface at Tedbury in much more detail in Chapter 3, which introduces some basic field observation techniques.

Why is it conserved?

The exposure of the unconformity surface is exceptionally good at the site, and this is the reason it is conserved.

How is it conserved?

See below.

Who uses the site?

Since it has been conserved (see below), the site has been used extensively by student parties and amateur geologists to demonstrate the features of a major unconformity.

How are conservation and other interests reconciled?

Following the cessation of quarrying at Tedbury Camp Quarry, the site was used as a hardcore dump. Subsequently, its educational potential was recognized and work undertaken to enable its use for teaching geology.

When the quarry was operational, limestone was extracted from a single quarried face, with processing plant fixed to the flat unconformity surface above. At the time it was abandoned the site had no apparent conservation value and the 3800m^2 of unconformity surface were seen as an ideal location for the long-term storage of hardcore and rubble. Consequently, the unconformity surface and overlying exposures of Jurassic limestone became almost totally obscured by tipped material, and, in parts, overgrown.

Early in the 1980s, geologists in the former Nature Conservancy Council (NCC) were carrying out field surveys in the east Mendips to identify sites for inclusion in a geological guidebook *New Sites for Old: a student's guide to the geology of the east Mendips* (K.L. Duff, A.P. McKirdy and M.J. Harley (eds), Nature Conservancy Council, 1985). During this reconnaissance work, Tedbury Camp Quarry was recognized as having tremendous educational potential. Negotiations with the Associated Roadstone Company (ARC) resulted in the NCC being permitted to develop the site for teaching geology. Contractors with heavy earth-moving machinery were employed to remove the now unwanted material from the unconformity. This was relocated against the main quarry face and graded so that a safe study platform was provided below the quarry edge, from where the unconformity and Carboniferous sequence could be seen in section.

Although it has no statutory protection, the site has since been conserved on a voluntary basis through the support of ARC and through its inclusion in the register held by Somerset Environmental Records Centre. Work parties have, from time to time, carried out routine practical management tasks, ensuring that the features seen at the site remain available for study.

Shap Quarry, Cumbria

Geology of the site

This is a large working quarry on the eastern side of the Lake District. Rock faces in the quarry expose good sections of the Shap granite, which has two main varieties, light and dark. Quarry faces are scientifically more valuable than many natural inland exposures where the effects of weathering makes features more difficult to see.

The Shap granite is an intrusive igneous rock. Igneous rocks form by the cooling and solidification of molten rock or *magma*. They may form as intrusive or extrusive rocks. Extrusive rocks form when magma pours out onto the Earth's surface as lava flows, which cool rapidly, and so the crystals in the resultant rock are usually very fine grained. Intrusive rocks are formed as magma cools beneath the Earth's surface after it has been intruded (i.e. forced) into pre-existing rocks (see Figure 2.9). If the intrusion is formed near the Earth's surface, it cools relatively quickly, and so its constituent crystals are relatively small, as in lavas. But intrusions like the Shap granite, which formed several kilometres beneath the Earth's surface, cool very slowly, and so their constituent crystals are easily seen with the naked eye, and can reach several centimetres in size (see Specimen F in the kit or Plate 2F in the colour plate booklet).

The Shap granite intrudes a series of Ordovician lavas (some 450 million years old) and slightly younger Silurian sediments. It is just one of a number of protuberances that project from a much larger mass of granite that underlies the Lake District. On a map (Figure 1.13(b)) the granite intrusion has a roughly circular shape, and is surrounded by a ring or aureole of baked rocks about a kilometre wide. These baked rocks are termed *metamorphic* rocks. In general, metamorphic rocks result from the alteration, by heat and/or pressure, of previously existing rocks – either sedimentary or igneous.

Box 1.5 Some subdisciplines of Earth science (continued)

Petrology is the study of rocks. It involves their description, which forms the basis for interpreting their origins in terms of past conditions operating both within and on the surface of the Earth's crust. This branch of Earth science is divided into igneous, metamorphic and sedimentary petrology.

The Shap granite formed 380 million years ago at the end of a major mountain-building episode that can also be identified in Wales, much of Scotland, Scandinavia, Newfoundland, Nova Scotia and the Appalachian region of the USA.

Why is it conserved?

The Shap Quarry provides fresh exposures of a granite that is probably typical of much larger masses of granite that occur beneath the Lake District and the Pennines. Its research value is that it enables igneous petrologists to study the origin of these granites, and the associated metal ore minerals that occur in small amounts within them.

(a)

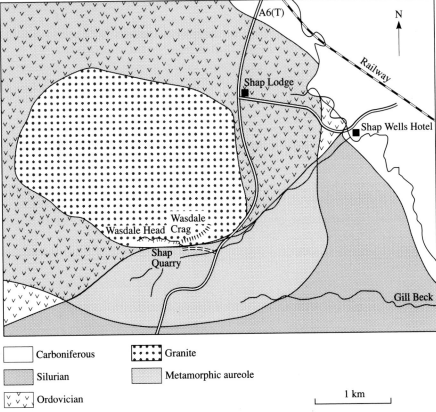

(b)

Carboniferous

Silurian

Ordovician

Granite

Metamorphic aureole

1 km

Figure 1.13

The Shap granite.

(a) View of Shap Quarry, showing vertical and low-angled joints (see Section 2.5).

(b) Map of the Shap granite and the surrounding rocks, showing the zone of baking or contact metamorphism that surrounds it.

How is it conserved?

The quarrying operations ensure that fresh faces are constantly available for research purposes. The operators of the site (Ready Mixed Concrete) are very amenable to educational visits, but for safety reasons do not allow students to work near the quarry faces. However, they have provided a display area in which very large blocks show the characteristic features of the granite.

Who uses the site?

In addition to researchers, numerous student parties (including Open University summer school groups) visit the site, so it also has significant educational importance. In fact, it is one of the most popular educational sites in Britain, and so the owners are forced to 'ration' the number of parties they can accommodate.

How are conservation and other interests reconciled?

The main issue at this site is the preservation of representative granite faces once the quarry has reached the end of its working life. Disused quarries often retain good faces for geological conservation purposes but may become unstable, hazardous or overgrown, preventing access to the site. Disused quarries often have after-uses which are detrimental to, or destroy, the geological interest. For example, landfill is an economically attractive use of an old quarry, but obscures all the faces.

In Shap Quarry, the application from the quarriers for an extension to the area of their planning permission was sent to English Nature as statutory consultees. English Nature suggested that to ensure the conservation of the site's long-term interest, any new planning consent should include advice on conserving representative faces in a safe and accessible manner. Minor engineering work was prescribed to address the safety issue, by making the final form of conservation faces stable and free of overhangs and loose blocks. This is achieved by blasting the face using a method known as 'smooth blasting'.

After negotiations, the final planning consent included the requirement that 'the extractive operators shall, towards the end of active extraction, prepare ... two or three "conservation faces" ... 20 metres in length, adjacent benches no less than three metres wide, to a maximum height of five metres, with a slope of four vertical: one horizontal in a smooth-blasted condition ... these faces should be confined to the upper levels of the quarry and include both Light Shap and Dark Shap varieties'.

Rhynie Chert site, Grampian Region

Geology of the site

The site is world famous because the rocks it conserves contain the oldest known fossil land plants in which full anatomical details are preserved. It is therefore of paramount importance to palaeobotanists in their understanding of the early evolution of land plants. In addition, the site is also important because it contains the earliest known insect and the finest fossils of tiny arthropods of Devonian age (see Table 1.1). Arthropods have external skeletons, and today include groups of animals such as crustaceans, insects, centipedes and millipedes.

The Rhynie Chert is a very hard siliceous rock originally deposited as peat. Soon after the peat was buried beneath younger sediments, it was replaced by silica (the compound from which glass is essentially composed) so that the plants and arthropods were beautifully preserved. A reconstruction of the environment of the deposition of the peat is shown in Figure 1.14(a).

Why is it conserved?

The variety of fossils, all preserved in very good detail, makes this one of the most important sites in the world for studies of evolution and palaeobiology (the interpretation of the biology of fossil organisms).

How is it conserved?

It is conserved by leaving the deposit in the ground, with permission to excavate it given only in very exceptional circumstances. Therefore it is the least spectacular site to visit of all those described in this chapter, for it is just an ordinary field! In 1988, permission was given to drill a borehole and obtain cores through the deposit for research purposes.

(a)

Lepidocaris (Crustacean) × 10

Rhyniella (Arthropod) × 11

Protocarus (Arachnid) × 70

Palaeocharinoiaes (Arachnid) × 12

(b)

Figure 1.14 *(a) Reconstruction of the Rhynie area at the time of formation of the Rhynie Chert. In the foreground the early plants* Asteroxylon, Rhynia *and* Aglaophyton *grow on a sandy substrate bordering a pool fringed by exposed mudflats with desiccation cracks. In the middle distance geysers and hot springs vent silica-rich water which deposits siliceous material around the vents and periodically invades areas covered in plants, causing them to be fossilized. Volcanic ash cones and lava flows lie along the line of a fault, beyond which uplifted older rock is being eroded and is supplying detritus to the area by the streams. (b) Some of the arthropod fauna preserved at Rhynie.*

How are conservation and other interests reconciled?

Apart from normal agricultural practices, no building or construction development can be permitted on the site, for this would remove irreplaceable material.

1.5 Some basics of Earth heritage conservation

Study comment

The ten sites you have studied in this chapter illustrate the variety of Earth heritage conservation sites, in terms of both the geological and geomorphological features they display and the means that can be used to reconcile conservation objectives with those of their owners. The last section of this chapter builds on what you have read. It introduces:

◆ the justification for conserving sites;

◆ the nature of sites in terms of whether or not they have statutory protection;

◆ the conservation classification of sites.

All these topics are followed up in more detail in Part 3.

Why should sites be conserved?

The justification for Earth heritage conservation rests on two main principles, both of which apply equally to all other spheres of conservation.

◆ We have a prime duty to future generations to preserve our heritage so that it may become theirs. This premise encompasses the scientist's argument that we should maintain the means to seek knowledge in the future.

◆ Conservation has direct and immediate benefits for humanity. The health of the natural world is inextricably linked with our own wellbeing and its resources underpin every aspect of our way of life.

The most direct link between everyday life and Earth heritage conservation is through the need to advance research and to train Earth scientists for industry. Sites have a major role in providing opportunities to acquire the knowledge and expertise for:

◆ economic and responsible exploration and management of mineral resources;

◆ safe and economic design of construction and waste disposal projects;

◆ safe management of groundwater resources and of environmental processes such as coastal erosion.

Other important facets of the need to conserve sites include:

◆ our international responsibility as the custodians of a particularly rich geological and geomorphological heritage, as illustrated by the case studies in this chapter;

◆ the inseparable blending of cliffs, coastal landforms and upland outcrops with their wider landscapes;

- the tremendous potential of Earth heritage sites for educational use in the modern curriculum;
- the rapid growth of fossil collecting, mineral collecting and caving as leisure pursuits;
- the fundamental connections between the Earth beneath us and our historical and archaeological heritage.

Sites of the kind illustrated in this chapter are used by five main categories of people:

- professional researchers and Earth scientists in industry (about 6000 people);
- students and staff in higher and further education (about 4000 specialist teachers and students reading for honours degrees, plus a much larger number of students studying geology as a subsidiary subject);
- tens of thousands of school pupils and teachers (Earth science is now a compulsory part of the National Curriculum for all state school pupils in England and Wales);
- amateur groups and collectors: hundreds of field excursions are undertaken every year by national and local societies;
- members of the general public and other interest groups: this form of use is difficult to quantify, for it includes the aesthetic, amenity, historical and wildlife value of sites, plus of course the link between geomorphology, geology and landscapes.

Visits to sites by the last two categories of users provides important opportunities to convince ordinary people with an interest in the natural world that conserving geological sites is just as important as conserving biological ones.

Site networks

In Part 3, the acronyms SSSI and RIGS will be used frequently; they were introduced briefly at the beginning of this chapter. SSSIs are Sites of Special Scientific Interest. They are selected by the country agencies (English Nature, Scottish Natural Heritage and the Countryside Council for Wales) on the basis of their research importance. As illustrated in some of the case studies, the country agencies have the legal right to object to any development that might detract from their scientific value. All the sites described in this chapter except Tedbury Camp Quarry are SSSIs.

Apart from SSSIs, the main network of Earth heritage conservation sites covers those selected for their importance at local level. These sites have been given the generic name Regionally Important Geological/geomorphological Sites (RIGS for short). They are chosen on the basis of their educational, research, historical and aesthetic importance, using less formal criteria than for SSSIs – more closely reflecting local use and interest. They do not have any statutory protection, but local planning officers are usually partners with local voluntary conservation organizations, and so will be aware of their local value. Tedbury Camp Quarry is included in the RIGS scheme established in Somerset.

Approaches to site conservation

In terms of methods of conservation of sites, there are two broad categories of site:

◆ *Exposure sites* provide exposures of a deposit which is extensive or plentiful underground. Usually the deposit or structure is widespread underground and is also certain to contain similar features to those visible at the site, but in practical and economic terms it can only be studied at the site because of the huge cost and difficulty of creating alternative sites. Exposure sites you met in the previous section include Barton Cliffs, Southerham Grey Pit, Tedbury Camp Quarry and Shap Quarry.

◆ *Integrity sites* contain relatively limited deposits or landforms that are irreplaceable. The active geomorphological sites (Morfa Harlech, River Feshie), the glacial sites (Achnasheen Terraces, Moor Mill), and Tynebottom Mine and Dump and the Rhynie Chert site fall into this category.

1.6 Summary

The description of the ten conservation sites in this chapter gave glimpses into episodes in the geological history of the British Isles, to which we will return in Chapter 4. These sites also demonstrated the rationale and methods of Earth heritage conservation, to which we will return in Part 3. At this stage of your study of this book, you should understand the following three key points.

1 Conservation of Earth heritage sites is justified primarily:
   ◆ because we are committed to preserving our heritage for the future;
   ◆ to allow research for the advancement of science and for the success of industry;
   ◆ to train Earth scientists;
   ◆ to provide an essential teaching facility for schools;
   ◆ as a focus for substantial leisure activities (collecting, caving, walking, etc.);
   ◆ because sites have aesthetic, amenity, historical, cultural and wildlife value.

2 The conservation sites are identified in terms of their research and/or educational importance. Sites of Special Scientific Interest (SSSIs) are of national and international research importance, and enjoy statutory protection. Regionally Important Geological/geomorphological Sites (RIGS) are valued in terms of local research and/or educational value, and are conserved by local voluntary organizations.

3 There are two basic types of conservation site:
   ◆ *exposure sites*, which are usually not harmed from a conservation viewpoint by removal of material by quarrying or erosion, but do need protection from being obscured by development such as landfill;
   ◆ *integrity sites*, in which the features are of limited extent, and so must be protected from extraction and constructional activities.

◆ PART 2 ◆

INTRODUCING GEOLOGY FOR EARTH HERITAGE CONSERVATION

Study comment

Part 2 introduces the basic geological vocabulary, concepts and skills necessary to appreciate the conservation value of sites, and to understand how geological histories can be interpreted from them. We begin in Chapter 2 by looking at Earth materials – minerals and rocks – which provide clues about the nature of processes that operated in or on the Earth in the past. This knowledge is then applied in Chapter 3 by reviewing observations and interpretations that can be made in the field when visiting sites. Finally, in Chapter 4 a very 'broad-brush' review of the geological history of the British Isles is given in order to put into context any site you might visit.

Suggested study times for the three chapters in Part 2 are:

Chapter 2: 8–10 hours

Chapter 3: 6 hours

Chapter 4: 2 hours

Chapter 2
MINERALS, ROCKS AND EARTH PROCESSES

Study comment

This chapter begins by introducing some of the commoner minerals and rocks. Next the processes that form rocks are reviewed. By understanding the nature of rocks and how they formed, you will have a better appreciation of why it is important to conserve rock exposures, including quarries. While studying this chapter you will need to examine the kit of mineral and rock samples and have handy the following items in order to investigate their properties:

◆ hand lens;

◆ cup or glass of water;

◆ penknife;

◆ copper coin;

◆ vinegar.

If you do not have access to the kit, you can use the photographs in Plates 1 and 2 in the colour plate booklet instead, although you will obviously not be able to carry out the investigations.

You will also need the geological map of Great Britain and Ireland (Plate 3 in the colour plate booklet).

If you do not have access to the kit of minerals and rocks, the samples are illustrated in the colour plate booklet.

2.1 What are rocks and why study them?

Have you ever wondered what rocks are or how they are formed? On holiday you may have noticed strange colours or patterns in the cliffs and wondered how they got there. Most people have at some time spent an enjoyable hour or two looking for or collecting shiny, rounded pebbles from the base of a cliff, a wave-washed beach or a rock pool. As a casual observer you could not be blamed for thinking that rocks are all much the same, but to a trained eye they can exhibit a wealth of clues about how they were formed.

ACTIVITY 2.1
COMMON ROCK NAMES

Write down some names of rocks commonly used in everyday language.

Then write down some commercial uses of rocks you can think of.

◆ ◆ ◆

Common rock names include granite, sandstone, slate, marble, limestone, coal, chalk and flint. Many of these names are familiar because they are used in the construction industry. You will have seen the polished slabs of marble or granite adorning the facades of shops, banks and offices. Such rocks are usually chosen for their ornamental qualities, but others are chosen for the ease with which they can be quarried, split and shaped, either into regular blocks for building stone (sandstone or granite) or into thin sheets for roofing (slate). However, these qualities alone are not the only consideration, since the rock should also be durable and resistant to the long-term effects of the weather, or abrasion if it is used as paving material.

Many other rocks are equally useful even though they may not appear as pleasing to the eye! Rock is quarried in large quantities for use as aggregate in road construction. Sand and gravel deposits are extracted for use in concrete, together with limestone, which is the main constituent of cement. Clay is used in the brick-making industry. Perhaps the most obvious example is coal, but others are just as important, such as ores, which are simply rocks which may be profitably mined for the purpose of metal extraction. The steel-making industry requires not only iron ore as a raw material, but also coal for energy and limestone as a flux in blast furnaces.

ACTIVITY 2.2
ARE ALL ROCKS COMPLETELY SOLID?

For this exercise you will need Specimens A and F from the kit, and a small jug of water. Ignoring what the rocks look like, pour a small amount of water on to both samples and observe what happens. Does the water soak in, run off, or sit on the surface?

◆ ◆ ◆

Water only soaks into Specimen A. It is a sandstone composed of small fragments between which there are spaces or pores (Figure 2.1). The water soaks into these

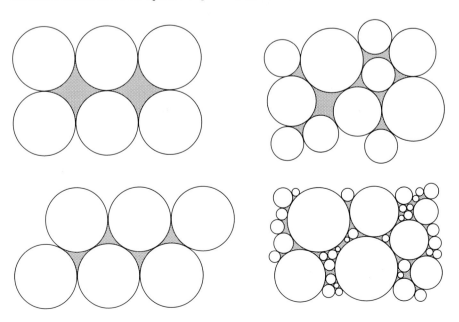

Figure 2.1
The effects of grain packing and the range of grain sizes on the porosity of sediments.

pores, rather like in a sponge, and can remain there for some time. Such rocks are said to be *porous* and some form underground reservoirs containing water, oil or gas. Just think what modern life would be like without such rocks in the UK. Much of the south-east of England would be desperately short of water, and we would have no North Sea oil or gas.

Specimen F is a granite collected from the SSSI at Shap Quarry in the Lake District (see Chapter 1). In this rock, the constituents (which, as you will see shortly, are crystals) are packed tightly together and interlock, so there is virtually no porosity. Such *crystalline* rocks can be polished and are resistant to weathering and abrasion, so are used as facing and paving stones.

Rocks are an important natural resource. Their occurrence can influence local employment and economies. Unfortunately, the mere process of extraction can affect, and in places completely change, the local landscape.

▼   Can you think of such an example close to where you live?

▲   You may have thought of a local quarry, an open pit or a mine.

Although such excavations are often regarded as scars on the landscape, they do provide excellent opportunities for examining and studying the local geology, and with careful management it is possible to restore the landscape while maintaining the usefulness of sites for research and education.

2.2 Rocks in the making

Most of the rocks we can study, including the samples in your kit, have come from near the surface of the Earth's thin outer crust (described in more detail in Section 2.10), for the simple reason that it is very difficult to sample the rocks at greater depths within the Earth. However, in spite of these seeming limitations, the study of rocks can give a fascinating insight into the various processes that have affected the Earth's crust, both at the surface and deep within it.

ACTIVITY 2.3
ROCK-FORMING PROCESSES

Can you think of any places where you might expect rocks to be forming at the present time? Look at Figure 2.2. Before reading the captions, consider what rock-forming processes might be occurring in the environments shown. Summarize your ideas in writing and then see how they compare with the information in the captions.

◆ ◆ ◆

As you would perhaps expect, the rocks being formed in such differing environments are correspondingly diverse. As you begin to study specimens from the kit, this will become more apparent.

When looking at any of the samples in the kit, many features will be much more obvious if you use a hand lens or magnifying glass. You should examine a sample

Figure 2.2 *Rocks in the making.*

(a) Masses of rock debris loosened by alternating freezing and thawing have accumulated beneath the steep valley side. Gravity has been responsible for movement of the debris after initial loosening from the parent rock by weathering. If this coarse angular debris were buried to become a rock, it would be called a breccia.

(b) Coastal erosion. The action of waves has resulted in the cliff line receding. Ribs of steeply inclined rock layers stand out above the beach sands. The sands on the beach are derived from the breakdown of solid rock: if buried, they would become sandstone.

(c) Deposition of sands and muds in an estuary. Reduction in the speed of river currents as they reach the sea causes rock debris (sand, silt and mud) to be deposited. In the future, if these deposits were to be buried, they would become new sedimentary rocks (sandstones, shales and mudstones). (a), (b) and (c) all show sedimentary rocks in the making.

(d) Outpourings of molten lava cool to form solid rock. All rocks formed from an original molten state (called magma) are termed igneous rocks.

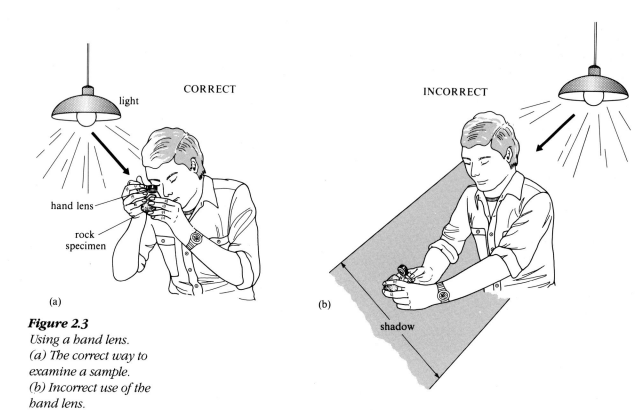

Figure 2.3
Using a hand lens.
(a) The correct way to examine a sample.
(b) Incorrect use of the hand lens.

in good light, ensuring that the light is to one side rather than from behind (Figure 2.3). You may find that you will have to move the sample or the hand lens around a little to get the sample properly into focus and to show it in the best light.

ACTIVITY 2.4
THE CONSTITUENTS OF ROCKS

For this exercise you will need Specimens A and F from the kit again, as well as a hand lens.

First take Specimen A. Rub your thumb back and forth across it. What do you notice?

Now examine Specimen A with the hand lens, paying particular attention to the nature and size of the grains.

Now take Specimen F. Try rubbing your thumb back and forth across it. Do you notice a difference compared with Specimen A?

Now examine Specimen F with the hand lens. How many different coloured constituents can you see, and what do you notice about the texture of the rock constituents? Are they rounded or angular, and do they interlock, or are they quite discrete as in Specimen A?

◆ ◆ ◆

You should have noticed that some of the fragments in Specimen A are easily dislodged. It's not difficult to see that it is made of small rounded grains or fragments of a pale material stuck together. This is a typical *fragmental* texture. The term 'texture' describes the size and shape of the particles a rock is made of. This rock is a sedimentary rock – a sandstone – and it has formed very simply by the cementing together of sand grains that occur in river, beach or dune sands. The term 'cement' is used in much the same way as you would do in everyday life: it refers to the minerals that grow later as the 'glue' that sticks the grains together.

It is impossible to dislodge individual grains in Specimen F since they seem to be tightly held together. You should be able to see that the rock is formed of closely packed, interlocking particles which fit together like a three-dimensional jigsaw. The particles in Specimen F are crystals that have grown together – each one interlocks with the others around it so that there are no spaces between them. This is why the rock did not soak up water when you tested it in Activity 2.1. The rock is said to have a *crystalline* texture. You should be able to see three different types of crystal here; some are white, others are grey and glassy and a few are black, shiny and slightly flaky. This rock was formed by slow crystallization from a molten mass several kilometres deep within the Earth's crust.

It should now be clear that rocks are aggregates of one or more types of grain or crystal. The grains or crystals are composed of different types of minerals.

2.3 Minerals: the building blocks of rocks

Minerals are naturally occurring substances with definite chemical compositions and physical properties. Minerals can have beautiful crystal shapes (Figure 2.4) which are related to their internal or molecular structure, although perfect crystal shapes are rarely seen, particularly when the minerals are found together as the components of a rock.

Figure 2.4 *Minerals can exhibit some beautiful crystal shapes if allowed to grow unimpeded in cracks and cavities in rocks.*

A few minerals are simply single elements, such as gold, copper and carbon (which may occur naturally as diamond or graphite, depending on the conditions of formation). Most minerals, however, are combinations of elements, i.e. chemical compounds. Certain minerals are rich in metals, which makes them economically important, and these are known as ore minerals.

The kit contains a selection of minerals, four of which are important rock-forming minerals, with the fifth being a common ore mineral, of iron. They are illustrated in Plate 2. The chemical names of these minerals are as follows:

Specimen	Mineral name	Chemical name
V	Quartz	Silica
W	Feldspar	Potassium, sodium or calcium aluminosilicates. The kit sample is a potassium-rich feldspar
X	Mica	Iron and magnesium aluminosilicates
Y	Calcite	Calcium carbonate
Z	Pyrite	Iron sulphide

A detailed study of the properties and chemistry of these minerals is beyond the scope of this text, but the commentary below on each specimen will give you an impression of the kinds of observations that can be made on them.

Quartz (Specimen V)

▼ Examine Specimen V and describe its crystal shape.

▲ You should be able to see that it forms long columnar (the technical term used is 'prismatic') crystals which are hexagonal when viewed end-on. Quartz can form good crystals such as these, but can also be found as shapeless 'lumps' or narrow strips or veins cutting across rocks. This mineral is commonly found in granites and as irregular or rounded grains in river, beach and dune sands.

▼ How would you describe its colour?

▲ This sample is transparent and colourless. You may be able to see a slight 'cloudiness' within the crystal but this is due to imperfections inside the crystal itself. You may also have noticed that this sample has a glassy look, rather like the reflection from the broken surface of a thick piece of glass.

Quartz can be colourless (transparent) like this, although when combined with other minerals in a rock it may look more grey in colour. When it is found in veins cutting across rocks it can be quite white. You may have seen such veins in pebbles and boulders lying around beaches.

▼ Now try to scratch the sample with a penknife.

▲ Impossible, isn't it? *Hardness* is an important property that helps to identify minerals. It can be measured using a qualitative scale (called Moh's scale) from 1 to 10, using common materials such as fingernails (2.5), copper coins (4.0), and steel, such as in a penknife (6.0).

Because it is so hard quartz is very resistant to weathering and erosion. This is one of the main reasons that it is one of the most common rock-forming minerals of sedimentary rocks. It breaks with an irregular, often curved, *fracture*. You may be able to see this at the broken end of your sample.

Feldspar (Specimen W)

▼ How does this specimen compare with the quartz that you have just looked at?

▲ It differs from quartz in that it is not transparent and glassy, instead being translucent with a less shiny, almost silky lustre.

This specimen is pale pink, but feldspar may also be deeper pink or off-white in colour. If you look carefully, using the hand lens, you should be able to see a series of parallel lines running through the crystal or giving a characteristic stepped appearance on the edge of the crystal, as seen in Figure 2.5(b). These lines and 'steps' indicate that the mineral contains *cleavage planes* along which it may split. These cleavage planes are related to the molecular structure of minerals, just as the crystal faces seen in the quartz specimen are.

▼ Now try to scratch the specimen with a penknife and then a copper coin.

▲ You might just be able to produce a scratch with the penknife, but certainly not with the coin.

Although feldspar is almost as hard as quartz, it is not as durable. This is because, unlike quartz, it has cleavage planes and is chemically less stable in damp or wet conditions, breaking down to very fine-grained clay minerals (such as the china clay of Cornwall, which was formed by the chemical breakdown of the feldspar in the adjacent granites). This process is known as *chemical weathering*. It occurs when minerals and rocks become exposed to the effects of water at normal temperatures and pressures at the Earth's surface.

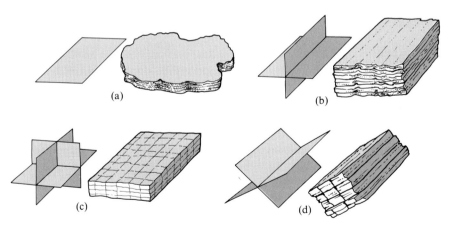

Figure 2.5   *Cleavage in minerals: planar surfaces along which a crystal splits. (a) cleavage in one direction, as in mica (Specimen X). (b) Two cleavage directions, almost at right angles, as in feldspar (Specimen W). (c) Three cleavage directions at right angles to one another, as in the golden iron ore mineral pyrite (Specimen Z), the lead ore mineral galena, and the well-known mineral fluorite (fluorspar). (d) Three cleavage directions not at right angles to one another, as in calcite (Specimen Y).*

Mica (Specimen X)

You should see immediately that Specimen X is quite different from the two minerals you have already examined.

▼ Ignoring the actual shape of the specimen (since it has been broken from a larger piece), what else do you notice about it?

▲ One obvious feature is its colour. This sample is dark brown with a shiny, resinous lustre, in places almost resembling a patch of oil lying on water, though some micas are colourless.

▼ Now look at the edge of the specimen for any evidence of cleavage.

▲ You should be able to insert a fingernail between the layers and split the specimen into thin, flexible sheets. This is because mica has perfect cleavage developed parallel in one direction (Figure 2.5(a)): this is a characteristic feature of the mineral. The development of this cleavage is related to its sheet-like internal structure.

▼ Now try to scratch the specimen with a copper coin.

▲ This you should be able to do quite easily because mica is much softer than quartz and feldspar; in fact you may even be able to scratch it with your fingernail.

Calcite (Specimen Y)

Specimen Y is another colourless to white mineral with a resinous or oily lustrous look to it.

▼ How would you describe the shape of the specimen? How many cleavage planes can you see and what angular relationships do they have to one another?

▲ You might have thought that the flat 'faces' on this specimen are faces of a single rhomb-shaped crystal, but they are not. In fact, the surfaces are cleavage planes. The mineral has three sets of cleavage planes, intersecting at 120°. They may be seen both at the edge of the sample and as parallel lines running through it (Figure 2.5(d)). Flat surfaces shown by the specimen are cleavage surfaces and not crystal faces. The most characteristic shape of calcite crystals is called dog-tooth spar, in which the crystals are hexagonal columns capped by six-sided pyramids.

▼ Now test its hardness, using the techniques with which you are now familiar.

▲ Because of its appearance, calcite can be difficult to distinguish from many other colourless or white minerals. However, there is one diagnostic test that can be useful.

▼ Try dropping a few spots of household vinegar on to Specimen Y and one of the other specimens. What do you notice?

▲ You should be able to see that the calcite specimen fizzes. This is because vinegar is a dilute acid and calcite reacts with it, giving off the gas carbon dioxide. This test is also useful if you are trying to identify a limestone, which is a rock composed of calcium carbonate.

Pyrite (Specimen Z)

Specimen Z is perhaps the most visually exciting specimen of all those in the kit. It is not a very common rock-forming mineral, but it is the commonest metal ore mineral.

▼ How would you describe its colour and lustre?

▲ It is yellow and shiny – almost gold in colour, and completely opaque (meaning that you cannot see through it) with a distinct metallic lustre. In places the crystal surfaces are quite tarnished.

Pyrite is often called 'fool's gold' because of its colour, and it may be found in veins associated with other ore minerals of economic importance. It may also be found as isolated crystals in some fine-grained rocks, such as slate (Specimen I), having grown within the rock.

▼ Can you notice any good cleavage?

▲ Depending on the specimen that you have, you may be able to see cleavage planes oriented at right angles on the edges of the specimen. This orientation is characteristic of cubic cleavage (Figure 2.5(c)).

Pyrite is frequently found as cubic crystals, sometimes intergrown with one another, but it may also be found in irregular lumps. Some of the crystal surfaces may exhibit peculiar parallel scratch-like marks or *striations* (Plate 2). Pyrite has a hardness of 6 and can just be scratched with a penknife. Like many of the other metal ores, it feels quite heavy because it is very dense.

You should now have a 'feel' for some of the properties that can be used to help identify minerals.

▼ Try listing some of these properties.

▲ The properties described in the commentaries included colour, shape (including crystal shape – but some minerals exhibit other shapes when many tiny crystals grow together), cleavage, hardness, and the 'acid test' (whether the mineral reacts with the dilute acid such as vinegar).

Look at rock Specimens A and F again. Specimen A is a sandstone composed almost entirely of grains of quartz that were derived by the breakdown (by chemical weathering and mechanical disaggregation) of pre-existing rocks containing abundant quartz – such as the granite illustrated by Specimen F. As stated earlier, Specimen F contains three minerals: quartz, feldspar and mica.

▼ Try to identify the three minerals in Specimen F.

▲ Mica is the easiest mineral to identify: the tiny black flecks scattered through the rock. Quartz shows up as the rather dull grey glassy areas, and feldspar as the pink and white constituents.

2.4 The three main types of rock

We have already looked at a few of the rocks in the kit when investigating the difference between fragmental and crystalline textures. So you should now be able to sort the collection into these two categories.

ACTIVITY 2.5
CLASSIFYING ROCKS: MAKING A START

Place all the rocks from the kit in front of you (Specimens A–K), or look at the photographs of them in Plate 1 of the colour plate booklet. You may be quite surprised at the wide variety of colours and textures they show.

Have a go at dividing them up into two groups according to whether you think they are fragmental or crystalline. Don't worry too much if you have trouble with this, but it is a good exercise in observation. When you have tried to sort the rocks into the two categories, look at the answers below.

◆ ◆ ◆

A–E are fragmental; F–K are crystalline. At this stage, do not worry if you could not classify specimens C, D, E, G and I.

In fact, rocks are divided into *three* major groups according to the way in which they were formed: sedimentary, igneous and metamorphic. The key to the geological map of Britain and Ireland in the colour plate booklet (Plate 3) uses these terms to divide up the rocks shown on the map.

Weathering and erosion of pre-existing rocks at the Earth's surface yields a vast amount of sediment that is subsequently deposited on to the surrounding land surface and, ultimately, into the oceans (Figure 2.2(a), (b) and (c)). After burial beneath further layers of sediment, these deposits become consolidated to give an important group known as the *sedimentary* rocks.

Rocks which have crystallized from molten material (magma), either at the Earth's surface, as in Figure 2.2(d), or deep within the Earth, are known as *igneous* rocks.

The final group are those rocks which are not in their original state, having been altered and recrystallized at depth within the Earth by temperature and/or pressure; these are known as *metamorphic* rocks.

These last two are both crystalline rocks.

Some of the more common types of igneous, sedimentary and metamorphic rocks are illustrated by specimens in the kit (Specimens A to K). The rock samples in the kit are taken from large blocks collected from quarries or freshly broken surfaces of natural rock outcrops. Some may have at least one sawn flat surface, which enables you to see certain features more clearly. For these reasons they may look different from the weathered exposures seen in quarries, cliffs and rock fragments lying around on the ground. To study a rock properly in the field it is best to ensure that you are looking at a freshly broken, unweathered surface and for this reason many geologists carry hammers. However, if everyone visiting an interesting geological site were to tap away at it with a hammer, it would not remain as an interesting site for long!

2.5 Igneous rocks and processes

Introduction

Igneous rocks form from molten magma as it cools and minerals crystallize from it. The size of the crystals within igneous rocks is related to the rate at which the rock cooled. If the rock cooled quickly as, for example, a lava erupted from a volcano at the Earth's surface, the crystals did not have have much time to grow and so the rock is fine grained. If, however, the rock cooled more slowly, at depth, covered by an insulating blanket in the form of overlying rocks, the crystals had a much longer time in which to grow to a larger size, and the rock will therefore be coarse grained.

▼ Examine Specimens G and H. Both are crystalline, but what can you say about their colour and grain size?

▲ They are both fairly dark in colour, although Specimen H is darker than Specimen G. They are both dark because they contain abundant dark, iron-rich minerals, but you may also be able to see some white crystals of feldspar, particularly in Specimen G. The most obvious difference between them is that Specimen G is fairly coarse grained, as individual interlocking crystals can be seen with the naked eye, while Sample H is fine grained, needing the hand lens to see individual crystals. These two rocks have the same chemical and mineral composition, but Specimen G cooled slowly at depth and Specimen H cooled quickly after being erupted as a lava. Therefore, despite having the same compositions, their origins are very different, and so they are given different names. Specimen G is a *gabbro* and Specimen H is a *basalt.*

As well as grain size, another important feature used when classifying the igneous rocks is their mineral content. The types of minerals present in a rock are related to its chemical composition. The amount of silica (the compound of which quartz and glass are composed) present in magmas is particularly important. Magmas with low silica contents, such as those that form basalt, flow freely (i.e. they have a low *viscosity*), and so are found in relatively harmless volcanic areas, such as Iceland and Hawaii. But magmas with high silica contents are very stiff or viscous, and so gas within them cannot escape easily and may build up. This produces highly dangerous eruptions such as Mount St Helens in North America and Mount Pinatubo in the Philippines in recent times, and Vesuvius in Roman times.

ACTIVITY 2.6

LOOKING AT IGNEOUS ROCKS

Compare Specimens F and G. Describe their grain size and colour and suggest whether they cooled fast or slowly, and on the surface of the Earth or at depth.

◆ ◆ ◆

Specimens F and G have similar coarse-grained, crystalline textures, indicating that both cooled slowly from a magma at depth. What about their colour? Specimen F is paler in colour than Specimen G, and if you look closely you should be able to see that the minerals are different in the two rocks. Specimen F contains the more silica-rich minerals quartz (grey and glassy) and mica (small black flakes) with white and pink feldspars. Specimen G contains darker, more iron-rich minerals with some paler greyish-white feldspar. The chemistry of the feldspar in the two rocks is also different. This difference in composition is also reflected in the density of the rocks: Specimen G is denser than Specimen F. As we saw earlier, Specimen F is a granite and Specimen G is a gabbro. As will be explained in Section 2.10, there are two distinctive types of the Earth's crust: continental crust is granitic in average chemical composition, whereas oceanic crust has a gabbroic composition.

There are, of course, many different types of igneous rock which can be classified according to their grain size and mineral content, and we have only introduced you to a few here. But the key point to remember about igneous rocks is that they have a crystalline texture, with interlocking crystals orientated in a random fashion resulting from the cooling of a molten magma.

The geological map of Great Britain and Ireland (Plate 3 in the colour plate booklet) shows igneous rocks at the base of the key in two colours: red for intrusive types, and purple for volcanic (or extrusive) types. The difference between these types is shown in Figure 2.6 and can be summarized as follows:

◆ intrusive rocks form from magmas forced into pre-existing rocks at depths ranging from a kilometre or so to tens of kilometres beneath the Earth's surface;

◆ volcanic rocks form when magma reaches the Earth's surface to produce lava flows, or is ejected explosively to form ash and large fragments of lava.

If you look at the geological map, you will see that there are significant areas of igneous rock (in red and purple) in south-west England, Wales, northern England, Scotland and Ireland. Complete volcanoes are rarely preserved in the geological record, since they are usually eroded away, but sometimes their solidified vents may be preserved if the igneous rock that finally plugged them is more resistant to erosion than surrounding rocks. Arthur's Seat in Edinburgh is a good example of such a volcanic vent (Figure 2.7(c) and (d)). The age of the igneous rocks is not shown on the map, but volcanic activity on the scale of recent spectacular eruptions (such as Mount St Helens and Mount Pinatubo) was characteristic of several episodes in the geological history of the British Isles (see Chapter 4).

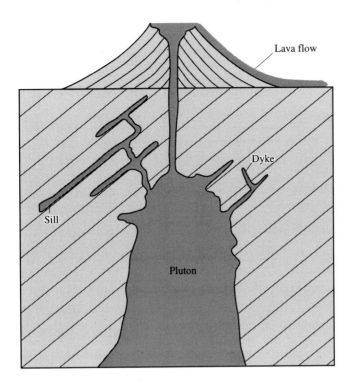

Figure 2.6
The principal occurrence of igneous rocks: lavas, sills, dykes and plutons.

Extrusive igneous activity

Lava flows are perhaps the most obvious extrusive features, but active volcanos emit various combinations of gas, lava and ash. The magmas from which these materials are derived vary in composition, and as we have seen this influences whether volcanism is explosive or relatively 'quiet'.

Lavas with a high silica content are quite 'sticky' and viscous (rather like treacle). When they are extruded on to the surface they resemble toothpaste being squeezed from a tube and tend to form steep-sided features called *domes*. If such viscous magmas have a high dissolved gas content, they erupt explosively to give huge clouds of ash and coarser debris. Pumice stone used in bathrooms is actually solidified lava that has been thrown out of an explosive volcano, the abundant small holes being the remains of gas bubbles trapped in the lava before it cooled. Explosive eruptions of this type were common in Wales and the Lake District 400–500 million years ago.

Less silica-rich lavas, such as basalt, are far more fluid and when extruded on to the Earth's surface flow for great distances, forming either very shallow-sloping volcanoes such as Hawaii or extensive flat lava plateaux. About 50 million years ago in the British Isles, such igneous activity formed the great plateau basalts of Northern Ireland (excellently exposed along the coastline of County Antrim and the Giant's Causeway) and Scotland (northern Skye and Mull, including Fingal's Cave on Staffa). In both these examples, the basalt exhibits a characteristic pattern of hexagonal cracks or *joints* which developed in the lava as it cooled (Figure 2.7(a)).

Figure 2.7
Three SSSIs showing Britain's volcanic past.
(a) 60 million year old columnar basalt lava flow, Giant's Causeway, County Antrim
(b) The defensive line of Hadrian's Wall (seen on the distant hill at the top left) follows the escarpment (in the foreground above the lake) produced by an almost horizontal sheet-like intrusion of basalt, the Whin Sill.
(c) Arthur's Seat, Edinburgh: an ancient volcano about 350 million years old.
(d) Sketch showing the geological interpretation of the photograph of Arthur's Seat.

(a)

(b)

(c)

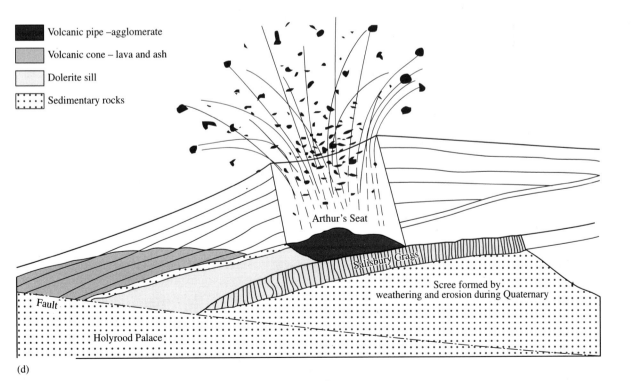

Volcanic pipe –agglomerate

Volcanic cone – lava and ash

Dolerite sill

Sedimentary rocks

Arthur's Seat

Salisbury Crags

Scree formed by
weathering and erosion during Quaternary

Fault

Holyrood Palace

(d)

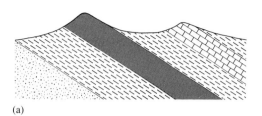 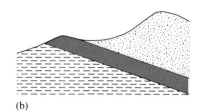 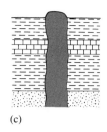

(a) (b) (c)

Figure 2.8
Sills and dykes.
(a) Cross-section of a sill. The beds above and below are likely to have been baked (light coloured zones) by the intrusion (dark coloured).
(b) A lava flow can be distinguished from a sill because baking only occurs below it, if at all.
(c) Cross-section of a dyke, showing baking on either side of it.

Intrusive igneous activity

Not all magma reaches the Earth's surface; in fact huge volumes solidify at great depths. The heat and fluids emanating from the cooling magma may also cause metamorphism of the surrounding rocks; this is called *contact metamorphism*. At their margins intrusive bodies may show the effects of rapid cooling.

▼ What feature would indicate rapid cooling?

▲ The rock at the margin of the intrusive body is likely to be finer grained than that in the main mass.

An igneous rock that is intruded as a sheet roughly parallel to the layering in sedimentary rocks is called a *sill* (Figure 2.8(a)). Sills are from a few metres to several tens of metres thick and may spread over a wide area at roughly the same level in a sequence of sedimentary rocks. A crack which cuts across the strata and is filled with magma is known as a *dyke* (Figure 2.8(c)). With a sill, the beds above and below are likely to have been baked by the intrusion, in contrast to a lava flow, which, although it may be found within a rock sequence once it has been buried, will only have baked the rocks lying beneath it, its uppermost surface having been exposed to the air when it was originally erupted (Figure 2.8(b)). With dykes and sills, the rocks on either side or above and below show the effects of baking.

Sills, dykes and lava flows are often hard resistant features that stand proud of the surrounding landscape (Figure 2.7(b)), or they may appear as eroded clefts, particularly in cliffs and other coastal exposures. Sills, in particular, may form resistant layers within a sequence of much softer sedimentary rocks, and when exposed in a river gorge or valley, may give a stepped outline or even be the site of a waterfall.

Larger, more irregular igneous intrusions, known as *plutons* or *batholiths* (Figure 2.9), may also cause baking of surrounding rocks but on a much larger scale than that caused by the minor intrusions because of the much larger volumes of magma. Thus surrounding rocks may be metamorphosed in zones around the intrusion, the degree of metamorphism decreasing with distance from the intrusion (Figure 1.12(b)).

Because of their sheer size these large intrusions may have a dramatic effect on the landscape, once uncovered from their original depths by erosion. For example, granite produces an acid soil, giving rise to vast expanses of exposed, boggy moorland, such as Dartmoor. As granite cools a well-developed system of roughly planar joints arranged horizontally and vertically in two sets approximately at right angles develops. As it is weathered preferentially along these joints, characteristic features known as tors develop (Figure 2.10).

Igneous intrusions of other rock types besides granite produce equally dramatic landscapes, often giving rise to great tracts of barren, desolate, upland areas, such as the gabbros of the Cuillin Hills of Skye.

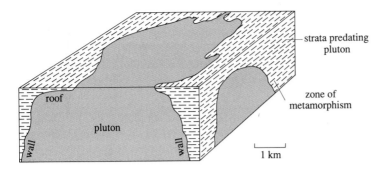

strata predating pluton

zone of metamorphism

roof

pluton

wall

wall

1 km

Figure 2.9 *Plutons/batholiths.*
(a) The zone of contact metamorphism around the igneous rock.
(b) The probable geometry of the batholith beneath the granite exposures of south-west England (see Plate 3 in the colour plate booklet for the appearance of these on the geological map of Britain and Ireland).

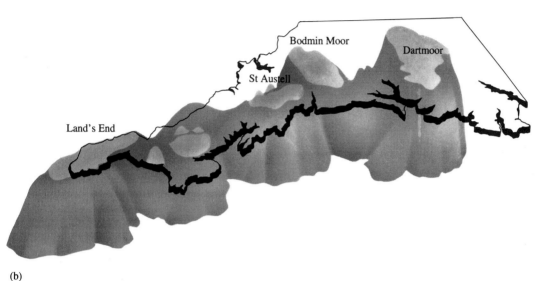

Bodmin Moor

Dartmoor

St Austell

Land's End

(b)

Figure 2.10 *Granite tors on Dartmoor. Chemical weathering may have occurred several tens of millions ago, with more recent erosion removing the weathered material to reveal relatively unweathered pinnacles of granite.*

2.6 Sedimentary rocks and processes

Study comment

As sedimentary rock is by far the most common rock type exposed in the British Isles, this section is longer than its igneous and metamorphic counterparts. After introducing some of the kit samples, it examines how sedimentary material is produced by weathering processes, and how it is then transported and deposited.

Introduction

Sedimentary rocks are mainly made up of mineral or rock fragments derived by the breakdown and erosion of pre-existing rocks and the transport of the resultant debris by water, wind or ice, eventually to be deposited in layers and then buried and consolidated. A few sedimentary rocks are formed by direct precipitation from sea water and may have a crystalline rather than fragmental texture. Others are formed from the dead remains of tiny organisms that float just below the sea surface (plankton), or from the shells and skeletons of animals such as sea urchins, shellfish and corals. The remains of these organisms accumulate on the sea floor and become consolidated and cemented into limestones.

▼ Compare Specimens A and B. They both have fragmental textures, but in what ways do they differ?

    _____

▲ Colour is perhaps the most obvious difference, but they are also quite different in grain size. The shape of the grains is also interesting.

▼ First look at Specimen A. You have already met this rock and been told that is a sandstone, probably transported by water and deposited as a sand such as might be found around present-day coasts.

    Describe the size and shape of the grains.

    _____

▲ The grains are very variable, ranging from 1 mm to 1 cm in size. There may even be some larger pebbles in your particular sample.

    This sandstone is therefore fairly coarse grained and poorly sorted (i.e. it contains a wide range of grain sizes). Some of the grains are quite angular, while others (usually the larger ones) are more rounded.

▼ What is the mineral that forms most of the grains?

    _____

▲ The grains are mainly quartz, but some white, clay-like material may have formed by the breakdown of feldspar grains.

▼ Now look at Specimen B. This is also a sandstone but it has quite a different origin.

    How would you describe the grain size of this rock?

    _____

▲ It is finer grained than Sample A and the grains are more equal in size. It is altogether a more well-sorted sediment (i.e. it contains a very small range of grain sizes).

If you look at it with a hand lens, you may also notice that the grains are more rounded. This is because this sandstone was deposited in a wind-blown environment and, unlike Specimen A, the grains were not cushioned from impact by water as they were transported by the wind. All the angular corners have been knocked off and individual grains have become very rounded.

The distinct red colouration of this rock is interesting. The grains themselves are quartz but they are cemented by a rusty coating of iron oxide, which gives the rock its distinctive appearance. The presence of this red iron oxide, together with the well-sorted, rounded grains, indicates that this rock was deposited in a hot, dry, wind-blown environment.

▼ Can you think where such conditions might be found?

▲ A desert is the most obvious suggestion, and ancient desert sandstones such as this are commonly found in parts of Devon, south Wales, northern England and around the Moray Firth in Scotland.

Look at Figure 2.2(c) (page 43). In addition to accumulations of sand, this photograph shows mud flats exposed in an estuary at low water. Both sand and mud can be carried in water but fine muds can be carried by currents that are not fast enough to carry larger sand grains. So finer muds are found in sheltered bays and estuaries, or carried out into the deep ocean where they settle very slowly. In fact, muds are by far the most common sediments accumulating today, and mud rocks are the most extensive of all sedimentary rocks.

Examine Specimen C, which is one variety of a mud rock: a shale. Other varieties include *clay* (which is plastic and can be moulded) and *mudstone* (which contains much less water than shale, and is massive rather than thinly bedded).

▼ What do you notice about its colour and grain size?

▲ It is dark in colour and extremely fine grained. Indeed, you may even have difficulty seeing individual grains with a hand lens. You may notice a few small shiny flakes of mica on flat bedding planes.

Because shales are so fine grained and thinly bedded they break up very easily, and are therefore not very resistant to erosion.

Geologists attach very precise meanings to the terms clay, silt, sand and gravel, as shown in Table 2.1. Sedimentary rocks may be classified on the basis of their particle size, the broad divisions being summarized in Table 2.1. Since sedimentary rocks are derived from pre-existing rocks of every type, they can contain an almost limitless variety of fragmental material, the mineral composition of which is the basis for classifying sandstones. However, such classifications are beyond the scope of this text.

Table 2.1 The names of sedimentary grains and sedimentary rocks defined on the basis of particle size

Grain size range in millimetres	Name of sedimentary particles	Name of rock composed of grains of different grain sizes
>256	Boulders	
256–64	Cobbles	Conglomerate (if particles are rounded) or breccia (if particles are angular)
64–4	Pebbles	
	Gravel	
4–2	Granules	
2–0.625	Sand	Sandstone
0.625–0.002	Silt	Siltstone
<0.002	Clay	Mud rock (clay when plastic; mudstone when not easily split; shale when easily split)

Limestones, though sedimentary in origin, sometimes show crystalline textures. This may make limestones rather difficult to identify as sedimentary in origin.

▼ Look at Sample D. What can you see?

▲ The rock seems to contain fossil-like fragments, although some surfaces may look more crystalline.

▼ Now try dropping a few spots of vinegar on to it.

▲ It should 'fizz' because it is composed almost entirely of the mineral calcite.

The fossils are fragments of organisms called sea lilies or crinoids. Sea lilies look rather plant-like but are actually animals. These organisms secreted skeletons made up of small plates, each of which is a single crystal of calcite. When the crinoids died, their skeletons broke up to give a deposit of calcite crystals, and so the resultant rock looks crystalline, even though it is made up of fragments of skeletal material. The rock was laid down in layers at the bottom of a clear, tropical shallow sea some 350 million years ago. A variety of other organisms living in this environment secreted calcitic skeletal material (Figure 2.11). Today limestones are forming in tropical locations like the Bahamas, the Arabian Gulf and the Great Barrier Reef of Australia.

▼ Now examine Specimen E. Put a few drops of vinegar on to it. What happens?

▲ It fizzes, indicating that it is composed of calcite.

This rock is a chalk; it forms the characteristic white cliffs along the south coast of England, and at Flamborough Head on the Yorkshire coast. It is composed entirely of tiny organisms that floated in the sea (Figure 2.12); when they died and decomposed the calcitic parts settled on the sea bottom to form a white ooze, which hardened when buried under younger rocks to produce chalk.

Figure 2.11 Reconstruction of a shallow sea in which abundant crinoids and other organisms flourished. This reconstruction is for the Carboniferous Limestone that was deposited over much of England and Wales about 350–325 million years ago. Key: A primitive shark; B crinoids; C and E colonial and solitary corals respectively; D and G brachiopods (two-shelled sedentary bottom dwellers); F sea snail; H trilobite (extinct arthropod).

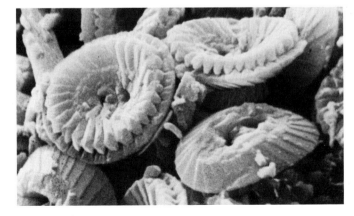

Figure 2.12 Microscopic organisms viewed under an electron microscope. Their dead remains accumulated to form chalk. These floating organisms (plankton), called coccoliths, were abundant in seas that covered much of northern Europe between 95 and 65 million years ago. Their average diameter is only a few thousandths of a millimetre.

Weathering

All the sedimentary rocks you have just examined owe their origin ultimately to processes whereby pre-existing rocks are broken down at the Earth's surface. These breakdown processes are known collectively as *weathering*. They include mechanical disaggregation or physical weathering and chemical degradation or chemical weathering.

One of the most important forms of *physical weathering*, which causes the break-up of large masses of rock into fragments, results from the repeated alternation of freezing and thawing of rainwater in cracks and fissures. Unlike most other substances, water *expands* on freezing, with an increase in volume of about 9%, and the resulting pressure on the pore spaces, joints and fractures causes them to split apart. The resultant pieces and blocks of rocks fall under gravity from rock faces and are shattered into smaller angular fragments, which accumulate as scree slopes. This process is called *frost shattering* and is responsible for the splitting of rocks into the broken slabby boulders shown in Figure 2.13. Shattering of rocks into fragments like this exposes a much larger surface area to rainwater, and so the fragments may soon undergo *chemical weathering*. This attack is enhanced by the presence of dissolved atmospheric gases such as carbon dioxide and sulphur dioxide in the rainwater, which make it slightly acidic. Chemical reactions may take place between the rock minerals and water, sometimes dissolving them completely and sometimes producing new mineral types.

Figure 2.13
Frost-shattered boulders. The cracks and crevices in which water collects can be seen clearly in the boulders, and the various stages in the break-up of the boulders are visible.

It is the products of weathering that eventually accumulate to form sedimentary rocks. When a rock is exposed to chemical and physical weathering, three basic products result (Figure 2.14).

◆ Substances that are soluble in water are carried away in solution by rainwater and rivers, and eventually enter the sea.

◆ New minerals are formed when soluble substances are leached out of existing minerals and their atomic structures partially collapse. An example of this process is the formation of clay minerals through the weathering of feldspars and micas in granite.

◆ Resistant minerals, such as quartz, are not chemically attacked at all.

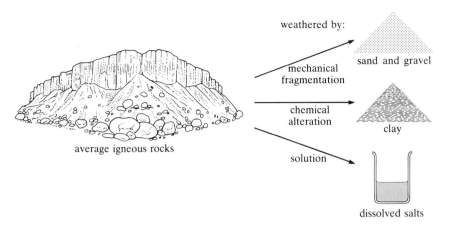

weathered by:

average igneous rocks

mechanical fragmentation → sand and gravel

chemical alteration → clay

solution → dissolved salts

Figure 2.14
The three basic products of weathering.

The weathering products of average igneous rocks are shown in Figure 2.14.

The new minerals and the resistant minerals are known as *residual minerals*. The most common of the resistant minerals is quartz, but if chemical weathering is not too prolonged, feldspar and micas will also resist chemical attack. These residual minerals are transported and deposited to form the sandstones and mud rocks (i.e. clay, mudstone and shale). The dissolved material is transported to the sea, and may eventually contribute to the formation of limestones, or of minerals formed by the evaporation of sea water, such as gypsum (calcium sulphate – used to make plasterboard) or rock salt (sodium chloride).

You should not get the idea that only igneous rocks are subject to weathering. As you will see in the next section, metamorphic processes lead to the formation of rocks at a wide range of temperatures and pressures (encompassing, at the upper limit, those of igneous rock formation), so they, too, are vulnerable to attack by weathering when subjected to the normal temperatures and pressures at the Earth's surface. Even sedimentary rocks themselves may be subjected to fresh cycles of weathering.

Transport

It is obvious that the soluble products of chemical weathering are easily removed by rainwater and rivers. However, the residual products of chemical weathering – mineral grains and clay minerals – and the larger fragments produced by physical weathering, are also removed by flowing water, and sometimes by wind or ice. The removal of weathered material is usually referred to as *erosion*.

Transport of sedimentary material by wind and ice is not significant in Britain at the present day. However, there is evidence in the geological record to show that there have been periods of time when Britain was subjected to wind erosion in desert conditions, and scoured by glaciers and ice sheets. But as it is water movement, either in rivers or in the sea, that concerns us in Britain today, we shall concentrate on this.

The transport of rock fragments and mineral grains by water involves either the bouncing or rolling of the material along the bed of a river or the sea as *bedload*, or the transport of the material within the water itself as *suspended load*

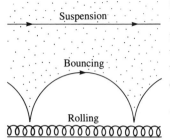

Figure 2.15

How sedimentary material is transported by water currents.

(Figure 2.15). If you take a spadeful of sediment and drop it into a moving stream, whether it is transported as bedload or suspended load depends on two factors: the size of the particles and how fast the stream is flowing. The coarser material will move as bedload, and only the finer sediment will be carried along within the water itself as suspended load. The largest fragments of all might well be deposited and remain immobile on the stream bed.

▼ If you repeated this experiment the following day when the stream was flowing much faster because of heavy rainfall overnight, would you expect the same result?

▲ In the broadest terms, yes. But now some of the coarser material previously carried as bedload will be lifted into suspension by the faster moving, higher energy water. This is important because it means that it is the *energy of the environment* that determines how a sedimentary particle is transported and, indeed, whether it is transported at all.

Water current speeds and changes in speed are largely responsible for the selective uptake and deposition of sediment grains, or the process of *sorting* a sediment, as well as whether it is coarse or fine grained. A well-sorted sediment has grains that are very similar in size whereas a poorly-sorted sediment has grains of various sizes. Coarse-grained sediments are found in high energy environments; fine-grained sediments are typical of low energy environments. There can be a good deal of variation in the type of sediment within a small area. For example, around headlands where wave action is concentrated, large pebbles and boulders are strewn on the beach, while in sheltered bays sands are deposited.

▼ Grains of silt size and below are deposited when there is almost no water movement at all. From general knowledge (and from Figure 2.2 at the beginning of this chapter), can you suggest any environment where this condition might be fulfilled?

▲ Suitable environments include lakes, river flood plains (after flooding has occurred and the river has returned to its normal channel, leaving vast pools of water on the flood plain), the parts of a river estuary or coastal mudflats that are covered by water only during the slack water at high tide, and the sea bed below the influence of normal wave and tidal action.

The sorting of sedimentary material is a progressive process. The further a mass of sedimentary material is transported, the greater is the chance that it will become separated out into fractions of different sizes. Sometimes this separation is aided actively by the way in which water moves. For example, the constant action of waves on a beach winnows out the finer sands and silts and keeps them in suspension to be deposited elsewhere where low energy conditions prevail, such as in sheltered bays or offshore.

Particles that have been picked up and transported are broken up and undergo changes in shape. It is fairly obvious that the longer particles are in motion, the more eroded they will become as edges and corners are worn away. It is perhaps less obvious that large particles are much more rapidly rounded than small ones. This is mainly because large particles have more momentum than smaller ones and can thus do more damage when they collide. The result of this is that rounded particles are more common in coarse-grained sediments deposited in a high energy environment than in fine-grained sediments deposited in a low energy environment. This is something you can confirm for yourself on a beach that has both pebbly and sandy parts. The pebbles are always smoothly rounded, but the sand grains are much more angular.

Deposition

Water

The nature of a sedimentary deposit depends upon whether the sediment is deposited directly from suspension (as is the case with very fine grains) or goes through a phase of bedload transport first (as with coarser grains). Fine grains fall out of suspension like confetti and come to rest on the bed beneath the water as very fine, flat and even layers, or *laminae*, usually only a millimetre or so in thickness. So fine-grained, laminated sediments are characteristic of suspension deposits (Figure 2.16(a)).

Coarser-grained sediments accumulate in thicker layers known as beds or *strata*. The surfaces that separate the beds are known as *bedding planes* (Figure 2.16(b)). Sediments which move in the bedload prior to final deposition do not form such neat layers. Often they are built up by the motion of the water near the bed into regularly spaced ridges and hollows, such as the ripple marks seen on beaches, and on sandbanks in estuaries at low tide. Once loose sediments have become compacted and cemented to form sedimentary rocks, ripples may be preserved. Ripples and larger sand dunes can migrate if sediment is deposited on their leeward sides. This produces *cross-bedding*, which leaves a record of past current directions. The way cross-bedding develops is shown in Figure 2.17, where the current is flowing from left to right, sweeping particles over the crest of the ripple to deposit them in the trough.

(a)

(b)

Figure 2.16 *Laminated and bedded sediments.*
(a) Alternating mud rocks and siltstones (see Table 2.1 for definition of these terms) deposited from suspension. The variation in grain size indicates slight variation in the speed of the water current from which the material was deposited. (b) Cross-bedded sandstones deposited by a relatively fast-flowing water current. The inclination of the beds indicates that the current flowed from right to left (Figure 2.17).

Figure 2.17
The formation of cross-bedding. The current is moving from left to right, moving material over the crest of the ripples (if the structures are small) or sand dune (if the structure is a metre high or larger) and depositing it on the leeward side. Eventually the material is buried by further advances of the ripple front.

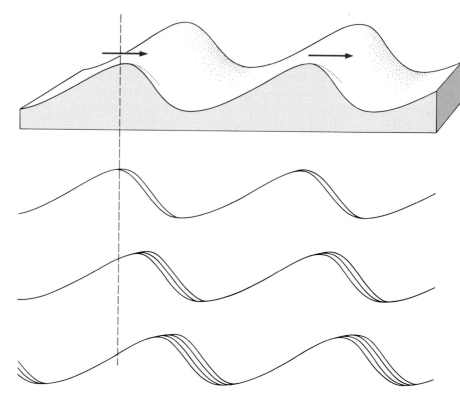

Wind

Although water is the most important medium for eroding and transporting sediments in Britain today, in other parts of the world, and at other times in Britain's geological history, wind transport was more significant.

▼ Can you think where conditions might be so dry that the wind becomes a more active transporting medium?

▲ Such conditions are found today in deserts such as the Sahara where rainfall is too low to compensate for the rate of evaporation.

Deserts do not necessarily contain vast quantities of sand, and they are not always hot (the Russian steppes, for example). In deserts, physical weathering is more important than chemical weathering because of the lack of moisture. The rate at which weathered material is removed may be high because of the lack of vegetation to help form and bind soils. Fine dust and sand are blown great distances by desert winds as bedload and suspended load. The difference from water is that moving air can only pick up a smaller range of grain sizes. You may have experienced the force of a sandstorm as the wind whips up loose sand-sized grains, but few people can testify to being the victim of a storm of pebbles!

Most transport by wind is in the form of bedload sweeping across the ground: only the finer dusts are lifted up into suspension. This usually means that after redeposition of the particles as wind speeds gradually fall, the resulting wind-blown sediments are usually very well sorted. The individual quartz grains are usually more rounded that those of water-transported sediments because the wind-blown grains collide without the cushioning effect of water, and so have their corners and edges worn down much more rapidly. The surfaces of the grains become frosted, rather like the frosted glass used in windows.

To most people, the most characteristic features of deserts are sand dunes. These produce cross-bedding on a grand scale. Ancient desert sandstones exhibiting such features are found in the Permian sandstones (about 280 million years old) in many places in England and Scotland (Figure 2.18(a)). There is a desert sandstone of this age (Specimen B) in the kit.

Figure 2.18 *(a) Cross-bedding in desert sandstones of northern England. The height of the face is about 3 m. (b)–(e) Formation of the cross-bedding. (b) Plan view of crescent-shaped sand dune with a steep face inclined in the down-wind direction. (c) Cross-section through the sand dune shown in (b) in a plane parallel to the wind direction, to show how new layers of sand are deposited on the down-wind side. (d) The three-dimensional structure of the sand layers that would accumulate if a series of dunes migrated up each other's backs (compare with (b)).*

(a)

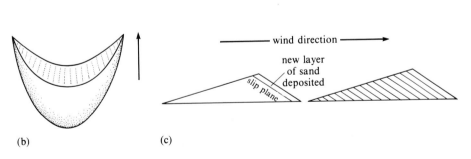

(b) (c)

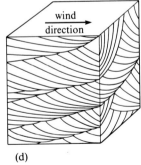

(d)

Ice

Today glaciers and ice sheets are confined to polar and high mountain regions, but although no longer active in Britain, the impact of ice on the landscape was considerable during the last 1.5 million years. During this period, there were several major advances of the polar ice sheet so that it covered much of northern Europe, including Britain (see Figure 1.4(b)). The growth and melting of ice sheets withdraws and releases large quantities of water from the oceans, causing rapid changes in sea level. The effects of this may be seen around the coastlines of Britain today in the form of raised beaches or drowned river valleys (Figure 2.19).

(a)

(b)

Figure 2.19 *Landscapes caused by changes of sea level.*
(a) The grass-covered slope behind a present-day beach in Scotland formed as a low cliff line when sea level was a few metres higher than today. The flat area to the left of the slope is an old wave-cut platform (see Figure 1.12(b)) cut when sea level was even higher.
(b) The mouth of a drowned river valley, Boscastle, Cornwall.

During the past ice ages in Britain, the main centres of ice accumulation were the mountains of Scotland, Ireland, North Wales and the Lake District. These areas have suffered heavy glacial erosion (Figure 1.4(a)), leaving jagged rocky peaks (*arêtes*), and U-shaped valleys and small mountain lakes (*tarns*) occupying hollows (*cirques* or *corries*) at the heads of valleys.

Moving ice transports anything from fine, clay-sized particles to large boulders. Some particles are picked up by the ice but larger boulders may fall from the sides of a valley on to the surface of a glacier. Such boulders sink through the ice as it melts below them. Once embedded in the ice, the fragments are not free to collide with each other and most will not be deposited until the ice melts, often many miles away from where they were picked up. Deposition takes place where debris is released from the ice, either at its contact with the underlying rocks or where it terminates. The most common sediment 'dumped' by glaciers is called *till* or *boulder clay*. Tills are virtually unsorted and consist of an unlayered mixture of grain sizes from clay particles to large boulders, depending on whatever the ice picked up on route (Figure 2.20). Many of the rock fragments may be angular and are relatively unmodified by physical or chemical action during transport.

Tills form thick featureless sheets blanketing pre-existing landscapes, but in some areas may have been moulded by the ice into clusters of small, low, elliptical mounds or *drumlins* (Figure 2.21).

Figure 2.20 *An exposure of boulder clay or till, showing a wide range of sizes of pebbles 'floating' in clay.*

(a)

(b)

Figure 2.21 *Drumlins. (a) A swarm of drumlins in Langstrothdale, Yorkshire. These features were moulded in boulder clay beneath a retreating ice sheet (Figure 2.22(b)). The elongated shape and gentler upstream slopes of the drumlins show that the ice was flowing from left to right when they were deposited beneath it. (b) Satellite view of the Lake District and adjacent areas showing numerous drumlin fields. Note how the elongation of the drumlins indicates the trend of the movement of the ice beneath which they were deposited.*

The meltwater streams that flow down crevasses in the ice sheets erode out tunnels in or at the base of the ice, from which streams eventually emerge at the ice front. Coarse sands and gravels are deposited on the floors of these tunnels when the flow slackens. When the ice finally melts these deposits are preserved as long, sinuous ridges called *eskers* (Figure 2.22(a)). Gravels from these eskers are frequently quarried as an economic resource, sometimes resulting in a conflict between extraction and conservation.

Other gravelly deposits may be deposited at the ice front and are known as *outwash fans*, which may build up as a series of terraces over a period of time. Deposits of gravel, originally formed on top of the ice surface, are dumped as ridges or small hills known as *kames*. These gravel terraces may be left along the sides of valleys where ice once stood, such as the Achnasheen Terraces in Scotland illustrated in Chapter 1 (Figure 1.5).

2.7 Metamorphic rocks and processes

Metamorphic rocks are those that have been formed by alteration and recrystallization, without melting, of pre-existing rocks. The firing of bricks and pottery from clay is analogous to metamorphism, although it only involves heat. In fact metamorphism may be the result of an increase in temperature or pressure, or a combination of the two. An increase in pressure results from the thickening of the Earth's crust during mountain building (see Section 2.10). Deep burial is also accompanied by an increase in temperature. However, an increase in temperature may also be related to the intrusion of hot magma into surrounding cooler rocks, but in this case the pressures usually remain relatively low.

The rock types that form as a result of metamorphism depend on the composition of the original rock before it was altered and on the conditions of temperature and pressure at the time of metamorphism. Metamorphic rocks are classified on the basis of their texture as well as any obvious minerals that may be present. As many metamorphic rocks were formed by squeezing under pressure as well as high temperature, during recrystallization the minerals that form often grew more or less parallel to one another (Figure 2.23).

▼ Examine Specimen I (slate). Ignoring the yellow crystals of pyrite, what is the grain size of this rock?

▲ It is very fine grained: the grains may even be too small to see with the hand lens.

The specimen has a characteristic tabular appearance because it has been split along the direction of alignment of its constituent minerals. This should be more obvious if you turn the sample sideways on. It does not need too much imagination to conclude that this rock probably formed by the metamorphism of a fine-grained sedimentary rock, such as a shale or a mudstone. Since it is still very fine grained, it has not been subjected to very high temperatures and/or pressures.

▼ Examine Specimen J. How would you describe its texture? What is the main dark-coloured mineral in this sample?

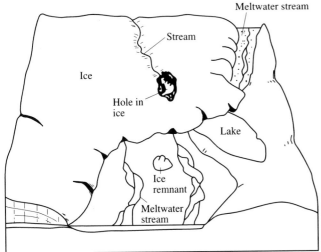

(a)

Figure 2.22 *Features of glacial deposition.*
(a) An esker, Kildremmie, Highland Region.
(b) The various features, including an esker, that form beneath and at the edge of an ice sheet.

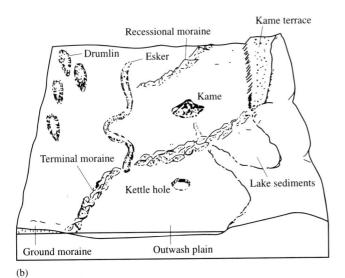

(b)

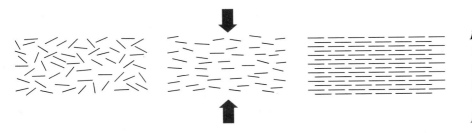

Figure 2.23
The development of mineral alignment as a result of recrystallization in the solid state under pressure.

71

▲ Specimen J is a coarse-grained rock. From the characteristic flaky appearance of the dark mineral you should be able to identify it as mica. You may also be able to see quite coarse crystals of grey or white glassy quartz. The parallel alignment of the mica flakes is characteristic of a *schist*.

Metamorphic rocks may be further classified in terms of the main minerals that may be visible in the sample. Thus one often finds references to quartz–mica schist, garnet–mica schist, and so on. The actual minerals present depend upon the composition of the original rock before metamorphism.

The ultimate stage in the metamorphic process only occurs under extreme conditions and may actually result in partial melting of the rock. Once a rock has *completely* melted, however, it forms a magma and on cooling this will crystallize out in the conventional way to give the crystalline texture of an igneous rock.

There are a few rocks, however, in which no new minerals are formed by metamorphism. These are the rocks made entirely of quartz (quartz sandstones) or calcite (pure limestones). Upon metamorphism, these minerals simply recrystallize and grow with a random orientation, without developing any alignment. Quartz sandstones become metamorphic *quartzites* and pure limestones become metamorphic *marbles*. You should be able to identify a marble in the kit by doing the 'acid test' that you have already applied to the limestone specimen. Specimen K is a marble – it will fizz if you drop vinegar on it. Ignore the shape of the sample, since it has been artificially cut this way. Examine its texture with the hand lens. It is finely crystalline and the crystals have a random orientation, formed by the recrystallization of calcite during the metamorphism of a pure limestone. You may be more familiar with the marvellously patterned, coloured marbles that are used for ornamental purposes. Such colours, patterns and streaks are simply the result of impurities in the original limestone.

Most of the metamorphic rocks described are the result of recrystallization due to increased pressure and temperature. However, if temperature alone is increased, as in the case of rocks intruded by a large body of molten magma, then a different type of metamorphic texture will result. As you can imagine, when hot magma is intruded into colder rocks, particularly sediments, the magma is chilled rapidly around the edges, giving a very fine-grained igneous rock, while the surrounding rocks are heated and 'baked'. This gives a characteristic hard, splintery rock. This is comparable to the way in which soft clay is transformed into brittle pottery when fired in a kiln. In the 'baking' process, new minerals may develop by recrystallization at random throughout the rock, giving it a characteristic spotted appearance.

Box 2.1 Rocks: a summary

By now you should be able to recall the key points about rocks that are summarized below, and begin to apply this knowledge by describing and attempting to identify rock samples you may encounter in future. In addition, you should be able to begin to interpret the processes that contributed to the formation of any rocks you examine.

◆ Texture is a term used to describe the size, shape and relationships between minerals or particles within rocks.

◆ Rocks are divided into two major groups on the basis of their texture: crystalline and fragmental.

◆ Crystalline rocks are composed of an interlocking mosaic of crystals.

◆ Fragmental rocks consist of crystals or fragments of other rocks that have been rounded to varying degrees by abrasion during transport by water and wind.

◆ Crystalline rocks may be of igneous or metamorphic origin.

◆ Igneous rocks formed from the cooling of magma. The grain size of igneous rocks is related to the rate at which they cooled: rapid cooling produces fine-grained rocks, and slow cooling produces coarse-grained rocks.

◆ Extrusive igneous rocks formed when magma cooled rapidly at the Earth's surface. Intrusive rocks were formed when magma was injected into pre-existing rocks. Intrusions may form sills (horizontal sheets), dykes (vertical sheets) or plugs (cylindrical) at relative shallow depths, and at great depths, large masses of magma cool to form batholiths.

◆ Metamorphic rocks form by the alteration of pre-existing rocks (igneous, metamorphic or sedimentary) caused by high pressures and/or temperatures.

2.8 The rock cycle

So far we have considered igneous, sedimentary and metamorphic rocks in separate compartments, but the processes that form them are linked together. These processes operate both within the Earth's crust and at its surface. This was recognized over two centuries ago by the pioneering Scottish geologist, James Hutton. In a book published in 1785 called, rather immodestly, *The Theory of the Earth with Proof and Illustrations*, he described what we now term the rock cycle. He showed how:

◆ igneous rocks may be eroded to form sediments by weathering and erosion;

◆ the sediments may become compacted into rocks;

◆ a later mountain-building event may then expose these sedimentary rocks at the Earth's surface, where they may be eroded away, thus forming a fresh generation of sediments.

The parts of the cycle are illustrated in Figure 2.24.

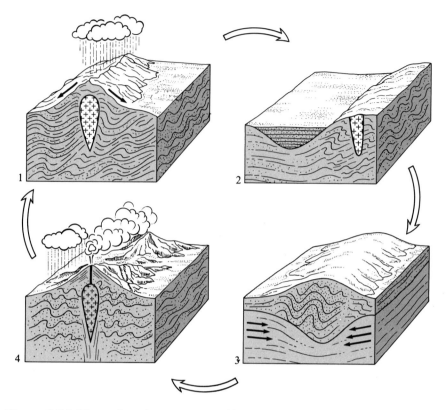

Figure 2.24 *The rock cycle, as envisaged by Hutton. Existing rocks are (1) eroded; (2) deposited to form sediments; (3) thrown up by Earth movements into a mountain belt; (4) subjected to igneous and metamorphic processes, and then eroded once more.*

In Hutton's day, many people believed that the Earth was only a few thousand years old. His work dealt a blow to the religious ideas of great catastrophes as an explanation of Earth history. Hutton's discoveries contributed greatly to the recognition that the Earth was immeasurably old, with '… no vestige of a beginning, no prospect of an end'.

If you find it difficult to understand this concept of cycles, consider one that affects our everyday lives: the water cycle. In this cycle water in the form of rain, hail or snow that falls on land is carried to the sea in rivers, and then evaporates, condenses, and falls again. This is illustrated in Figure 2.25.

▼   A cycle of any kind requires an energy source to drive it. What energy source drives the water cycle?

▲   The energy source driving the water cycle is the heat of the sun.

Because it drives the water cycle, solar heat helps drive the rock cycle. This is because moving water plays a major part in the formation of sedimentary rocks. Equally important, however, is the Earth's internal heat, which is responsible for driving movements in the Earth's crust, including the formation of mountain belts.

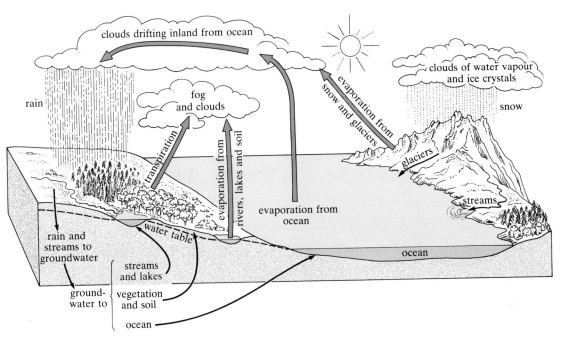

Figure 2.25 *The water cycle. Movement of water into the atmosphere by evaporation, mainly from the oceans, is matched by precipitation as rain and snow.*

Figure 2.26 is a more detailed summary of the rock cycle than that shown in Figure 2.24. It shows how the water cycle is linked to the weathering, erosion, transport and deposition of sediments and how, on burial, these become sedimentary rocks, and in some cases are transformed into metamorphic rocks. This diagram also shows what is termed the tectonic cycle – the process by which rocks are buckled and fractured, and by which huge masses of rock are moved to different depths within the Earth's crust. The processes that lead to the buckling and fracturing of rocks are outlined in Section 2.9.

2.9 Tectonic processes: folding and faulting

Introduction

Tectonic processes are concerned with the mechanical deformation of rocks. The word 'tectonic' is derived from the Greek word for builder. It is used to describe the mechanical processes which deform rocks. Almost all rocks are deformed in some way, although this may not always be obvious. As soon as one layer of sediment is deposited on top of another, the lower layer will be squashed and compacted. Sometimes it is reduced by as much as 80% of its original thickness. When sedimentary rocks are subjected to sideways compression they may crumple to form folds.

When sediments are deposited, they build up in distinct layers that are generally horizontal in the first instance (Figure 2.27), with the oldest deposits at the bottom and the youngest at the top. Frequently however, beds are tilted (as at Tedbury Camp Quarry, see Chapter 1), folded or faulted.

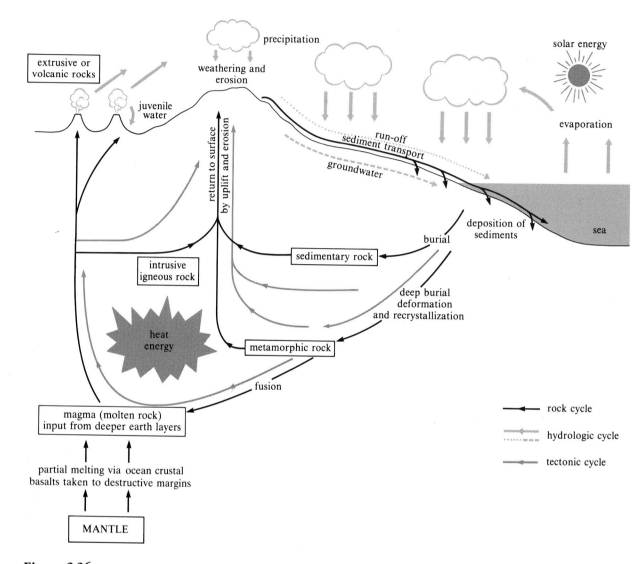

Figure 2.26

A diagramatic summary of the rock cycle, showing the roles of igneous, sedimentary and metamorphic processes.

If rocks are stretched (extended) or squeezed (compressed), they are deformed in different ways. Several factors control the way in which the rock will be deformed:

◆ the nature of the rock itself (for example, a clay will deform easily, but a granite will not);

◆ the temperature of the rock;

◆ the time over which extensional and compressional forces are applied.

It is common sense to think that if a rock specimen is stretched or extended, it will eventually break cleanly apart. Under compression, the rock may be ruptured, though not with a clean, smooth fracture (Figure 2.28(a)). When rocks respond to deformation by snapping or rupturing, this behaviour is known, not surprisingly, as *brittle deformation*. At low temperatures, rocks usually behave in this way. At higher temperatures, however, rocks behave rather differently. Under tension,

Figure 2.27
A cliff exposing a series of horizontally bedded strata.

low temperatures   high temperatures

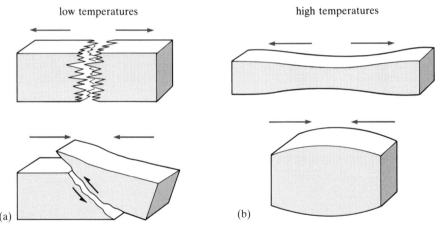

(a)   (b)

Figure 2.28
The deformation of rocks. (a) At low temperatures a rock specimen subjected to tension will snap; under compression it will rupture along an inclined failure surface. (b) At high temperatures the same specimen is more likely to stretch under tension, or bulge under compression.

they will tend to stretch and become thinner rather than snapping apart, whereas under compression they will not rupture, but will merely bulge outwards like a beer barrel (Figure 2.28(b)). This is called *plastic deformation*, and a temperature of over 100 °C is usually required to bring it about. The higher the temperature, the more easily the rock is deformed plastically.

Structures produced under tension

Structures produced under tension are perhaps the simplest and most widespread rock structures. After solidification from magma, igneous rock continues to cool. As it does so it shrinks slightly, and this causes tensional stresses which produce a well-defined pattern of polygonal fractures known as *joints* (Figure 2.7(a), page 54).

Figure 2.29 Joints in limestone. This photograph (taken in the Isle of Purbeck in Dorset) shows how the limestone was quarried for building stone by taking advantage of the horizontal bedding and the vertical joint patterns within the rock. The cave mouth is about 2 m high.

Joints are simply cracks in the rock where it has split or fractured w*ithout* any movement taking place *along* the crack. They are extremely common in all kinds of rock, and can be seen in almost any outcrop. Joints form even in apparently undeformed sedimentary rocks (Figure 2.29), and indicate that they have in the past been subjected to slight tension on a regional scale.

Faults are planar fractures running through rocks where, unlike joints, movement has taken place along the fracture plane, causing a relative offset between features on different sides of the fault. By far the most common faults are those called *normal faults*, where the rock on one side of the fault has simply dropped down relative to that on the other side (Figure 2.30).

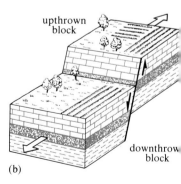

upthrown block

downthrow block

(a)

(b)

Figure 2.30 Normal faults. (a) A typical small-scale normal fault in layered sedimentary rock. The fault is in the centre of the photograph and runs from top left to bottom right. The rocks on the right hand side of the fault have moved down relative to those on the left of the fault, by a distance of about the length of the geological hammer, say 30–50 cm. (b) A block model showing the formation of a normal fault. Compare this with the fault in (a).

▼ Are faults of the type shown in Figure 2.30 formed in rocks under tension or under compression?

▲ Normal faults form under tension.

Structures produced under compression

When rocks are squeezed hard, especially at low temperatures, they rupture. High-angle compressional structures are known as *reverse faults* (Figure 2.31(a) and (b)). A *thrust* is produced when a large mass of rock breaks along a gently inclined plane and the upper block overrides the lower one (Figure 2.31(c)). Some of these moving blocks may be huge (of the order of kilometres), and cases are known of thrust blocks moving for tens and even hundreds of kilometres.

(a)

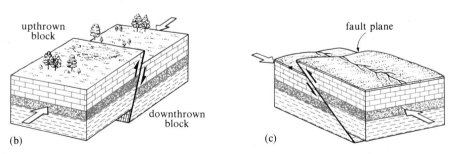

(b) (c)

Figure 2.31 *Reverse faults. (a) A typical small-scale reverse fault. The rocks on the left-hand side of the fault have moved* up *over those on the right of the fault. (b) Block model showing the formation of a reverse fault. Compare this with the fault shown in (a). (c) Block model of a thrust fault, where the angle that the fault plane makes with the horizontal is much lower than for the reverse fault in (a) and (b).*

When rocks are subjected to compression at higher temperatures over long periods, they will not fracture but *fold* instead. This is particularly evident when layered sedimentary rocks are involved. The overall shortening of the layers accommodates the compressive stress. Many kilometres of shortening can be seen in mountain chains such as the Alps and, on a smaller but still impressive scale, in many British sea cliffs (Figure 2.32).

Figure 2.32 *Folding at Stair Hole, west of Lulworth Cove in Dorset.*

2.10 The Earth as a machine

Study comment

Now that you have been introduced to a variety of Earth materials (minerals and rocks) and processes, you are equipped to consider how they, and the landscapes sculptured from them, are made. As you will see, the Earth is far from static: it is a machine, driven by internal and external sources of heat, that is continually processing rock material. This section starts with a brief description of the gross structure of the Earth, and poses the question 'why are there continents?' This leads to a consideration of how the Earth's outer layer, the crust, behaves, and how the processes you have studied in previous sections relate to this behaviour.

Earth structure

In order to understand some of the ideas introduced in this section you need to be aware of the meaning of the terms used to describe the internal structure of the Earth. This structure has not been directly observed, but is a *model* based on observations concerning the way in which earthquake waves travel through our planet (a subject beyond the scope of this book).

Figure 2.33(a) shows that the Earth has a concentrically layered structure consisting of an upper *crust*, a middle *mantle* and a central *core*. So the Earth is rather like a spherical avocado pear. The thin green skin represents the crust, the yellow flesh the mantle, and the hard stone at the centre the core. In this section we are concerned with the crust, which is the very thin outer skin (seldom thicker than 60 km). Imagine a scale model of the Earth in which its 6370 km radius is scaled down to a half-metre diameter beach ball. On this scale, even the deepest mines and boreholes have not penetrated the plastic to let the air out! But as we

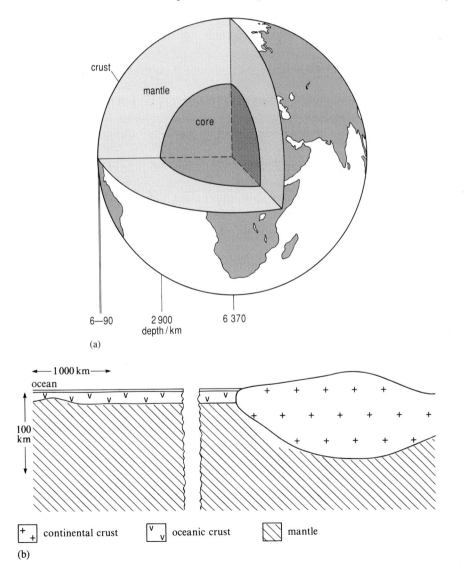

Figure 2.33
The structure of the Earth. (a) Diagrammatic section through the Earth showing the core, mantle and crust. The crust is too thin to show to scale on this diagram; variations in its thickness are depicted in (b). (b) Generalized section through the Earth's crust showing variations in thickness of continental and ocean crust. Oceanic crust is between 2.8 and 2.9 times as dense as water and has a chemical and mineral composition similar to basalt and gabbro; continental crust is less dense (2.6–2.8 times as dense as water) with a composition similar to granite.

81

shall see, much has been discovered about the workings of this outer skin. In Figure 2.33(b) the crust can be seen to be thinner under the oceans and thicker under the continents – especially under mountain ranges. The base of the crust is marked by the Mohorovicic (generally known as the Moho) discontinuity, detected by earthquake studies.

▼ Why are there continents?

▲ You might expect the concentric pattern for the whole Earth to continue into the detailed structure of the Earth's outer skin. But this skin, consisting of gabbroic and granitic material, and covered by the oceans and gaseous atmosphere, does not show a regular layered structure (Figure 2.33(b)). We find that the less dense granitic material is dotted about the Earth's surface in slabs of irregular thickness with water occupying the hollows in between, instead of being spread uniformly over the globe as a single, shoreless ocean (Figure 2.34). This irregular distribution of crustal materials implies that something must have separated the lighter continental crust into slabs at some stage during the Earth's history.

We know that continents were formed very early during the Earth's history. The Earth is considered to have formed approximately 4500 million years ago and the oldest rocks found on the continents have been dated at 3800 million years. So it seems that continental crust has existed for a vast period of time. The present volume of land above sea level is about 130 million cubic kilometres, and it is estimated that 13.6 cubic kilometres of rock material are removed from the land to the oceans every year by erosion (Figure 2.2). If this were the only geological process operating on the continents, how long would they last? If the erosion continued at the same rate until they were planed flat, the continents would be covered by the sea in slightly less than 10 million years – yet they have lasted thousands of millions of years (over two orders of magnitude longer than the estimate suggests). In reality, erosion would not continue at the same rate but would slow down because as irregularities in the surface (called the 'relief') of the continents were diminished, rivers would flow more slowly, and so carry less material. Nevertheless, if erosion continued – albeit at a diminishing rate – other processes must have operated to maintain the relief of the continents through the vast span of the Earth's history.

Figure 2.34 When the structure of the outer 'skin' of the Earth is examined, the idea of a model consisting of concentric shells breaks down. Instead of granitic and gabbroic crust and the overlying ocean forming successive shells of uniform thickness (b), the base of the crust mirrors, in an exaggerated way, the surface relief of the Earth (a).

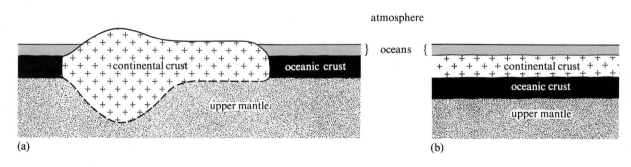

The discussion in the previous two paragraphs provides a brief glimpse of the problems posed by the nature and distribution of the features of the Earth's solid surface. It is clear that the processes that drive the rock cycle have operated, and still are operating, to maintain the relief of the continental crust. This is in marked contrast to the situation on the Earth's nearest neighbour, the Moon (Figure 2.35). The lunar surface not only looks different from that of our home planet, but is dominated by immensely old rocks – older than 3000 million years. The Moon's surface has altered little in this vast period since the rocks were formed, whereas the Earth's outer skin has been reworked by geological processes time and time again so that over three-quarters of its surface is less than 200 million years old. You have already met all these processes except that which causes major movements of the crust – plate tectonics.

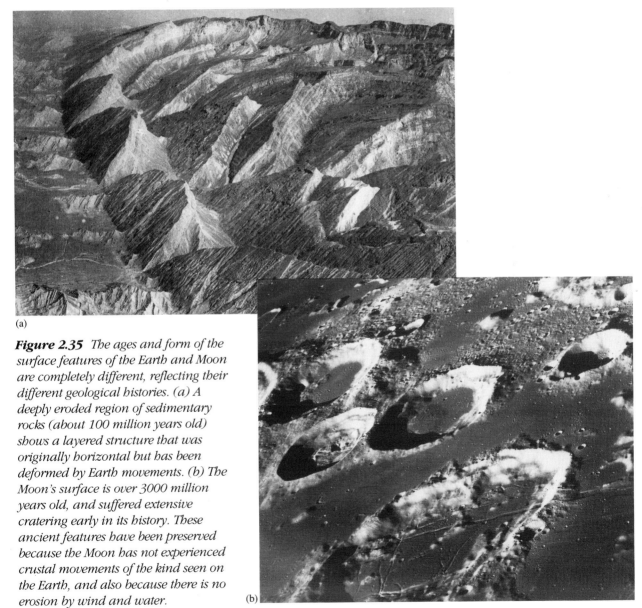

(a)

(b)

Figure 2.35 *The ages and form of the surface features of the Earth and Moon are completely different, reflecting their different geological histories. (a) A deeply eroded region of sedimentary rocks (about 100 million years old) shows a layered structure that was originally horizontal but has been deformed by Earth movements. (b) The Moon's surface is over 3000 million years old, and suffered extensive cratering early in its history. These ancient features have been preserved because the Moon has not experienced crustal movements of the kind seen on the Earth, and also because there is no erosion by wind and water.*

The crust in motion: plate tectonics

The Earth's crust varies in thickness, being thinner under the oceans and thicker under the continents, especially under mountain ranges (Figure 2.33(b)). Continental crust is less heavy and dense than ocean crust and much less dense than the mantle beneath it. As such, continental crust tends to 'float' on top of the mantle, rather like a piece of wood floating in water or an iceberg in the sea.

One piece of evidence that supports the idea that the crust 'floats' on the mantle is the observation that parts of Britain and Scandinavia are rising by small amounts each year (Figure 2.36(b)). This is because in the relatively recent past (in the geological sense) both areas were covered in thick ice sheets several kilometres thick. When these existed, the weight of them depressed the crust, just as it does in Greenland and Antarctica today (Figure 2.36(a)). After the ice sheets melt, the

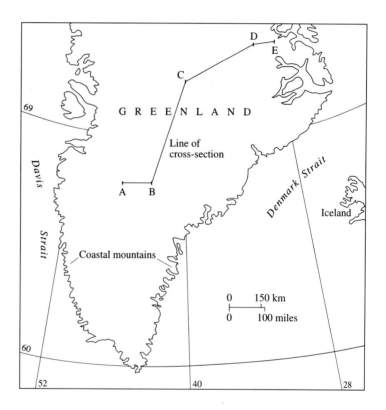

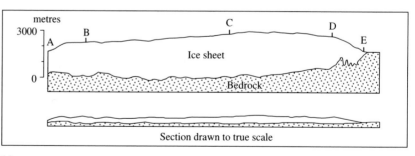

Figure 2.36 *Ice sheets and crustal rebound. (a) Cross-section across Greenland showing how the crust has been depressed into a saucer-shaped depression.*

(a)

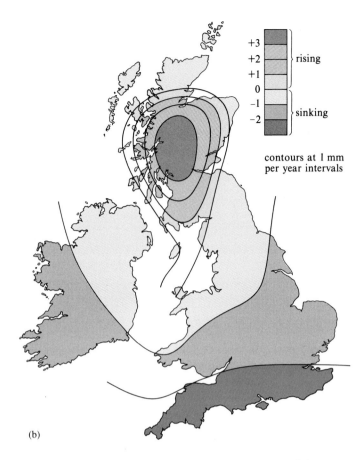

Figure 2.36 (b) The current rate of rise and fall of the crust around the British Isles caused by the removal of the thick ice sheet that capped the northern areas 100 000 years ago.

crust slowly rebounds. This is similar to what happens if you place a weight on a wood block floating in water, and then remove it.

We now know from a variety of lines of evidence (including, recently, by direct measurement from satellites) that horizontal movements occur in the Earth's crust. Discussing the evidence is beyond the scope of this book, but you should be aware in broad terms of the nature of the model Earth scientists have devised to explain the workings of the crust. Put simply, the crust consists of a series of slabs or *tectonic plates*, each moving in a different direction. Where they collide or move apart, there are zones of geological activity, but there is virtually no activity away from the boundaries between the plates.

▼ What form do you think this activity takes?

▲ Volcanoes and earthquakes mark the boundaries of the moving plates.

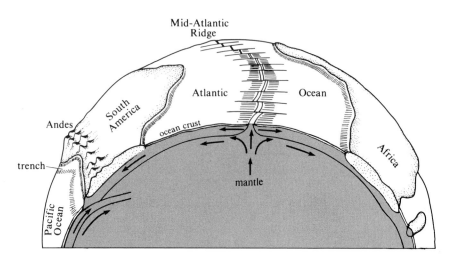

Figure 2.37 *The relationships of three crustal plates in the Earth's southern hemisphere. The thickness of the crustal layers is not to scale.*

Figure 2.37 shows plate boundaries associated with South America and Africa, two continents which are moving slowly apart at about four centimetres per year. This is twice the rate that our fingernails grow. This means that the South Atlantic is getting wider. In fact, new oceanic crust is being formed along the Mid-Atlantic Ridge as basaltic magma wells up from the mantle to form both intrusive and extrusive igneous rocks. The ridge is associated with a narrow zone of shallow earthquakes.

To the west of South America, the Pacific oceanic crust is moving eastwards, and diving down beneath the continental crust. As it does so, it enters hotter regions, and begins to melt. The resultant magma rises upwards, melting some of the continental crust on its way to produce granites. Some of the magmas, which are very viscous, do reach the surface and cause explosive volcanic activity. This plate collision zone is also characterized by an inclined zone of earthquakes plunging beneath the Andes, and by ocean trenches.

Figure 2.38 shows the distribution of the crustal plates around the world. Most of the plate boundaries shown on this map fall into two categories, constructive and destructive, but there is a third type termed a conservative plate boundary. The main features of the three types of plate boundary are as follows.

◆ *Constructive plate boundaries*: where basaltic magma (cf. Specimen H, basalt, and Specimen G, gabbro) rises from the mantle to form ocean ridges such as that running down the middle of the Atlantic. They are also characterized by shallow earthquakes (down to 5 km depth).

◆ *Destructive plate boundaries*: where oceanic crust plunges beneath continental crust. This process is called *subduction*: it is associated with deep ocean trenches and an inclined zone of earthquakes down to depths of several hundred kilometres. Subduction results in the melting of crustal material to produce viscous magmas which cause explosive volcanic activity. Destructive plate boundaries occur where two slabs of continental crust collide (such as the

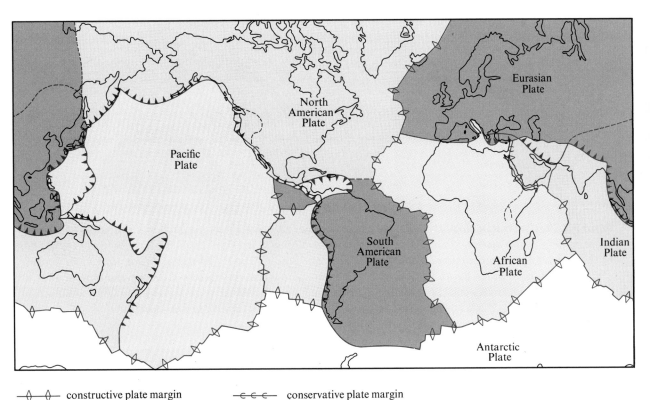

—◇—◇— constructive plate margin	—c—c—c— conservative plate margin
—▲—▲—▲— destructive plate margin	- - - - - - - plate boundary uncertain

Figure 2.38 *The distribution of crustal plates and the earthquake activity at their boundaries. All the plate boundaries are regions of shallow earthquakes: deeper-focus earthquake zones mark the sites of destructive plate boundaries. The rates at which ocean crust is forming at constructive plate boundaries are shown schematically by the width between the parallel lines used to show them. The directions of plate movement are shown by arrows, the lengths of which are proportional to the rate of movement: the shorter the arrow, the slower the plate is moving.*

Himalayas). Most of the Pacific Ocean is ringed by destructive plate margins; on its western side many such margins are marked by ocean trenches and associated volcanic islands arranged in an arc-like plattern, such as the Japanese islands.

◆ *Conservative plate boundaries*: where plates slide past each other, causing shallow earthquakes (the best known example is the San Andreas Fault in California).

What causes the movement of crustal plates? Basically, plate movement is the mechanism by which the Earth loses its internal heat generated by the breakdown of radioactive elements present in the crust and mantle. The internal heat drives a series of convection currents in the mantle which in turn drive plate movement (Figure 2.39), although the exact linkage between the currents and the plates is not clear. Are they pushed apart along constructive boundaries, or pulled down along destructive boundaries? As yet there is no consensus among Earth scientists.

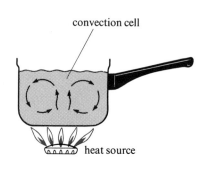

(a)

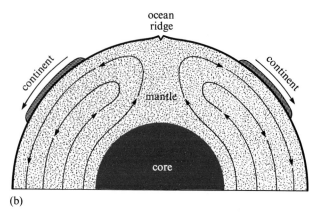

(b)

Figure 2.39 *Convection currents and plate movement. (a) An analogy: in the kitchen a saucepan of soup or jam simmers, and a system of convection currents is established. Heat from the hob enters the system at the base of the pan, and is carried upward by the less dense, hotter liquid. Heat is lost at the surface, and so the cooler, denser liquid sinks. In the Earth, the heat source is from radioactive materials in the crust and mantle. (b) Convection currents in the mantle: their rising limbs are postulated to occur under ocean ridges (constructive plate margins) and the descending part beneath the ocean trenches (destructive margins).*

Plate tectonics is the driving force behind the rock cycle. The formation of new oceans and their subsequent closure produces a variety of rock types and structures that enable past plate tectonic processes to be interpreted from the rock record. At destructive plate margins, sedimentary rocks are folded, thrusted, and deeply buried, leading to metamorphism. Igneous processes along such margins result in the formation of huge masses of intrusive igneous rocks above which explosive volcanoes occur. All these processes result in the thickening of the crust, which then rides higher on the underlying mantle to produce mountain belts. Such uplift increases rates of erosion, and sediments accumulate on the margins of the newly deformed continental crust.

The rock record of the British Isles reveals that two episodes of ocean opening and subsequent closing occurred before the present-day Atlantic Ocean began to open; these are discussed in Chapter 4. But at this point an important indicator of past episodes of plate collision, not described earlier in this chapter, needs to be explained. This feature is an *unconformity*, an example of which was illustrated in Chapter 1 at Tedbury Camp Quarry (Figure 1.12(a)). Figure 2.40 shows, in cross-section, an idealized sequence of events in a cycle of ocean opening and closing, culminating in mountain building. As the mountain belt is uplifted it is eroded, and sediments derived from it are deposited in neighbouring lowland areas, or in new oceans formed nearby if the continental crust splits up once more. As the mountains are lowered by erosion, they become partly covered by sedimentary rocks which overly the older deformed rocks with an angular discordance, producing a major unconformity. The unconformity surface may represent a major 'time gap' of tens of millions of years (as at Tedbury). Thus major unconformities are an indication of mountain building, or rather the end of it (Figure 2.41).

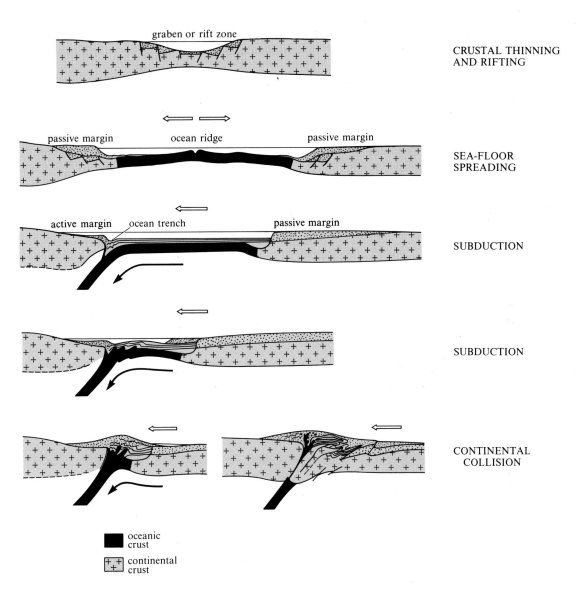

Figure 2.40 *Sequence of events in a cycle of ocean opening and closing, culminating in continental collision. It is possible for both margins of an ocean to be subjected to subduction, although this is not shown here.*

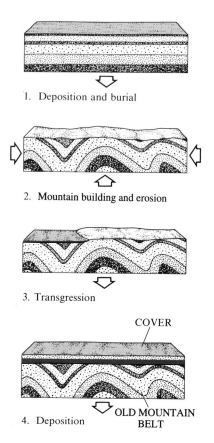

1. Deposition and burial

2. Mountain building and erosion

3. Transgression

COVER

4. Deposition OLD MOUNTAIN BELT

Figure 2.41 *The development of a major unconformity. After deformation of earlier successions of strata by mountain building, erosion and flooding by the sea may occur. Major unconformities often mark the end of one plate tectonic cycle that culminates in both continental collision and mountain building (see Figure 2.40).*

Now that you have been introduced to some of the basic geological vocabulary and concepts, we can proceed to show how this knowledge can be applied in the field when examining exposures (Chapter 3) and how field and other types of observations can be integrated to unravel the geological history of the British Isles (Chapter 4).

Chapter 3

FIELDWORK: LOOKING AT SITES

Study comment

The assumption made in this chapter is that the sum total of your geological training is contained in Chapters 1 and 2 of this book. So if you have experience of geological fieldwork, you may prefer to scan the chapter for information on the conservation interest and issues at the two localities to be explored. This information can be found in appropriately headed sections.

Two 'armchair fieldtrips' are presented in order to give you a feel for the scope of observations that can be made in the field, and how they can be used to interpret events in the geological history of the areas visited.

3.1 Introduction

Chapter 2 discussed how rocks, sediments and landforms evolve and what they look like. However, Earth heritage conservation is essentially about fieldwork, since the purpose is to conserve sites for research, education (in its broadest sense) and public enjoyment. So the next step is to go out into the field to see what Earth scientists actually do when faced with a cliff, quarry, road cutting or geomorphologically interesting landscape. The way we will approach this task is through two contrasting fieldwork simulations which should give you confidence to do some real fieldwork.

You will be equipped with:

◆ some essential terminology in the form of a glossary;

◆ colour photographs (in the colour plate booklet) of localities which are both case study sites from Chapter 1;

◆ background information about the geological interest of each site;

◆ additional illustrations of the sites in the text.

Your aim in each simulated excursion is to end up with a systematic description of site geology which is sufficient on the one hand to give you an understanding of the importance and interest of the site, and on the other to serve the purposes of conservation. In doing this you will be achieving something equally important – a generalized understanding of the mental processes and physical activities appropriate to this kind of fieldwork.

When you have studied this chapter, you should know how to:

◆ produce a useful sketch of a site;

◆ differentiate between different rock units using simple criteria;

◆ understand and apply some of the basic concepts of stratigraphy;

- understand and correctly use the terms bed, bedding plane, joint, fault, dip, unconformity, intrusion, phenocryst, groundmass;
- measure the thickness of beds and record vertical changes in a sedimentary sequence;
- describe and sketch individual features such as cross-bedding;
- make simple interpretations of the geological history of a site;
- follow safety procedures;
- identify some conservation problems and solutions.

You will probably be pleasantly surprised at how much you can achieve in the way of 'fieldwork' through this paper exercise, but bear in mind the old saying that 'the best geologists have seen the most rocks'. When you find yourself in the field for real there will be many features which you will have to rely on a trained geologist to interpret. However, what we hope you will have after working through this chapter is a good understanding of procedures – the rest is a matter of experience and continuing interest.

The fieldwork sites were introduced in Part 1. They are:

- a quarry in sedimentary rocks: Tedbury Camp Quarry;
- an upland outcrop in hard rock: Shap Quarry.

Each simulation will follow more or less the same pattern.

1 A brief introduction detailing general geological information which you will read about before the site visit.
2 An exploration of the features which should be included in a sketch of the whole site, using the colour photographs provided.
3 Step-by-step investigation of rock types, mineralogy or sediments using photographs and diagrams to provide a more detailed view.
4 The production of field sketches and notes which you make for yourself.
5 An interpretation of the site based on your own observations in the form of a brief geological history.
6 A summary of conservation interest and issues.
7 A view of investigative procedures, data recording, equipment and safety awareness.

3.2 Making a start

Good field notes and sketches should be usable by anyone else who wants to visit a site subsequently, so clarity and precision are very important (see Box 3.1). They are the raw data for the designation of RIGS (Regionally Important Geological/geomorphological Sites) which, apart from statutorily designated Sites of Special Scientific Interest (SSSIs), are the main vehicle for ensuring conservation and the continuing development knowledge of our geological heritage. You will find more about the nature of such sites in Part 3.

Box 3.1   Making notes in the field

One of the most important aspects of fieldwork is observation, and recording as much of what you see as possible so that you can refer to it later. This is more important than trying to suggest complicated interpretations of what you see. Beware of jumping to conclusions too soon.

Taking notes

To obtain the maximum benefit from fieldwork you have to take accurate notes in the field. This is essential whether you are an experienced geologist or a beginner. Good field notes provide a store of information on which you can draw. We suggest you adopt a standard format for your notetaking: it is even worth learning the list of data you should record at each locality, because, for the beginner, this is the only way of making sure that you do not forget to record anything. Note that all features may not be relevant to every locality, but they are included here for completeness. Each day start by noting the date and general area to be visited. Then at each locality record the information indicated in Table 3.1 overleaf.

Obviously this list is predominantly for sedimentary rocks, but you will find that much of it also applies to igneous rocks. It may help to make a list of the main points to record at each locality in the back or front of your field notebook, as a check for each outcrop.

Making field sketches

Field sketches always form an important part of any field notes. The best field sketches are not perfect artistic drawings. The idea is that they should show the significant large-scale geological features of an outcrop correctly.

To make best use of your sketches it may be necessary to annotate them extensively. Don't forget to include a rough scale and north point as well as to label or number any detailed notes in your field notebook. The very act of sketching (even if you are not very good at it) should make you think about interpreting the geology of the area you are examining.

Taking photographs

Remember to record the details (e.g. film number, frame number, locality, orientation of view) for each locality. Photographs are not a substitute for a field sketch.

Table 3.1 Checklist for field notes

1	Locality	Grid reference or locality name or number
2	Rock lithology	Texture (crystalline or fragmental)
		Minerals present (grain size and shapes)
		Rock identification and brief description, with sample number if taken
3	Bedding	Measure inclination (dip) of bedded sedimentary rocks
		Thinly or thickly bedded?
		Any minor features, e.g. ripples or cross-bedding?
4	Tectonic structures	Joints ⎫
		Faults ⎬ Record orientation if present
		Folds ⎪
		Cleavage ⎭
5	Fossils	Note abundance and variety of fossils and trace fossils
6	Other features	Note any obvious features, such as mineral veins and any cross-cutting relationships
7	Sketch and/or photograph	Particularly useful if a variety of rocks are present or if there are clear structures such as folds or faults; label all sketches/photographs with the locality

You will also become aware that there are simple ways of observing and recording in a systematic manner. What you have learned about the origins of rocks and how to look at rocks in hand specimens in the preceding chapter will come in very useful. However, fieldwork introduces new dimensions to your knowledge of the Earth sciences. For instance:

◆ the appearance of weathered rocks in the field can be very different to the fresh specimens in the kit;

◆ in the field you are concerned not just with individual rocks but with the way they relate to each other (see the definitions of stratigraphy, unconformity and field relations in Box 3.2);

◆ you need to identify not just a rock type but structures within it which are only observable on a scale larger than a hand specimen;

◆ at geomorphological sites you will be looking at sediments (sand, gravel, clay, etc.) and/or entire landforms rather than the underlying rocks.

One question which always arises for those going out on a first field visit is: what equipment do I need? The answer is, mainly, your eyes and a notebook and pencil. There are equipment checklists given for both excursions. But first, a word of caution. Most people's mental picture of a geologist would include a hammer – and it is true that many of us feel empty-handed without one in the field and that they are often useful and sometimes essential. However, professionals use them sparingly: only when they have to see a fresh rock surface and none is to be found, and only, of course, when they know what hammering is permitted. Finally, hammering is not a macho pursuit whatever the big guy with the beard tries to tell you! Normally it is technique rather than brute force that does the trick.

Box 3.2 Useful terms

There are a number of terms related to fieldwork which you will probably want to familiarize yourself with. The glossary below can be used for reference as you work through the rest of this chapter.

Bed (= stratum, plural strata) – the smallest unit in a sequence of sedimentary rocks, bounded by bedding planes (linear discontinuities) at its upper and lower surface (Figure 2.27). Most beds are originally laid down in a roughly horizontal position, but may be tilted by subsequent movements of the Earth's crust. The main exception is **cross-bedding**.

Body fossil – the lithified (i.e. turned into rock) remains of the hard parts of an organism or a mould of its shape. Other fossils such as leaves or even jellyfish may be preserved as surface impressions on a bedding plane.

Correlation – linking sediments of the same type and/or age in different places.

Cross-bedding – sedimentary layering within a bed which is inclined at an angle to its bedding planes; indicates sediment deposited from flowing water or moved by wind (Figure 2.16(b)).

Cross-lamination – a small-scale version of cross-bedding with individual layers only a few millimetres thick; often formed by the migration of small ripples.

Dip – the inclination, measured in degrees, of rock bedding. In many exposures apparent dip is visible in rock faces; true dip is defined as the inclination of strata measured at right angles to the direction along which the dip reading is zero (i.e. the **strike** direction).

Exposure – bedrock visible *in situ*, not as loose pebbles or boulders: for instance the walls of a road cutting, a quarry face, a rocky surface on a hillside, a coastal cliff or a rocky beach.

Fault – a more or less planar fracture or fracture zone across which Earth materials have moved up and down or sideways relative to each other (Figures 2.30 and 2.31). Displacement can be anything from centimetres up to kilometres (or tens of kilometres in the case of lateral movement). Large faults may juxtapose very different types and ages of rock. Faulting occurs in all types of rock and also, on a small scale, in unlithified sediments (i.e. those which have not been cemented together to form solid rock).

Field relations – the structural, genetic and age relationships of different rock types and units to each other.

Groundmass – see **phenocryst**.

Horizon – a usefully vague term which can be used to designate a zone (either sharply or gradationally delimited) within a larger rock unit, for example 'a pebbly horizon' within a bed or 'a biotite-rich horizon' within a unit of metamorphic rock.

Intrusion – a body of igneous rock which cuts across any other type of rock. Minor intrusions, as distinct from large intrusions many kilometres across, termed **pluton**s or batholiths, are small bodies of igneous rock such as dykes, sills and veins. Intrusions can often be dated in millions of years by analysing the amounts of radioactive elements in their constituent minerals. They can be used for relative dating: any rock they cut through must have been in existence before they formed; any overlying rock not intruded by them must postdate the activity which produced them (Figures 2.6, 2.8, 2.9).

Joint – a normally straight fracture surface in a rock formed when the body of rock was subjected to systematic stresses, often appearing on a rock face as discontinuous lines when seen in cross-section or as parallel plane surfaces (Figure 2.29). A joint set is a group of more or less parallel joints with a locally characteristic spacing of anything from a few centimetres to a few metres and a consistent **strike** and **dip**. Joints occur in all types of rock.

Outcrop – often used synonymously with **exposure**, but strictly speaking an area where rocks exist at or near the surface. The rock may be exposed or may be hidden beneath postglacial sediments, soils, vegetation or buildings.

Phenocryst – a crystal in an igneous rock which has grown much larger than the other minerals which form the remainder of the rock (known as the groundmass). For instance, we can talk of feldspar phenocrysts in a groundmass of quartz and mica (Plate 1F).

Pluton – a massive igneous intrusion which has crystallized some kilometres below the surface of the Earth (in the realm of Pluto, the god of the underworld; Figure 2.9).

Rockground – a rocky, shallow sea floor which has been encrusted and bored into by marine organisms before being preserved in the geological record.

Section – a horizontal or vertical **exposure** of part of a stratigraphic sequence.

Stratigraphic column – the depiction of geological time as a sequence (as a table or diagram) of named and dated sections, such as Table 1.1 and on the back cover. The oldest rocks are Precambrian (older than about 600 million years and stretching back to over 3000 million years); the youngest are Pleistocene (formed in the last two million years). Note particularly the Carboniferous and Jurassic Eras in the stratigraphic column on the back cover as these are the ages of the rocks exposed at the first site.

Stratigraphy – the study of strata and their correlation from place to place, leading to the interpretation of rocks as successive events in geological history.

Strike – the direction along which a bedding surface has zero **dip**, i.e. is horizontal.

Trace fossil – the traces left by the activities of an animal, for example dinosaur footprints or worm burrows.

Unconformity – a break in the stratigraphic sequence representing a (perhaps very long) period of erosion (Figures 1.12(a), 2.41). Thus rocks of very different ages and origins can be superimposed at unconformities. Exposures which demonstrate this may be on the scale of the landscape or be revealed in a small section, perhaps only a metre or two long. An angular unconformity is so called because strata dip at different angles above and below it.

3.3 Fieldwork simulation 1: Tedbury Camp Quarry

Background information

Before 'visiting' Tedbury Camp Quarry it would be useful to reread the case study in Part 1. Some additional background information is given below.

The Carboniferous and Jurassic (in fact, Middle Jurassic) rocks at Tedbury Camp Quarry are limestones formed in warm shallow seas like those forming in tropical areas today. (The ages of these periods of geological time were introduced in Chapter 1 are shown in Table 1.1 and on the back cover.) Indeed, during Carboniferous times this area of continental crust lay close to the equator. Since then, the cumulative effect of various movements of crustal plates has ensured a gradual progress to northerly latitudes. The rocks at Tedbury are also interesting because they form a *rockground* – a record of repeated colonizations during the Middle Jurassic of a rocky sea floor by numerous encrusting and boring worms, bivalve shells and other rock-encrusting organisms (Figure 3.1(b)). If you imagine an area of rocky sea floor richly populated at and just below the surface with organisms with shelly hard parts, you have the basis of a rockground.

The Carboniferous and Jurassic rocks at Tedbury Camp Quarry are separated by a clearly exposed *unconformity*, making it an excellent candidate for conservation as a Regionally Important Geological/geomorphological Site (RIGS). This site is invaluable for education purposes, acting as a window into the remote history of the east Mendips, and demonstrates fundamental geological concepts in a safe and easily accessible context.

ACTIVITY 3.1
DESCRIBE AN UNCONFORMITY

To make sure you are clear what this 'excursion' will illustrate, explain in your own words what an unconformity is.

Check your answer with the glossary description in Box 3.2.

◆ ◆ ◆

Figure 3.1

The rockground at Tedbury Camp Quarry. (a) The rockground, showing borings filled with lighter coloured sediment. (b) Above: An idealized sketch of the rocks exposed in the quarry. Below: a reconstruction of the surface of Carboniferous strata when it formed a rocky sea floor in Jurassic times. The organisms shown are: A bivalve shell that bores into hard rock; B encrusting oyster, cemented to the rockground; C boring tube worms; D marine snail; E sea lilies (crinoids); F colonial corals; G brachiopods (two-shelled organisms fixed to the rockground by a tubular ligament); H belemnite (extinct relative of squids).

(a)

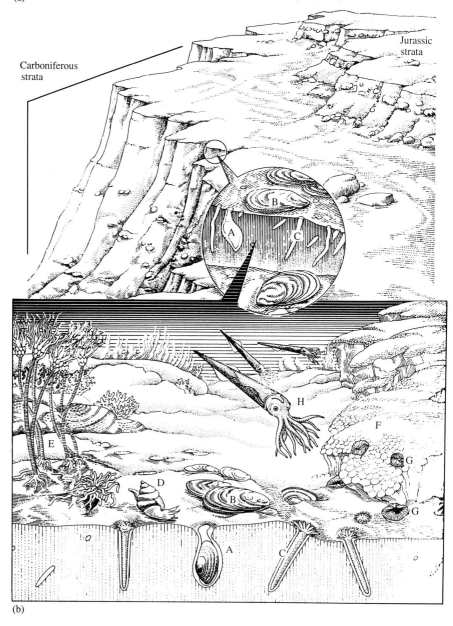

(b)

In the field

The equipment needed for a real field trip is reviewed later. The list below refers to the simulation exercise:

◆ colour photographs (Plate 5);

◆ notebook (A5 is a convenient size for outdoor work);

◆ sharp pencil;

◆ eraser;

◆ squared or graph paper (useful for keeping sketches in proportion and noting dimensions).

You are now ready to study the photographs (Plate 5) of Tedbury Camp Quarry.

The first thing to put in your notebook is the date, the name of the site and its grid reference which is, in this case, ST746489. Read Box 3.3 (overleaf) if you are unfamiliar with giving grid references.

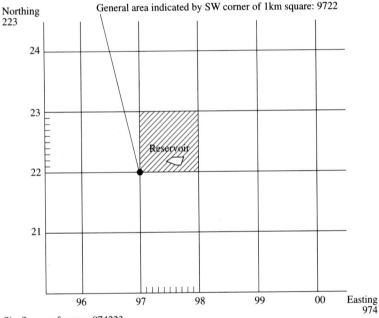

Six-figure reference: 974223

Figure 3.2
Obtaining grid references for a landmark, and for a general area.

The next step at any site is to find a spot where you have a good general view. This has been done for you in the two colour photographs (Plates 5A and 5B). If you rush in with hammer and hand lens you may not see the wood for the trees (or perhaps the rocks for the fossils would be more apt). So the first thing to do is stand back (or in this case, sit back) and sketch the major features. To make a useful sketch you have to be absolutely clear about what its purpose is. Field sketches have two functions:

◆ they force you to observe in a disciplined way, selecting geologically important features (or those which are relevant to conservation);

◆ they provide an essential record of the site and enable others to verify or make use of your observations.

One of the most satisfactory methods of citing a map reference is by using co-ordinates. One co-ordinate, in a west to east direction (left to right), is known as the *easting*; the other is a south to north (bottom to top) co-ordinate called a *northing*. These co-ordinates divide the map up into small squares known as a *grid*. In Britain the Ordnance Survey uses one-kilometre squares, and the country is covered by the *National Grid*. It is usual to use six-figure grid references – these can locate places on a map to within 100 metres. The grid reference for a reservoir on a map is shown in Figure 3.2. If the area in which the reservoir is situated needs to be indicated on a map, one of the 1 km squares may be used by quoting the co-ordinates of its *south-west corner*.

Field sketches do not require artistic ability; a simple line drawing with a sense of perspective is all that is required. Photographs can provide a useful supplementary record, especially if annotated to show the main geological features. Several photographs taken over time can be used to record changes of the outcrop if it is in a quarry or a coastal cliff. Your sketch will have lots of descriptive labels, so choose a scale which leaves room for them on the page. Always indicate:

◆ the orientation of the sketch (approximately SE–NW, from left to right, in Plates 5A and 5B);

◆ the length and width of the view (about 20 m at the front of the photo, and 50 m for the low cliff at the rear);

◆ the height of the outcrops (the cliff at the back of the photo is about 5 m high, that at the front about 2–2.5 m high).

If you were actually in the field, you would probably need to measure dimensions accurately at some point with a tape measure. Plate 5A shows two rock units. The lower, light grey one shows beds inclined to the right (north-west), and is overlain by a cream-coloured rock unit in which the bedding is horizontal. Plate 5B shows that there is a large flat surface on top of the inclined grey rock, and that the cream-coloured rocks rest on top of this surface; the horizontal bedding of the upper unit is clearer in this photograph.

What features will you sketch? That is, what is geologically significant about the view? You can start to answer this question by asking yourself some additional straightforward questions.

▼   Are you looking at more than one rock unit?

▲   The different bedding orientation and different colours suggest that there are two main rock units. The beds in the lower cliff produce a more angular pattern, whereas the upper cliff is more rubbly in appearance.

ENVIRONMENTAL SCIENCE
SCHOOL OF APPLIED SCIENCE
WOLVERHAMPTON UNIVERSITY

▼   What is the nature of the boundary between the two rock types? Is it sharp or gradational, flat or irregular?

▲   It seems to be the flat surface of the quarry floor, and so is sharp and flat.

▼   Could the flat quarry floor be the unconformity surface?

▲   It does seem to disappear under the base of the vertical rock face at the rear of the quarry, which could be composed of Jurassic limestone. That would mean that the rock forming the quarry floor and everything below that level is Carboniferous.

▼   What are the vertical lines running through the rock in the rear cliff? These are visible in Plate 5A.

▲   They are joints.

▼   What are the parallel lines running away from you across the unconformity surface in Plate 5B? Are they continuous features?

▲   At first sight (especially if you had not seen the lower quarry face) it would be difficult to decide if they were bedding planes or joints. The parallel lines are in fact produced by inclined bedding planes intersecting the flat surface in the quarry.

▼   What are the short lines or breaks orientated at right angles to the inclined beds in the lower part of the quarry?

▲   They are joints. Figure 3.3 is a close-up view of the bedding and joints in the lower limestone.

Figure 3.3
Close-up view of dipping beds and inclined joints in the lower limestone unit (Carboniferous Limestone) at Tedbury. The beds dip to the right (north-west) and the joints are perpendicular to the bedding surfaces.

So, geologically significant features include:

◆ changes in colour and orientation of the beds of rock which enable two different rock units to be identified;

◆ a horizontal plane separating the two rock units: this is the unconformity;

◆ vertical or diagonal lines you see running through the rock: these are joints;

◆ the different appearance of the two cliffs – one angular and the other rubbly – indicating that the lower one is more resistant to weathering.

Now complete Activity 3.2.

ACTIVITY 3.2

MAKING A FIELD SKETCH

Sketch the quarry faces from Plate 5A. Distinguish where possible between continuous and discontinuous lines in the faces and do not attempt to draw every detail; rather, search for features which seem characteristic and illustrate them where they are most clearly displayed. If, on closer inspection, a feature can be found throughout the site or only on a particular section, you can annotate your sketch to that effect later. Finally, mark in approximate dimensions and indicate vegetation at the margins of the exposure. You may want to amend your sketch when you have a more precise idea of what you are looking at, so it is perfectly acceptable to put a question mark beside a feature you think, from a distance, may be a joint or a significant boundary or a separate rock unit – or simply something you can not put a name to yet. Label the features you can identify on your sketch.

◆ ◆ ◆

Now, with the overall picture on paper, in your imagination walk slowly across the quarry floor shown in Plate 5B. It is clear and rather smooth (thanks to the quarriers having exposed it and conservationists clearing any remaining rubble). Its most striking feature is its flatness, although there are some ridges and furrows. How did it get that way? This needs thinking about (or maybe there is some written information available which you can consult later). If you have never previously contemplated the flatness of an exposure as something extraordinary and interesting, try to visualize a few hectares of rugged rock and ask yourself what forces and processes could reduce it to something like a gigantic billiard table. In pursuit of this thought perhaps you can recall Lewis Carroll's poem *The Walrus and the Carpenter*, which describes two creatures 'walking on the strand':

'If seven maids with seven mops swept it for half a year,
Do you suppose', the walrus said, 'that they could get it clear?'
'I doubt it,' said the carpenter, and shed a bitter tear …

The poor carpenter might well have found more consolation had his friend been a geologist instead of a walrus, since the former would probably have replied, without a thought for poetic metre, 'Good question!' or 'Yes! Given enough time and energy'. For it is precisely by processes such as the movement of many grains of sand over immense periods of time (albeit in quantities and over timespans longer by several orders of magnitude than those encompassed by the imagination of the walrus) that hills can be reduced to plains – and unconformity surfaces formed. Look again at Figure 1.12(b), which shows an exposure of Carboniferous Limestone on the coast of the Gower Peninsula in South Wales. The unremitting action of waves and tides acting over thousands of years has worn away the rock to produce a large wave-cut platform which is colonized by a variety of marine creatures.

▼   Where can you best see the dip of the limestone beds in this photograph?

▲   In the cliff forming the headland.

▼   What are the remarkably long straight lines running across the wave-cut platform?

▲   They are bedding planes, seen at an oblique angle on the flat surface because of the dip of the beds.

The similarity between the Gower wave-cut platform and the unconformity surface at Tedbury Camp Quarry is striking. So it is very likely that the flat surface at Tedbury is a wave-cut platform. Now imagine that the sea level were to rise a few metres around the Welsh coast so that new sediments started to accumulate on top of the Gower wave-cut platform. If, in the distant future, these sediments were to be turned into rock, the present-day wave-cut platform at Gower would also become an unconformity surface, separating rocks of even greater age disparity than at Tedbury.

But back to observable facts at the quarry. Exactly what kind of rock are you looking at? You already know that there is limestone of Carboniferous age, but 'limestone' is a very general description in something, in the same way as terms such as 'bird of prey' or 'woodland' are general categories which need further definition.

▼   How can you check that a rock is a limestone? Think back to a test referred to in Chapter 2.

▲   See if it fizzes with acid. A dropper bottle of dilute (10%) hydrochloric acid is a useful field tool, but if you use it, take great care that it does not leak, and avoid getting any acid on your skin.

So far, you have identified two limestone units, separated by an angular unconformity ('angular' because the lower unit has beds inclined (dipping) off to the right, whereas the beds of the upper unit are horizontal).

So, you have now accumulated evidence which is the basis for interpreting four major events in the geological history of Tedbury Camp Quarry.

▼   Describe the four major events.

▲   1 The lower grey limestone was formed from sediments deposited in a shallow tropical sea, and later cemented to make a hard rock.

2 The limestone unit was subjected to Earth movements so that the beds were tilted quite steeply.

3 Erosion by the sea produced the flat planar surface.

4 Much later, younger limestones were deposited on top of the flat surface.

With more sophisticated observation and background knowledge an experienced geologist could say a lot more – but this is an excellent start.

Now label the flat surface as an unconformity on your sketch and indicate probable areas of Jurassic and Carboniferous Limestone.

▼ How thick are the exposures of Jurassic and Carboniferous Limestone respectively? How can you measure them?

▲ The Jurassic limestone is horizontally bedded. Its thickness can simply be measured vertically from the quarry floor to the top of the cliff with a ranging rod or metre stick. The Carboniferous Limestone dips at about 45° so some simple trigonometry and a calculator are called for, as shown in Figure 3.4. But as long as you note the dip angle and the length of the exposure the calculation can be done later. For the moment, simply note that it is a lot thicker than the Jurassic in this exposure.

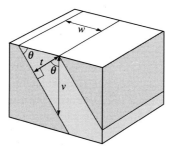

Figure 3.4

Calculating the thickness of a dipping sequence of sedimentary rocks.

Block diagram showing the relationship between dip (θ), width of out-crop (w), true thickness (t) and vertical thickness (v).

$$t = v \times \cos$$

Up to now, you've been making quite a lot of assumptions on the basis of background information, so bit more detailed observation is needed to give you confidence in what you are sketching and noting. So look around carefully, searching for any variations in colour, texture and structure. On closer inspection, some thin horizons and lenses in the Carboniferous Limestone seem to have a different, very fine-grained composition and lighter colour, as shown in Figure 3.5. The rock forming these horizons does not fizz with acid and it is harder than limestone because it can only be scratched with difficulty with a steel penknife. It seems to lie parallel to the limestone bedding and is associated with some low ridges which run across the unconformity surface, confirming that it is in the form of thin beds which are more resistant to weathering than the limestone.

Figure 3.5 *The Lower Carboniferous Limestone unit at Tedbury Camp Quarry. The hammer rests on a bed containing a thin, light-coloured band that is much harder than limestone. Bands such as these form low ridges across the unconformity surface (see Plate 5B).*

▼   You cannot identify this rock, so do you guess that it is volcanic in origin, pretend you haven't seen it, or make accurate field notes, sketches or photographs and take a sample (if you are sure that hammering is permitted) to show to a more experienced geologist?

▲   You need help, so the third alternative is the obvious choice. In fact the rock in question is chert, the same type of silica which forms flints in the Chalk. The silica was derived from the siliceous skeletons of animals which were exceedingly plentiful in the warm sea from time to time. During burial of the limestones the siliceous fossils were dissolved and the silica concentrated in the bands of chert we see today.

You now need to consider two basic questions about the Carboniferous Limestone:

◆   Does the rock exhibit any features which are clues to the environment(s) in which it formed?

◆   Is it homogeneous throughout the exposure?

Thinking back to what you've learned about how rocks form, can you suggest any categories of feature which could act as palaeoenvironmental indicators?

Limestone is a sedimentary rock, so the nature of the particles of which it is composed will provide information about the environment in which it formed. Any sedimentary structures such as cross-bedding will provide further clues to the physical conditions of deposition. Fossils of creatures known to require certain conditions such as clear water or a rocky bottom in shallow water will enable additional deductions to be made.

(a)

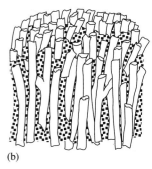
(b)

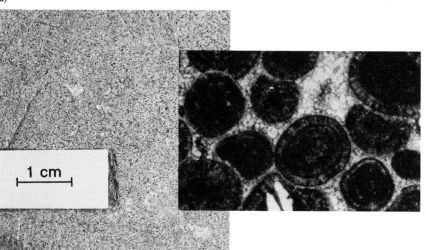
(c)

1 cm

(d)

Figure 3.6 *Close-ups of three types of Carboniferous Limestone at Tedbury Camp Quarry. (a) Limestone containing fossil corals (the rubbly looking material on either side of the hammer), with (b) a sketch of a well-preserved specimen. (c) Close-up of oolitic limestone; the small round particles consist of concentric layers of fine-grained calcite that accumulated as the particles rolled around on the bottom of the Carboniferous sea. Inset shows cross-section of ooids (about 0.5 mm diameter) as seen under a microscope. (d) Limestone containing abundant fossil brachiopod shells, seen in cross-section as thin curved lines to the right of and below the hammer head.*

In keen pursuit of scientific knowledge you crawl around a bit on the unconformity (an important field technique unless your eyesight is particularly acute) but quickly realize that not much in the way of fine detail is visible on the dusty, scuffed surface (which you have previously referred to as clean and flat). You have not brought a stiff brush to clean it with and it occurs to you that this procedure might be even less rewarding in heavy rain on a cold day.

▼   Where might you be able to see things better?

▲   On the low vertical face at the front of the quarry where you can see the beds in cross-section. The best place to start is at the base of the sequence with the oldest stratum and work your way up, charting any changes through time.

▼   How can you tell which is the top and which is the bottom of the Carboniferous sequence?

▲   If you have any difficulty answering this question, look at your sketch of the bedding planes, mark in the dip angle if you haven't done so already and mentally swing the beds back to the horizontal. It should now be obvious that the base of the Carboniferous Limestone is on the left of the view in the photograph.

If you found it difficult to understand the explanation above, make a small stack of thin books. Each book represents a limestone bed with the oldest one deposited first (at the bottom of the pile). Tilt them to the right so that the 'bedding planes' between the books mimic those in the rock in Plate 5A. The 'oldest' book, (the one at the bottom of the pile) is on your left. You have now demonstrated a simple and useful rule: strata normally get younger in the direction of dip (unless they have been turned upside down). In other words the oldest beds are on the left of the photograph, the youngest on the right because the beds dip to the right.

Figures 3.5 and 3.6 shows the main types of Carboniferous Limestone visible on close inspection of the low, vertical face at Tedbury Camp Quarry. Our samples were obtained by cracking open pieces of fallen rock or hammering off a bit to see a fresh surface which is a clean mid-grey, unlike the weathered 'rind' visible in the colour plate. The photographs show that it is not homogeneous, which indicates that more than 300 million years ago environmental changes took place from time to time.

The fine-grained limestone containing no large fossils (Figure 3.5) probably formed from deposits of lime mud precipitated by chemical and biological activity in clear, shallow seas. The mud must have settled in a low energy environment such as a shallow lagoon or in open sea at a water depth below the influence of wave-generated currents. We do not have enough evidence to determine which of these two alternatives is correct, so 'low energy environment' is as precise as we can be.

Figure 3.6(a) shows fossil corals preserved within the Carboniferous Limestone. Such organisms require warm shallow tropical conditions to flourish, and so provide an important clue about the nature of the sea that covered the Mendip area in Carboniferous times.

The oolitic limestone (Figure 3.6(c)) consists of millions of tiny limestone 'beads' called ooids (literally, egg-shaped stones). Ooids are forming today in shallow sandbanks in the Bahamas. Their limey concentric layers grew steadily thicker as they were rolled backwards and forwards in shallow water by vigorous waves and currents in sea water saturated with calcium carbonate. This is just one example of how we can confidently attribute forms and structures preserved in ancient rocks to specific physical processes and environments.

The shelly limestone (Figure 3.6(d)) occurs as layers of brachiopod shells resting at various angles. The animals which secreted them needed a firm sea bottom to attach themselves to. They fed by filtering fine suspended organic matter from the surrounding water. So neither soft mud nor a sandbank of shifting ooids would have suited them.

The four types of limestone now preserved in a vertical succession indicate the successive development of different types of physical and biological environments in the same place at different times. With more detailed observation the past environments can be reconstructed in great detail, as shown in Figure 2.11. Moreover, providing there is a good network of conserved geological sites, we could show how the area represented by Tedbury Camp Quarry was linked to, or decoupled – perhaps by a major fault – from other sites, and the geological processes and events recorded in them. Perhaps you can now begin to see how, if geological sites are not conserved, we can neither refine our understanding of Earth history nor train new Earth scientists who may re-evaluate current theories and interpretations in the light of new knowledge and techniques.

ACTIVITY 3.3

COMPLETING YOUR FIELD NOTES

We have come a long way from identifying sets of lines running across rock faces and finding bits of shell in a hard grey rock. We can now review what further observations and information should be recorded in your notebook as sketches and notes. Take time now to check that you have indeed recorded all relevant detail by checking against Table 3.1 and the example of a field sketch and notes given in Box 3.4 on page 111.

◆ ◆ ◆

If you cannot identify fossils in the field you should, if possible, sketch, photograph and describe them accurately, noting that broken bits of fossils or specimens crushed badly as the rock was compacted during burial may difficult to recognize even by experts. Three very useful and inexpensive books for identifying fossils are *British Paleozoic Fossils*, *British Mesozoic Fossils* and *British Caenozoic Fossils*, published by the Natural History Museum. It should also be clear by now why a complementary description of the rock in which the fossils occur is necessary. A fossil without a rock is, to a geologist, very much what a coin found by someone with a metal detector is to an archaeologist: no use out of context.

If you were actually at Tedbury Camp Quarry the next step would be to examine the junction between the Carboniferous and Jurassic rocks at the base of the cliff to confirm that the bedding planes really do continue right up to the base of the cliff and thus, presumably, beneath it. You can take it that they do, which is another bit of proof that the story of Jurassic sediments being deposited on an extensive wave-cut platform cut long after the limestones of Carboniferous age were deposited and tilted is correct. You would also want to check that the junction between the Carboniferous and Jurassic sequences is abrupt (as opposed to gradational), as would be expected at an unconformity which represents a long period of erosion. After that, a detailed look at the Jurassic sediments would be necessary to establish their characteristic features and fossils and see how they contrast with the rocks beneath the unconformity. We shall not stop to do this just now because the point of the exercise is not to teach you about the Jurassic limestones but to let you see what type of question geologists must ask themselves when faced with a rock exposure, why these questions are important, and how to find answers to them. But note in passing that particular fossil assemblages can be used to allocate rocks to particular divisions of geological time and sometimes to date them quite accurately (see Chapter 4, Section 4.1).

ACTIVITY 3.4
ASKING QUESTIONS IN THE FIELD

Can you classify the questions asked and answered so far in a way which would help you know what sort of questions to ask at a different site? Take a little time to think about this before reading the comment.

One kind of question is aimed at producing a broad overview of geological structures and units at the site.

◆ Is there more than one kind of rock?

◆ How thick are the different units?

◆ What boundaries are visible between the units?

◆ Are the units horizontal or dipping?

◆ Are joints visible?

Other questions seek information which will confirm and bring to life things you have read or been told about the site in advance (the type of rock present, structures within it, its fossils).

Yet others help to turn the outline plot (an unconformity separates Carboniferous and Jurassic limestones) into a story (a succession of different limestone types formed in changing sedimentary environments during the Carboniferous; much later in the Jurassic the Carboniferous rocks lay in an intertidal area and were planed to a wave-cut platform). Moreover, the story is only a small chapter in a huge novel, though you cannot verify this for yourself at a single site. All the same, it makes you aware of the importance of a network of sites for education and research.

Now that you have obtained and recorded the necessary information it is time to tell the story properly. This you start to do by going back to your original viewpoint and writing the heading 'Geological history' on a fresh page of your notebook.

Geological history

Most of your observations, questions, notes and sketches of Tedbury Camp Quarry have had one aim: to work out the geological history of the rocks exposed there.

ACTIVITY 3.5
WORKING OUT A GEOLOGICAL HISTORY

Starting as always at the base with the oldest events, use your notes and sketches to elaborate the list of the successive geological events recorded in the rocks at Tedbury Camp that you made earlier. See how far you can get without looking at the version below.

(If your notes and sketches do not seem equal to the task in hand, take time to go back over the text and see if you can fill in the gaps.)

1 During the early part of the Carboniferous, calcareous sediments formed in the warm, shallow seas that teemed with life (Figure 2.11). Most of the limestone was produced by organic activity. Later, as the limestone sediments were buried, they became compacted and cemented to produce the succession of limestones we see today (Figure 3.7(a)).

2 Major earth movements tilted the Carboniferous Limestone about 45° to the north-west. In fact compressional forces folded the limestones. The dipping beds at Tedbury are part of a large fold structure.

3 There was a major period of erosion. We cannot be precise about its duration from the evidence at Tedbury. But elsewhere in the Mendip area we know that deposition went on virtually continuously for another 40 or 50 million years until nearly the end of the Carboniferous Period. Therefore the Earth movements must have happened after this interval. In fact, evidence from around Britain indicates that the movements occurred around 290 million years ago. Over the next 70 million years or so, erosion removed great thicknesses of Carboniferous rocks (Figure 3.7(b)). The Middle Jurassic limestones are about 160 million years old, so the time gap represented by the unconformity is about 140 million years.

4 In Middle Jurassic times, a shallow sea with a rich benthos (population of bottom-dwelling creatures) repeatedly colonized the surface of the Carboniferous Limestone, forming a sequence of rockgrounds on an extensive wave-cut platform.

5 After some time, deposition resumed (because either the sea level rose or the land surface began to sink; we cannot say which because we have no information), resulting in a sequence of fossiliferous sediments which now form the cliff at the back of the quarry (Figure 3.7(c)).

6 A renewed episode of uplift and erosion has prevented further preservation of rocks at this site for the last 160 million years or so.

7 Thin soils have formed since the last ice age and cap the Jurassic limestones, so there is another major unconformity in the making on the top of them.

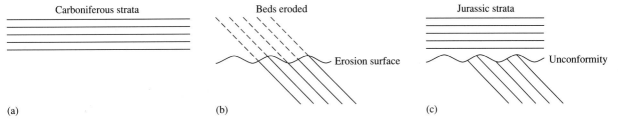

Figure 3.7 *Stages in the development of the unconformity at Tedbury Camp Quarry. (a) Depositions of successive beds and Carboniferous Limestone. (b) Tilting of Carboniferous beds (the dipping beds are part of a later fold structure) and subsequent erosion. (c) Deposition of Jurassic limestones on top of hardground surface Carboniferous.*

Box 3.4   An example of a beginner's field sketch and notes for Tedbury Camp Quarry

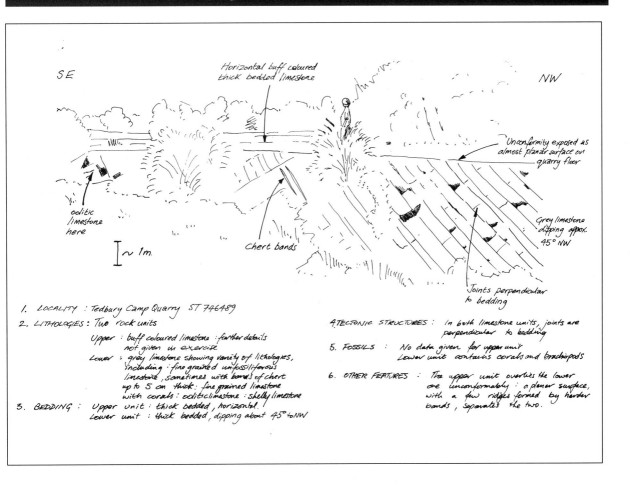

Fieldwork review

Before you 'leave' the quarry review what you have done, as it may be difficult to arrange to come back and check anything you have forgotten. Besides, on the basis of a much improved understanding of what there is to be seen, you may want to modify some initial observations as recorded in your sketches and notes.

Go back to the original viewpoint (Plates 5A and 5B) and look critically at your site sketch. Have you included all the significant features? Have you labelled everything clearly? Could someone else with a comparable knowledge of geology to your own use your diagram next week (or next year) to orient and inform themselves at this site? Have you recorded in writing all the additional information you've gathered in a form that they could use? Remember that it is more important to sketch and describe than to name. A good description can be matched by other workers against the name of the structure or fossil. A good description with a question mark or a field name such as 'green rock spotted with crystals of whitish mineral' or 'spiny tube fossil' is much more useful than a guess at a name which may be wrong.

Before reading on, check that your sketches and notes are as clear and useful as possible, preferably by showing them to someone else and checking they can understand them. Compare your notes and sketch with the version given in Box 3.4.

Site conservation at Tedbury Camp Quarry

When Tedbury Camp was a working quarry, the softer Jurassic limestone was stripped off so that the quarriers could blast the Carboniferous Limestone which forms hard, angular fragments ideal for use as hardcore in road building and other engineering works. The fortuitously exposed rockground was later used as a flat surface on which to dump hardcore and rubble when quarrying ceased. As a result, the rockground and overlying Jurassic limestones became almost completely obscured by tipped material and vegetation. However, in the early 1980s a survey of sites by Nature Conservancy Council (NCC) geologists for a new geological excursion guide to the east Mendips revealed the quarry's educational potential. Negotiations with the owners resulted in the NCC being able to arrange for material to be scraped off the rockground and relocated against the main working face, the top of which is the low cliff of Carboniferous Limestone in the foreground of the site in which you examined joints and bedding (Figure 3.8).

Although it has no statutory protection, the site has since been conserved on a voluntary basis through the support of the quarry owners and through its inclusion in the RIGS register held by the Somerset Environmental Records Centre. From time to time, work parties have done practical maintenance to ensure that features at the site remain available for study. The need for RIGS registration is underlined by the fact that Tedbury Camp Quarry, as is the way with quarries, has recently come into the hands of new owners. If developments damaging to conservation interests were to be proposed at any time in the future, the recording mechanism would provide a good basis for negotiation of an outcome acceptable to both developers and conservationists.

Figure 3.8
Work in progress cleaning the unconformity surface at Tedbury Camp Quarry. The quarry face is in Jurassic limestone, and the material tipped on the quarry floor is being removed to expose the unconformity surface on top of the Carboniferous Limestone.

At Tedbury Camp Quarry conservation work has been done already, so the full story of the geological past recorded here is easily accessible. But if you are actively involved in site conservation you will certainly come across sites where the outcrop is obscured by landslipping or vegetation or where the conservation interest is threatened by development or changes of use. In such cases you will need to make additional field sketches and notes showing clearly what the problem is.

A review of equipment, procedures and safety

In this section your fieldwork at Tedbury Camp Quarry is reviewed under two main headings, equipment and procedures. A final part deals with the safety aspects of site visits.

Equipment needed (or useful) in the field

You will need:

◆ notebook;
◆ pencil;
◆ eraser;
◆ squared or graph paper;
◆ OS map;
◆ compass-clinometer;
◆ hand lens;
◆ tape measure (preferably steel and several metres long), or metre stick.

You might also have a camera, a clipboard to hold papers down in the wind, a 1:50 000 Geological Survey map, a geological excursion guide if one is available, an acid bottle, a reference book for identifying fossils and a geological hammer.

Procedures for fieldwork

Your approach was systematic.

1 You recorded the date of your visit (quarries and landscapes can change over time), and the grid reference.

2 You found a good viewpoint which you identified with a compass orientation, and then analysed the main features and structures. Sketching them served both as part of the analytical procedure and as a record of observations. You recorded the number of major rock units and the relationship between them (bedded unit horizontally laid down on top of dipping beds, the tops of which are planed flat). The sketch was modified and labels added as you obtained more detailed information.

3 Starting with the rocks at the base of the sequence and looking around to make sure you understood what was typical and what was unusual or variable, you recorded the following information:

   ◆ colour of the rock units;

   ◆ large-scale internal structures such as erosion surfaces, chert bands, dip of the beds and joints;

   ◆ rock types and texture;

   ◆ fossils;

   ◆ weathering characteristics.

   You recorded quantitative data such as compass orientations, thicknesses, dip in degrees wherever possible.

4 Contrasting structures, features and fossils in the overlying rocks visible in the low cliff at the back of the quarry were examined next, although we did not go into full detail.

5 These systematic observations enabled you to conclude that the flat surface forming the upper surface of the Carboniferous Limestone is an angular unconformity.

6 You then confirmed that what you were calling Carboniferous Limestone really was a limestone and that it recorded a succession of environmental changes.

7 Once you had recorded the data you were able to do some simple paleoenvironmental reconstructions by relating features of the rock to physical settings in which they could have formed.

8 Finally, you produced a summary geological history of the site by interpreting the events recorded in the rocks.

Safety on site

Since your fieldwork has been done sitting in a chair the question of safety did not arise. But there are some commonsense rules (Box 3.5) which make the possibility of accidents remote. No-one engaged in fieldwork can afford to ignore them.

Box 3.5 The rules of geological fieldwork

Don't visit sites, especially either working or disused quarries, without prior permission from the owner.

Don't go by yourself.

Wear strong boots with non-slip soles to protect toes and ankles.

Always carry extra warm, waterproof clothing if you plan to spend several hours in the field.

Wear a hard hat when working near rock or soft sediment faces.

Be aware that collapses of sand and gravel faces or heaps can occur.

Never hammer hard, splintery rock without wearing glasses or goggles – and without warning other people to turn away.

Don't visit coastal sites without checking tides.

Use binoculars rather than clambering around on steep faces.

Take sensible safety precautions *always* – not sometimes.

3.4 Fieldwork simulation 2: Shap Quarry

Study comment

The next excursion is to a very different locality. Information given in the previous section on Tedbury Camp Quarry which applies generally to fieldwork will not be repeated, so you may wish to refer back to the glossary (page 95) and to advice about making field notes and sketches (particularly Table 3.1, page 94). Before you start, mentally review the simple procedures which allowed you to extract so much information from the rocks at Tedbury Camp Quarry.

Prepare yourself for this armchair excursion by gathering together the appropriate equipment and colour photograph (Plate 6). You will get most out of the exercise if you have access to the granite specimen in the kit and a hand lens or magnifying glass (alternatively, look at Plate 1F). You should also reread the case study in Chapter 1.

Allow at least two hours' study time and aim to work with one or two others to allow group discussion if this is feasible.

Background information

From the discussion in Chapter 1, you know that Shap Quarry is situated in a granitic intrusion.

▼   Can you state in one or two sentences how and where granites form?

▲   A granite is an intrusive igneous rock, originating some kilometres beneath the surface of the Earth in a molten or semimolten state, that is, as a *magma*.

Its subsequent history is likely to involve cooling and consequent joint formation. If the granite magma was very hot compared with the country (i.e. surrounding) rock into which it was intruded, the immediately adjacent country rock will have been baked.

▼   Do you recall what this baking is called, and what appearance the affected rocks will have?

▲   A zone of *contact metamorphism* is produced in the country rock where it is in contact with the hot granite, forming what is known as a metamorphic aureole. The affected rocks are often hard and splintery and new minerals, characteristic of the rock chemistry and temperatures involved, may be distributed randomly throughout the affected zone.

The Shap granite has a metamorphic aureole, the extent of which is shown in Figure 1.13(b). Most granites, and Shap is no exception, are also cut by one or more sets of veins or other minor intrusions where hot fluids circulating through cracks in the rock have cooled and precipitated various minerals.

The country rocks round the Shap granite are folded and metamorphosed Ordovician and Silurian sediments and volcanic rocks as shown in Figure 1.13(b). Note in passing that the Carboniferous Limestone is not far away either, lying unconformably over older sediments. It was laid down in the same seas that, for millions of years, washed over both Tedbury Camp and the area which is now northern England. This is evidence for the submergence of large parts of England during Early Carboniferous times. Beneath the Carboniferous Limestone there are a few metres of sandstones and conglomerates which contain feldspars derived from the Shap granite. This indicates that the granite was exposed at the surface in Carboniferous times.

The Shap granite was one of the intrusions generated within what is now the British landmass towards the end of a lengthy episode of mountain building along the margins of colliding continents, something akin to what is happening in the Himalayas today as India drives slowly but inexorably northwards into Asia. The granite appears to be one protuberance of an enormous batholith which underlies most of the Lake District. The presence of granites such as the Shap bears witness to particular physical and chemical conditions in the Earth's crust characteristic of past collisional or destructive plate boundaries (see Figure 2.40). The episode of plate collision or mountain building to which the Shap granite belongs is known as the Caledonian Orogeny (Caledonian because it greatly affected many of the rocks which now form northern Scotland; orogeny from the Greek word *oros*, meaning mountain). The Shap granite has been dated at about 393 million years using information from the decay rates of long-lived radioactive minerals, and is thus Lower Devonian in age.

Further information about intrusive igneous rock was given in Chapter 2, Sections 2.5 and 2.10; the Caledonian Orogeny is discussed in Chapter 4.

In the field

You will need the same equipment as for Tedbury Camp Quarry, together with Plate 6. The initial entries in your notebook will also be similar. The grid reference for Shap Quarry is NY561082 and the view from left to right in the photograph runs approximately west to east. Although this is only a simulated visit, bear in mind that Shap is a working quarry where the two unbreakable rules are that you wear a hard hat and go only where you are specifically permitted, even though you may suppose other areas to be safe. Binoculars are useful when you cannot get close to the rock faces.

ACTIVITY 3.6

MAKING A SKETCH OF SHAP QUARRY

Study the general view of the quarry (Plate 6) preparatory to sketching it. This is a partial view of the very large quarry whose dimensions can be worked out using a 1:25 000 (or larger) scale map. So for the moment just make sure that proportions of height, length and width are approximately correct. Make your outline sketch now.

◆ ◆ ◆

You should be wondering whether there are any large-scale structures or geological boundaries which will provide information about field relations or about processes which have acted on the rock.

▼ Is there only a single rock type, or is any of the country rock exposed?

▲ It is difficult to say without getting close up. No country rock is exposed as quarriers do not waste money hacking their way through unwanted rock if they can avoid it.

▼ Are there any faults or joint sets?

▲ Yes, joints are present.

You are not wasting time asking questions to which the answer is 'no'; such questions are an efficient way of narrowing down possibilities and focusing on important features.

Add joints to your sketch. You may be able to make out one horizontal set, two vertical and at least one oblique.

▼   There's not much more you can do at a distance, so what is the next question?

▲   You want proof that all the rock you're looking at really is granite! That means picking up some samples and having a close look.

If access to the quarry faces is permitted, checking the nature of the rock *in situ* is essential, but in any quarry there are always innumerable rock fragments lying around. Granite is clearly defined in terms of its origins, texture, mineralogy and chemistry, but a wide variety of grain sizes, minerals and predominant colours is possible. The Shap granite is so distinctive that a piece carried off to someone's garden hundreds of miles away is instantly recognizable to those who have studied it.

▼   What are the general characteristics of granite? How can we tell it is igneous, not metamorphic?

▲   Granite is a coarse-grained igneous rock whose predominant minerals are quartz, feldspar and mica. It can be distinguished from a metamorphic rock because the crystals are randomly oriented. Igneous rocks do not show the alignment and banding of minerals often discernible in those which have been subjected to high temperatures and pressures.

ACTIVITY 3.7

EXAMINING SHAP GRANITE

Look now at Specimen F in the kit, which is a typical piece of Shap granite. Make notes on the colour, the grain size and the principal minerals. If necessary, first refresh your memory of how to identify quartz, mica and feldspar as described in Chapter 2. Even if you do not have a kit sample, make a labelled sketch based on Plate 1F, showing the large well-formed pink feldspar crystals, quartz and mica.

The very large, well-formed pink feldspar crystals in the Shap granite are unusual. Judging by both their size and the straight edges which reflect their well-defined crystal shape, they were not competing for growing space with other crystals.

▼   Do you think that these pink feldspar *phenocrysts* are more likely to have been formed when the magma was cooling relatively rapidly, or during a long period of chemical and thermal stability?

▲   It is reasonable to suppose that these crystals have grown slowly in a magma of just the right temperature and chemistry for precipitation of feldspar but not suitable for the growth of much mica and quartz. The size and shape of the crystals implies that they had a long period of time in which to grow so large and perfect.

Figure 3.9 shows photographs of dark patches of material within the granite. They look like foreign bodies of some kind that have somehow found their way into the granite. These are called 'enclaves'. This is a neutral term which does not suggest anything about their origin. Quarriers call them 'heathens'.

ACTIVITY 3.8

ENCLAVES IN THE SHAP GRANITE

Study the photographs in Figure 3.9 describe the differences between the two types of enclave shown in (a) and (b). You do not have to use technical vocabulary: concentrate on their shape and any differences you can see in mineral composition expressed by their relative dark or light appearance and the presence of visible crystals. If you have any thoughts about the origin of the two types of enclave, note them as well.

◆ ◆ ◆

The biggest difference between the two types of enclave is that one has a very angular shape with a very abrupt contact with the surrounding granite, whereas the other is rounded, with a slightly 'fuzzy' boundary with the granite.

The angular enclave is very dark in colour and must be fine grained as no individual mineral grains are visible and it contains parallel laminations. This enclave is a fine-grained sedimentary rock – shale – derived from the country rocks surrounding the granite. It must have broken off the margin of the intrusion and settled down through it for some distance before the magma had completely solidified.

Figure 3.9
Enclaves in the Shap granite. (a) Angular enclave, showing parallel laminations. (b) Rounded enclave containing large feldspar crystals.

(a)

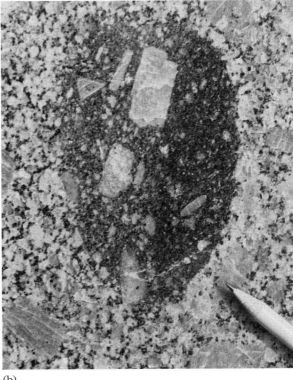

(b)

The rounded enclave is much coarser grained than the angular one, as it is possible to see light and dark coloured minerals within it. However, it is much finer grained than the surrounding granite. On close inspection, the junction between the granite and the enclave is seen to be transitional, with small crystals of quartz and feldspar mixed with the darker minerals of the enclave over a few millimetres. One of the most puzzling features is the large feldspar phenocrysts within the enclave: they seem to be identical to those within the granite.

Explaining the origin of the rounded enclaves is not so easy as it was for the angular ones. The questions we choose to ask next will determine the quality of our understanding of this phenomenon. Where did this dark rock come from? How did it get caught up in the granite? Why does it have a rounded shape whose edges grade into the groundmass of the granite, whereas the boundaries of the angular enclave are so sharp? What process allowed the same large pink feldspar crystals to grow in the enclave and in the granite itself?

One line of argument begins from the explanation of the origin of the angular enclaves as a piece of country rock that dropped into the granitic magma. Could the rounded enclave have a similar origin? This is unlikely, as it cannot be matched with any of the surrounding country rocks. And even if it were a solid piece of country rock, how could the large feldspars grow within it?

The discussion above is a good example of many instances in geology when it is not possible to explain with certainty the origins of features of rocks seen in the field. In the case of the rounded enclaves at Shap, and their feldspar phenocrysts, two hypotheses to explain their origin have been proposed.

◆ The enclaves are fragments of country rock that have been heated by the granite magma to become plastic rather than liquid. The heating caused recrystallization to the coarser texture seen today. The feldspar phenocrysts in the enclave *and* the granite formed after both had cooled down by growth in the solid state by some kind of metamorphic process.

◆ The enclaves formed as 'blobs' of magma that was more iron and magnesium rich than that which cooled to form the pink Shap Granite. These blobs, having a different chemical composition, could not completely mix with the main bulk of the Shap magma. The phenocrysts grew early on in the cooling of the blob, just as they did in the main mass of the granite. This idea of two magma types is consistent with the fact that the Shap intrusion contains two granite types: the pink one you have examined and a darker one.

Do not spend time trying to resolve the argument – professional geologists are still trying to do so! In fact, the controversy is one of the reasons why Shap Quarry has been designated an SSSI – a site statutorily protected because of its national research value.

Geological history

The complete geological history of the Shap granite, like any igneous rock, is not very easy to unravel simply on the basis of field observation of an outcrop. However, you can make a very useful start.

ACTIVITY 3.8

HISTORY OF THE SHAP GRANITE

Using your notes and sketches and the background information given, make a summary of what you know of the geological history of the Shap granite. Number each event as you did for the history of the rocks at Tedbury Camp quarry.

1 In Early Devonian times the Shap granite was emplaced into folded and metamorphosed Ordovician and Silurian country rocks (this event has been dated at about 393 million years). These were relatively cold, since a metamorphic aureole formed as heat and fluids were emitted by the new, hot intrusion and angular fragments of these rocks broke off and settled through the magma.

2 More than one magma type appears to have been incorporated into the intrusion.

3 The magma may have cooled very slowly at first to allow the growth of numerous, well-shaped phenocrysts. Even when the granite was entirely solid, further cooling resulted in the formation of joints. (Other features of the granite, including the formation of small veins of fine-grained intrusive rocks, and mineralization along the joints, are not discussed here.)

4 Uplift and erosion occurred in Devonian times, followed by deposition of Carboniferous sediments unconformably over the granite and its country rocks.

5 Post-Lower Carboniferous uplift and erosion (we cannot be any more precise on the evidence available) raised the granite to its present position at the surface.

6 After glaciation, thin, poorly-drained soils developed on the surface.

Site conservation at Shap Quarry

The main issue at this site is the preservation of representative faces once the quarry has reached the end of its working life. Quarry faces are scientifically more valuable than many natural inland exposures where weathering has obscured features of interest. However, disused quarry faces may become overgrown or unstable and hazardous. Moreover, after-uses such as landfill are economically attractive but may destroy geological interest.

At Shap Quarry, the application from the quarriers for an extension to their planning permission area was sent to English Nature as statutory consultees for work proposed in an SSSI. English Nature's response was that any new planning consent should require conservation of safe and accessible representative faces when quarrying terminates. This entails minor engineering work using smooth blasting to leave faces stable and free from overhangs and loose blocks.

As described in Chapter 1, the final planning consent included the requirement that the quarriers should leave these conservation faces in a pre-split or smooth-blasted condition. This is clearly a satisfactory outcome which can be achieved with little cost and difficulty, satisfying both economic and conservation interests.

Shap Quarry: a review

Fieldwork

Think over what you have achieved by way of fieldwork at this locality:

◆ you asked and answered questions about major units and structures;

◆ you studied and interpreted rock textures, some of which were enigmatic;

◆ you noted features which provided information about the relative ages of bodies of rock;

◆ you gleaned as much background information as possible;

◆ you brought all these observations to bear on producing an outline geological history of the Shap granite.

Another time, with more experience, you could look for additional interesting rock textures, identify vein minerals (for instance, there is a lot of pyrite at Shap), learn about their sources and examine the actual junction of the intrusion with the country rock, which can often reveal a great deal about the processes of emplacement.

Field notes

Take an honest look at your sketches and notes – or better still swap them with a fellow student in order ask for, and offer, helpful comment. Are basic data about the locality (dates, dimensions, grid reference, etc.) clearly recorded? Do they contain all the salient points you've learned as well as questions to be followed up? Have you added a potted geological history? Would you or someone else find your field notes useful in six months' time?

Equipment

If you had really been at Shap quarry, what equipment would you have found essential or very useful? Make a list then check it against the comments on field equipment at this locality and Tedbury Camp Quarry.

Safety

Glance at the colour photograph of the quarry again and record, in the form of brief notes, the advice you would give a colleague about to visit it. If safety precautions don't spring readily to mind, reread the notes on safety from this section and the previous one on Tedbury.

Conservation

Shap Quarry is an SSSI and a satisfactory management agreement has been worked out with the present owners.

You have now investigated quarry exposures in sedimentary rocks and igneous rocks and seen how field observation and interpretation can piece together the geological history of an area. In Chapter 4, an outline of the geological history of the British area is presented. This story is based largely on detailed field investigations of the kind you have just experienced.

Chapter 4

HISTORICAL GEOLOGY –
A BRITISH PERSPECTIVE

Our geological past involves a barely believable story of whole continents moving around like croûtons floating on a bowl of thick soup, of great oceans forming and disappearing like seasonal puddles, of mighty mountains being thrown up and worn down, of formidable glaciers and ice caps advancing and retreating behind mile-thick walls of ice as they melted and reformed again. Scotland itself has been a desert, a swamp, a tropical rainforest and a desert again; it has drifted north over the planet with an ever-changing cargo of lizards, dinosaurs, tropical forests, giant redwoods, sharks, bears, lynx, giant elk, wolves, and human beings.

(Magnus Magnusson, Chairman of Scottish Natural Heritage, *Earth Science Conservation*, No. 32, 1993, p.4.)

Study comment

The quotation above is applicable to the whole of the British Isles. You have already been introduced to snippets of the geological history of Britain in the case studies of conservation sites given in Chapter 1, and the two substitute field trips to sites in the last chapter. This chapter gives an overview of the main geological events that contributed to the evolution of the Earth's crust beneath the British Isles.

We begin by reviewing how the study of fossils contributes to our understanding of Earth history by providing important clues to the nature of past environments, and enabling rocks to be dated in relative terms. Next we examine the fundamental role played by several British scientists in laying the foundations for the modern approach to studying the geological history of different regions of the Earth, and indeed the history of the entire planet. In a conservation context this is very important, for British rocks were the field laboratories in which important new ideas were forged, and so British localities have a special global significance, not the least of which is that the names of several geological periods originated here.

The last two sections look at the British rock record. Firstly, we explore some of the geological patterns that can be seen on the geological map of Britain (Plate 3), and explain how they were produced by major events involving the collision and growth of crustal plates. Secondly, we look in a little more detail at these events and their relevance to sites described in Chapter 1.

4.1 Fossils, past environments and geological time

In Chapter 2, the processes that form the major rock types were explained. As you saw in Chapter 3, this knowledge is used to interpret the geological history of individual localities. The study of fossils adds to the precision of such interpretations of sedimentary rock successions in two ways:

◆ by providing additional information about the nature of past environments through palaeoecological interpretations;

◆ by enabling rock successions to be dated and correlated to successions of the same relative age in different parts of the country and around the world.

What are fossils?

▼ Write down your own definition of fossils.

▲ Fossils are the remains of ancient organisms preserved in rocks.

Figure 4.1 shows examples of present-day organisms and the marks they leave, which, if buried beneath layers of sediment, might become fossils. Fossils may be preserved as *body fossils* or *trace fossils*. Body fossils are the hard parts of organisms. Sometimes the original mineral matter making up bones or shells may be preserved. But usually such material has been altered or replaced by other minerals, or moulds or casts are formed in the sediment in which they were buried (Figure 4.2).

Preserved soft parts or whole organisms are extremely rare but may sometimes be found. Trace fossils can be found as footprints, crawling tracks, burrows and borings into rock and other shelly forms. Such fossils are the record of animal movements or dwelling habits.

Figure 4.1

Potential fossils on present-day beaches. (a) A pile of shells: a future fossiliferous sandstone? (b) A gastropod (a marine snail) has left a trail across ripple marks; the shell could become a body fossil, and the trail a trace fossil.

(a)

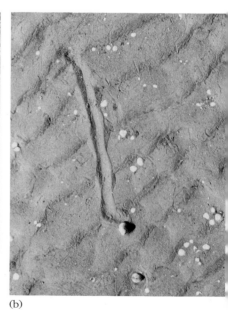
(b)

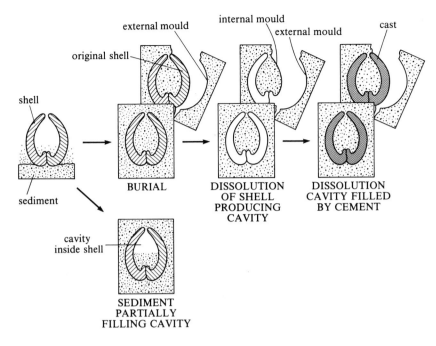

Figure 4.2 How the hard parts of organisms may be fossilized as moulds and casts. Along the centre is shown the sequence of events that may follow burial of a shell – dissolution of the shell and filling of the resulting cavity by cement. The diagrams behind show what is revealed if the rock is broken open at different stages. The diagram at the bottom shows how a partial sedimentary fill of a cavity between two shells can produce a sort of 'spirit level'.

Fossils are usually only found in sedimentary rocks, but they may sometimes be preserved in metamorphic rocks if they have not been too highly deformed (Figure 4.3).

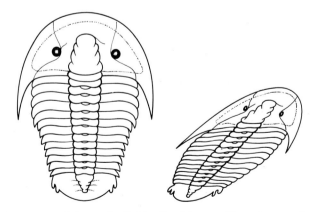

Figure 4.3 An undeformed trilobite fossil in a sedimentary rock, and a distorted specimen in slate, which was deformed when the slate was formed by lateral compression during metamorphism. Trilobites are an extinct group of arthropods.

Fossils and past environments

Figure 4.1 shows some organisms characteristic of present-day beach environments. If similar organisms, preserved as body and trace fossils, were to be found in a sedimentary rock, it would be reasonable to assume that the rock was deposited in a similar type of environment, especially if the size and sorting of its constituent sand grains were similar to those in present-day beaches.

Plants and animals do not live alone but together in communities which are characteristic of particular habitats. Communities are dependent on each other and the world around them. One community will be confined to areas where there is well-sorted sand and where the water is clear and warm, and a completely different one will occur where there is muddy sediment, and the water is cloudy and cold. If we assume that past geological environments were as varied as present-day ones and were the result of similar processes, then studying present-day organisms in relation to their environment can give us many clues about the likely habits of organisms preserved as fossils. More formally, the approach is known as the *principle of uniformitarianism*. It is based on the premise that the laws of physics and chemistry, which describe the forces controlling the processes that can now be observed on the Earth's surface, are applicable throughout the history of the Earth. This commonsense approach to the interpretation of past geological events may seem very obvious today, but it was revolutionary when it was first presented over 150 years ago. The reconstruction of the Carboniferous and Jurassic environments at Tedbury Camp Quarry is based on this method.

Fossils and geological time

To make any sense of the rock record in terms of successive events in Earth history, it is essential to be able to place rocks in any part of the world in a relative order, and to be able to identify rock units of the same relative age at different localities around the globe.

The whole of geological time is divided into major divisions called *eras*. The three most recent of these were defined and given their names from the general character of the contents of fossils in the rocks of each one long before geologists knew anything about the timescales involved. The three eras and their timespans are:

Cainozoic	0–65 million years ago
Mesozoic	5–250 million years ago
Palaeozoic	250–570 million years ago

These three eras are shown in Table 1.1 and on the back cover. They were named according to the fossils each one contains. In the Cainozoic (recent life), life was very much like that of the present-day Earth; the similarities become progressively reduced further back in time during the Mesozoic (middle life) and Palaeozoic (ancient life). As we saw in Chapter 1, this crude three-fold division has been considerably refined.

To understand the ways in which geological events can be ordered in time can be explained by two analogies.

Consider first the recent past. Various objects have been found in old refuse dumps near mining camps in North America, and seven examples of these are shown in Figure 4.4(a) overleaf. Their distribution in three boreholes in one dump is shown in Figure 4.4(b). The dates of manufacture of bottles, cans and nails are known from their makers' old records, and so a 'range chart' can be worked out showing the duration of manufacture of each item. You will realize that some of these articles can be used to give a fairly exact age to a part of the dump because they were in use for only a few years, while others were used over a long time and so are not as valuable for dating. Some groups of articles were only in use together for a short time, and so an assemblage of these found together can tie down the age of the dump very precisely. For example, finding items 3 and 4 together would indicate a date of 1900.

▼ With the aid of the range chart in Figure 4.4(a), work out the ages of the rubbish in boreholes A, B and C in Figure 4.4(b).

_____

▲ Column A is pre-1900: it contains square-headed nails (6), bottles with hand-finished necks for corks (3), and soldered tin cans (1): all of these are pre-1900 materials. Column B is 1900–1920: it contains items 4, 7 and 1. Column C is 1920–30: it contains items 2, 7 and 5.

In a directly analogous way to the dating of the mine dumps, many sedimentary rocks can be dated by the fossils they contain. Fossils are now widely used to determine the relative ages of rocks and place them in their correct order, that is their correct *stratigraphic sequence*. But how was this sequence originally worked out? Two early 19th-century geologists, William Smith (1769–1839) in England, and Georges Cuvier (1769–1832) in France, discovered that overall there is a sequential order of fossils through time; the biological explanation of this came later, particularly as a result of the work on evolution by Charles Darwin (1809–1882). William Smith is now recognized as the father of stratigraphy, and his work is discussed in more detail in the next section.

Much of the general course of evolution can be verified by the study of fossils. By careful collection, palaeontologists have discovered a succession of different fossil assemblages in the rock record from the beginning of the Cambrian Period (about 570 million years ago) to the present. The evolutionary order of plants and animals can be used to establish the relative ages of rocks because we assume that, in general terms, evolution proceeds from simpler to more complex organisms; for example, the evolution of the vertebrates followed the sequence from fish to amphibians to reptiles to mammals. If we place this sequence in stratigraphic order we have:

Youngest beds	Fish	Amphibians	Reptiles	Mammals (220 million years)
	Fish	Amphibians	Reptiles (330 million years)	
	Fish	Amphibians (370 million years)		
Oldest beds	Fish (400 million years)			

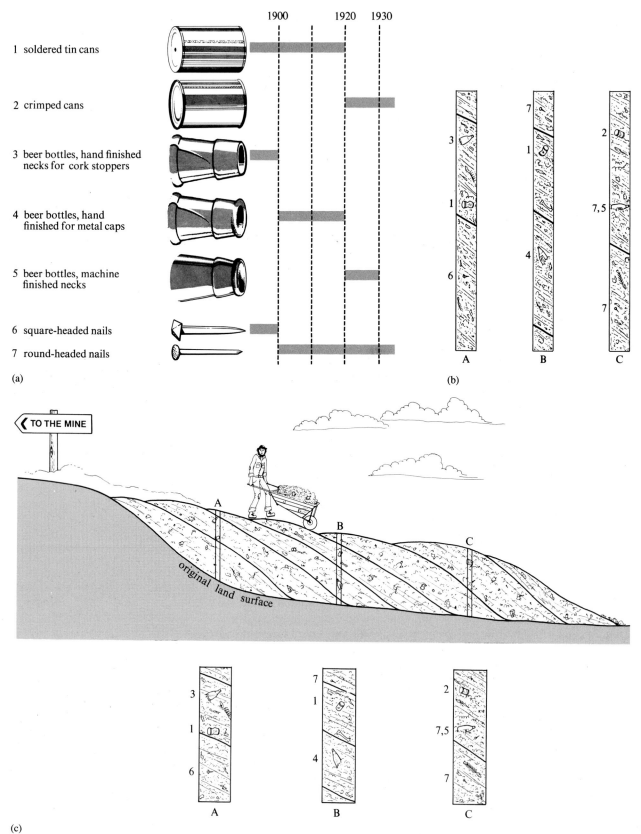

1 soldered tin cans

2 crimped cans

3 beer bottles, hand finished
  necks for cork stoppers

4 beer bottles, hand
  finished for metal caps

5 beer bottles, machine
  finished necks

6 square-headed nails

7 round-headed nails

(a)

1900   1920 1930

(b)

A   B   C

TO THE MINE

original land surface

A   B   C

(c)

Figure 4.4 *Finding out the age of layers in an American mine dump.*
(a) Chart showing the dates of manufacture of cans, bottles and nails prepared from historical records. Each article is given a number, and these numbers are used in (b) to show how the articles were found in the boreholes. (c) Rubbish dump of old American mining camp, to show the distribution of cans, bottles and nails in the rubbish tipped on the original land surface.

400 million years ago the only vertebrates were the fish, but by 220 million years ago all four groups had evolved. Thus the oldest rocks in this sequence will contain only fossil fish and the youngest, besides containing mammals, will also yield fossils of the three other groups. This example only permits the relative dating of rocks in a very broad way. Using other fossil groups which evolved much faster enables correlation to be achieved from place to place with much finer resolution. Figure 4.5 illustrates the degree to which the different fossil groups are useful in determining to which geological period rock sequences around the world belong, and the degree to which they are useful in correlating rocks from place to place. To be an effective correlation 'tool' around the world, a fossil must be:

◆ a member of a group of fossils that evolved rapidly through time;

◆ relatively common and easy to identify;

◆ present in a wide variety of rock types.

It was not possible to assign absolute ages to the geological periods when they were defined during the first half of the 19th century. It must be stressed that the quantitative definition of the time periods spanned by the geological periods was not known at that time. Measuring the ages of rocks only became possible after the discovery of radioactivity and the realization that some radioactive elements decay over various periods of time, some of which are on a geological timescale of tens or hundreds of millions of years. Once it became possible to measure the tiny amounts of radioactive decay products within rocks, the true immensity of geological time was realized.

Figure 4.5 *The age range of major fossil groups. The width of the bars indicates relative abundance through time; dashed lines suggest probable evolutionary relationships.*

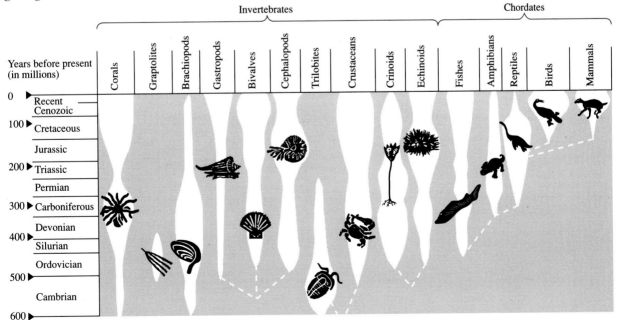

129

Figure 4.6

Diagrammatic section of strata (after Cuvier) showing how particular fossils are associated with particular horizons in the sequence of strata. Breaks in the sequence where erosion of the underlying beds occurred before subsequent beds were laid down can be seen in several places, perhaps best where strata with a walking vertebrate (shown by vertical ruling) are overlain by a horizontally shaded bed.

4.2 The founders of historical geology

Georges Cuvier (1769–1832) was one of the first to describe systematically the skeletal remains found preserved in rocks as fossils, to interpret them in terms of the living organisms they represented, and to work out their succession in Earth history. He studied the fossil plants and animals in the Tertiary rocks of the Paris Basin and concluded that older fossils differed more from living creatures than did younger ones. He summarized his conclusions diagrammatically by sequences of strata, such as those shown in Figure 4.6. He deduced from these that some older forms of life had become extinct and that the extinct forms had been replaced by newer forms.

But some of Cuvier's conclusions were not correct. For example, in his answer to the question of how new species arose, Cuvier believed that each old species was wiped out by a universal catastrophe followed by the 'special creation' of new species.

Catastrophism is the name given to the hypothesis that geological history can be explained by a series of catastrophic events. Starting from the biblical idea of Noah's flood, Cuvier invoked similar 'deluges' to explain each break in the series

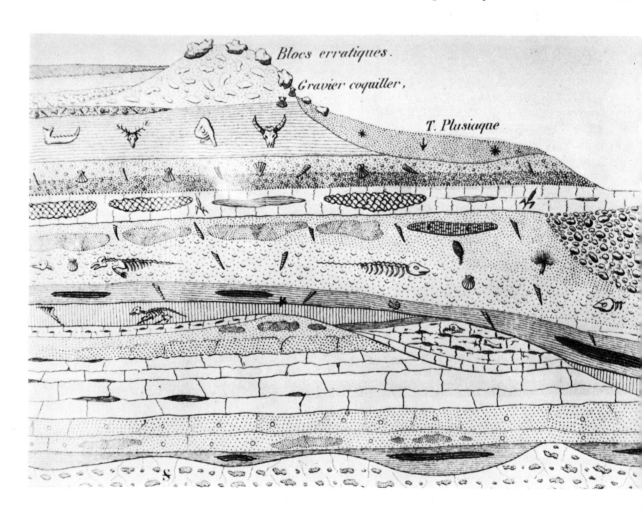

Figure 4.7
The Asiatic Deluge, from Louis Figuier (1869) The World before the Deluge.

of fossils in his sequence of sediments. Since he was not able to find intermediate species connecting the fossils at different levels in the stratigraphic column, and since, moreover, there was often evidence of a break in the deposition of the sediments themselves, marked by changes in rock type which coincided with the faunal changes, it was logical to invoke a new 'deluge' for each break. Geological history then was thought to be a whole series of deluges which killed off all life, each followed by special creation of a whole new fauna. During the 19th century there were many graphic representations of 'deluges', one of which is shown in Figure 4.7.

Cuvier noticed that very often the breaks in the sequence of strata and fossils were marked by a horizon where there was evidence of erosion of the underlying beds before deposition of the next layer, and that the beds immediately above contained pebbles. Indeed, this was powerful evidence for the 'deluge'. We saw in Chapters 2 and 3 that such breaks or unconformities usually represent a long interval of time during which sedimentation ceased and erosion occurred because the area had risen above sea level. Several unconformities are shown in Figure 4.6.

In the last years of the 18th century an Englishman, William Smith (1769–1839), an engineer and surveyor who worked on canals, roads and drainage schemes all over England, found that he could recognize distinctive beds within rocks such as the Chalk on the North and South Downs, or within the coal-bearing strata in widely separated coalfields, and that *each group contained a particular assemblage of fossils quite distinctive from those of the strata above and below.*

Smith began to correlate apparently dissimilar sedimentary strata *because they contained similar fossils.* Furthermore, he found that there was *the same succession of fossil assemblages from older to younger beds in different parts of the country.* He concluded that each stage of this succession of fossils represented a particular span of geological history, or a discrete period of time, and that rocks formed during that time would contain the same fossils wherever they occurred geographically. This he called the *principle of faunal succession*, and, using it, he was able to correlate widely separated exposures of rock by the fossils they contained.

By using these fossil assemblages as a method of correlation, and applying the hypothesis that each faunal assemblage represented a unique time interval that could be recognized anywhere, Smith was able in 1815 to produce the first geological map of England and Wales and part of Scotland. On a scale of five miles to the inch, it measured about 2 m by 3 m. He took an existing geographic map and showed the outcrops of each stratum by painting them in watercolour. Painting the geology onto a geographic base remained the main method of producing geological maps for more than a hundred years until it was superseded by colour printing.

Having produced the map, Smith was then able to draw a geological section across it along the road from London to Snowdon, to show the relationship between the different strata. A simplified version of his 1817 section is shown as Figure 4.8(a).

If you look at Figure 4.8(a) you can see that a journey from London to North Wales would take you on to progressively older rocks. You can also see that each range of hills is caused by a particular geological unit that is more resistant than the softer rocks forming the lowlands between. For example, the journey from London to Oxford starts and finishes on soft clays, the high ground of the Chilterns between being produced by the harder Chalk.

Now that you have looked at the section, you can appreciate how Smith was able to produce the first nearly complete stratigraphic column for Britain, which accompanied his large map. We have produced a simplified version of this stratigraphic column as Figure 4.8(b). Many of the terms he coined for rock strata are still in use today, although some have been modified. Once such a rock succession has been established, the study of the features of each unit (rock type, and fossils if it is a sedimentary rock) can be interpreted to determine the nature of

Figure 4.8 *William Smith's geological cross-section and stratigraphic column. (a) Geological cross-section from London to Snowdon. The original hand-painted colours have been replaced as well as possible by two-colour printing. The solid line represents the road surface, whose gradients appear much steeper here than they actually are because of the enormously exaggerated vertical scale which Smith used (see the right-hand side of the figure). The succession of strata is shown accurately below the road. Above the road Smith gave an indication of the size of adjacent hills and of the rocks of which they were formed. (b) Stratigraphic column compiled by Smith (simplified after his original, which accompanied his 1815 map). The ornaments used here have been changed from his original colours. The column consists of a sequence of rock strata that Smith recognized from his fieldwork, with observations about their character, uses, and effect on the landscape. It is not drawn to scale accurately, but in broad terms, relative thicknesses of the rock units are depicted. The whole column represents a total vertical thickness of well over 15 km of strata.*

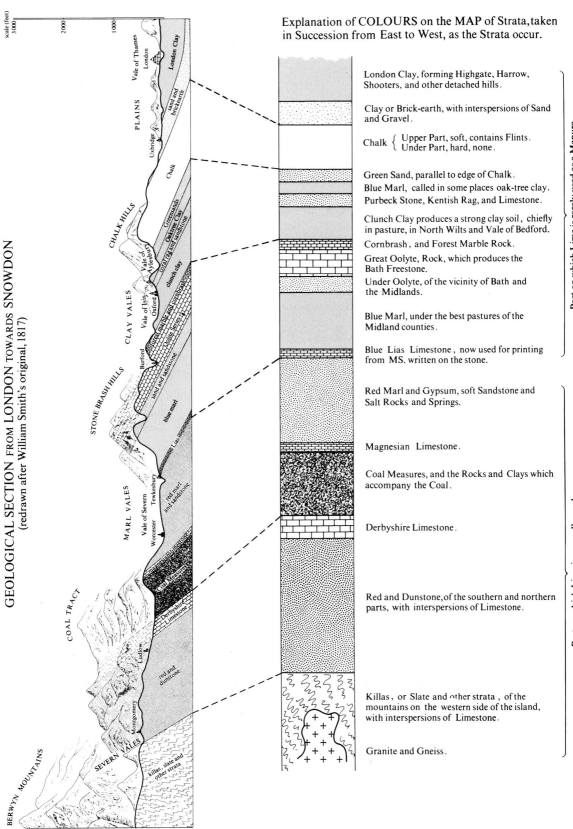

the processes that produced it. As we saw in the previous section, such interpretations are based on the premise that processes operating today to shape the Earth's crust were also operating in the past. This *uniformitarian* approach – that the present is the key to the past – was first formulated by James Hutton (1726–1797). His work contributed a great deal to the unravelling of the Earth's history, and dealt a great blow to the religious ideas of great catastrophes as an explanation of the Earth's history. Geologists now use observations of igneous and sedimentary processes which they can observe today, together with models for processes occurring at depth, to infer events that occurred millions of years ago. We also apply the plate tectonic model in this way, as you will see in the next section.

The stratigraphic column was introduced in Chapter 1 (Table 1.1, page 11), but now the time has come to become more familiar with it. You may be puzzled why geologists do not use dates like historians do. There are two main reasons. One is that the periods within each of the eras were recognized by the early stratigraphers before there was any agreement about the age of the Earth, or the duration of the periods. The advent of methods of dating rocks using the small amounts of radioactive elements present in them enabled the relative scale of the periods to be calibrated in time. But even today, this calibration is not very precise because of experimental errors and the different versions of such calibrations in use! So this is the second reason we use the names of the geological periods rather than dates – for once it is less confusing than using numbers.

When looking at Table 1.1, you may have wondered how the names of the geological periods were first established. We will examine just one part of the column to give you an insight into some of the problems that arose.

The Palaeozoic Era is composed of six periods. The three lower ones were first recognized in Wales, but not without some controversy between Adam Sedgwick (1785–1873) and Robert Murchison (1792–1871). Both began mapping the undifferentiated 'Killas, or Slate' at the base of Smith's column (Figure 4.8(b)). Murchison started with the distinctive Old Red Sandstone of Devonian age (Smith's 'Red and Dunstone') in south Wales and established a sequence of strata, each group characterized by particular fossils, working down the stratigraphic column. For this sequence he introduced the name Silurian, from the name of a tribe, the Silures, who inhabited part of south Wales at the time of the Roman occupation of Britain. Sedgwick concentrated his studies in north Wales. He was at a disadvantage compared with Murchison because he did not have a reference level to work from in the stratigraphic column like the Old Red Sandstone. But after several years he was able to work out a succession of the strata that he was mapping for which he proposed the name Cambrian, after Cambria, the Roman name for Wales.

At the time these two periods were proposed, neither Murchison nor Sedgwick had any clear idea how they related to each other. It was discovered some years later that the lower part of Murchison's Silurian contained the same fossils as those in the upper part of Sedgwick's Cambrian. This discovery led Murchison to conclude that all of Sedgwick's Upper Cambrian was merely a part of the Silurian – a conclusion strongly opposed by Sedgwick. The argument turned a warm friendship into enmity that lasted the lifetime of the two men. Finally, in 1879, after both were dead, another geologist, Charles Lapworth, proposed the name Ordovician, after a tribe which had occupied north Wales, to include the Upper Cambrian of Sedgwick and Lower Silurian of Murchison. The proposal was accepted and so the Ordovician Period now separates the periods of the two rivals in the stratigraphic column.

If you are interested in the origins of the other period names, have a look again at Table 1.1. The periods, once they had become established, together with other stratigraphic names, became part of an international geological terminology which could be and still is applied all over the world.

4.3 The geological map of Britain: exploring some geological patterns

Despite being a very simplified version, the geological map of Britain and Ireland shown in Plate 3 in the colour plate booklet contains a considerable amount of information which you can explore as we begin to trace the geological history of the British Isles. The map shows what kind of rock actually occurs at the surface, or would do so if sediments deposited in the last 1.5 million years or so by rivers and ice were stripped away. The key on the left side is arranged in chronological order (apart from the igneous rocks), just like the stratigraphic column. Igneous rocks were formed in nearly every period, so it would be impossible to assign different colours to depict their different ages.

▼ What do you notice about the shape of the rock outcrops shown on the map? Do some areas show simpler patterns than others?

▲ In southern and eastern England, there are very broad strips of Jurassic, Cretaceous and Tertiary rocks. In the south they trend roughly E–W, but in the Midlands and Yorkshire, the trend is almost NW–SE.

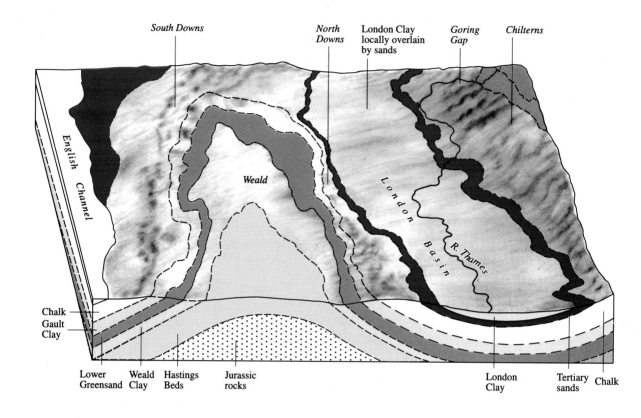

Figure 4.9 *The structure of the London Basin and the Weald. Compare this with the corresponding part of the geological map shown in Plate 3.*

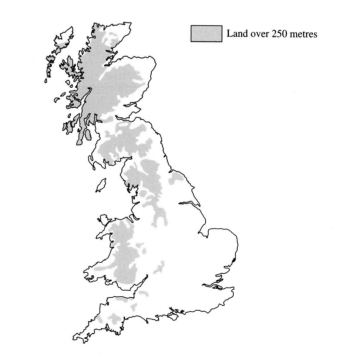

Land over 250 metres

Figure 4.10
The areas of higher ground in Britain.

As you can see from William Smith's cross-section (Figure 4.8(b)), to the north of London the NW–SE pattern described above is due to the strata being inclined or dipping very gently to the south-east. The reason London is flanked to the north and south by Cretaceous rocks is because it is situated in a broad saucer-shaped structure known as a *syncline* (Figure 4.9, overleaf). The Weald is a shallow domal structure, or *anticline*, and another syncline in Hampshire preserves Tertiary rocks around Portsmouth.

▼ Where do the oldest rocks of all occur in the British Isles?

▲ In north-west Scotland and the Outer Hebrides, where the metamorphic rocks known as the Lewisian, parts of which are nearly 3000 million years old, are exposed.

▼ Look at Figure 4.10, which shows the areas of higher ground in Britain. Comparing it with the geological map, to which of the main rock types or geological eras (Cainozoic, Mesozoic, Palaeozoic) can these areas of high ground be related? Why do you think this is so?

▲ All the mountainous and high ground of Britain is underlain by Palaeozoic or older rocks, or by metamorphic or igneous rocks. This is because they are generally much harder and more resistant to erosion than Mesozoic and Cainozoic sediments.

▼ We have already noted the NE–SW and W–E 'grain' to outcrops of Mesozoic and Tertiary rocks in southern and eastern England. Can you see any other areas where a definite trend in outcrop strips is noticeable?

▲ From south to north the following outcrop trends are discernible on the map:
   ◆ Southernmost Ireland, south-west Wales, Devon and Cornwall: Devonian and Carboniferous rocks trending almost W–E.
   ◆ Mid-Wales, south-east Ireland (south of Dublin), the Southern Uplands of Scotland and adjacent Ireland, the Midland Valley of Scotland: Lower Palaeozoic (Cambrian, Ordovician and Silurian) rocks trending roughly NE–SW.

You may have noticed that the rocks in all the areas listed (apart from southern Ireland) contain granites.

▼ With what type of crustal plate boundary are granites associated? If necessary, turn to page 86 for a reminder.

▲ Destructive plate boundaries.

In answering the last two questions, you have recognized some of the evidence that has enabled geologists to determine that two major periods of plate collision occurred to form mountain chains across parts of Britain. The older mountain-building episode culminated about 400 million years ago, and exhibits the NE–SW

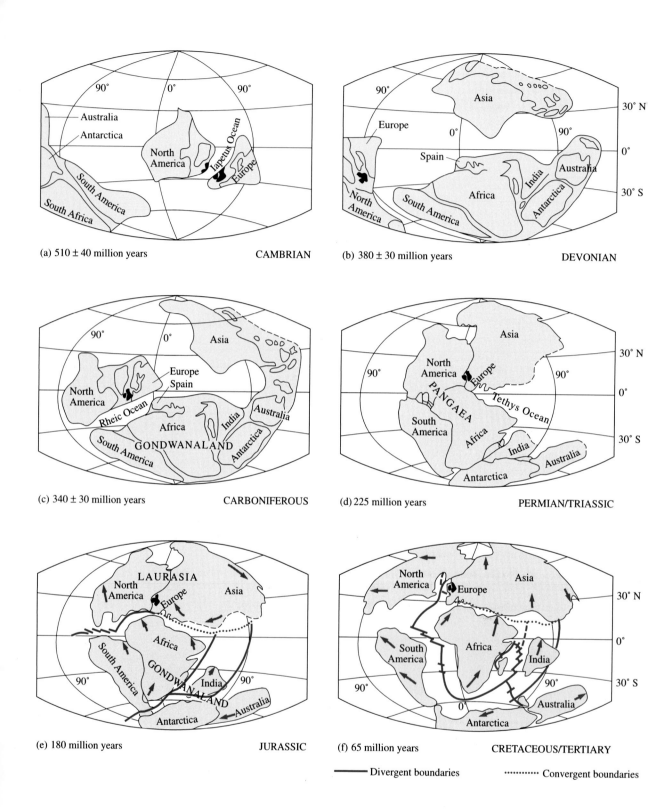

(a) 510 ± 40 million years   CAMBRIAN

(b) 380 ± 30 million years   DEVONIAN

(c) 340 ± 30 million years   CARBONIFEROUS

(d) 225 million years   PERMIAN/TRIASSIC

(e) 180 million years   JURASSIC

(f) 65 million years   CRETACEOUS/TERTIARY

——— Divergent boundaries   ·········· Convergent boundaries

Figure 4.11 *Reconstructions of past continental configurations. Note how the British Isles (black) were once split between two separate continents/tectonic plates. The names of two oceans that once divided Britain (the Iapetus Ocean in (a)) and bordered it to the south (the Rheic Ocean in (c)) are shown. The present-day Mediterranean is the final vestige of the Tethys Ocean that formed a huge embayment in the supercontinent of Pangaea in the Permian (Triassic) and began to close from the Jurassic onwards (e–f).*

grain seen in Wales, Scotland and Ireland. The younger episode culminated 300 million years ago and imprinted the W–E grain on the rocks of southern Ireland and south-west England. Both of the episodes were associated with the opening and subsequent closing of major oceans.

The maps in Figure 4.11 show how areas of continental crust have moved around the planet during the past 500 million years. An ancient ocean known as Iapetus is shown splitting the British area into two parts, with Scotland and the northern part of Ireland attached to a continental mass which includes North America! By Devonian times (380 million years ago) Europe had collided with North America. In Figure 4.11(c), the Rheic Ocean is shown; it had closed by about 290 million years ago. In fact at this time all the continental areas had amalgamated into one supercontinent called Pangaea. This began to split up about 250 million years ago.

Chapter 2, Section 2.10 describes the sequence of events in a cycle of ocean opening and closing, culminating in mountain building (turn back to Figure 2.40 on page 89 if you need to refresh your memory about this). The mountains are then eroded, and sediments from them deposited in neighbouring lowland areas, or in new oceans formed nearby if the continental crust splits up once more. Therefore major unconformities are another indication of mountain building, or rather the end of it (Figure 2.41). Major unconformities can be identified across the British Isles, separating four structural storeys (Figure 4.12 and Plate 4). These structural storeys were introducd at the end of Chapter 2, and their ages are summarized on the back cover; they are described in the next two sections.

Miocene–Quaternary
Younger cover, Permian–Oligocene,
in part folded 25 million years ago

Older cover, Devonian–Carboniferous,
folded 290 million years ago during the
Variscan orogeny

Caledonian, Lower Palaeozoic, folded
400–500 million years ago during the
Caledonian orogeny

Basement, Precambrian, folded at
various times up to 600 million years ago

Figure 4.12
The four crustal units or 'geological storeys' of Britain, shown schematically as a column. The distribution of these structural storeys is shown as a map in Plate 4.

4.4 The Basement

The Basement is the oldest of Britain's structural storeys. It contains rocks ranging in age from 600 to 2800 million years old. As shown on Plate 4, it is most extensive in north-west Scotland and the Hebrides, but smaller areas occur in North Wales, south-east Ireland and Shropshire. There are also some tiny outcrops in the English Midlands, most notably at Charnwood near Leicester. The Basement rocks record early events in the complex development of continental crust underlying the British Isles which is beyond the scope of this book. The history of the Scottish Basement and that in England, Wales and southern Ireland is totally different. This is because the former is a fragment of what was once North American continental crust, whereas the latter is European. They were once separated by the Iapetus Ocean (Figure 4.11(a)), and were brought together as the Iapetus closed and the Caledonian mountain belt formed. In Scotland, the relationships between the Basement and this mountain belt is spectacularly exposed (Figure 4.13(a)). Figure 4.13(b) is an east–west cross-section illustrating the relationship between the different rock units.

ACTIVITY 4.1

KEY EVENTS IN THE GEOLOGICAL HISTORY OF THE COASTAL REGION OF NORTH-WEST SCOTLAND

Using the cross-section in Figure 4.13(b), and the description of the rock units given in the caption, list the major geological events you can interpret from this data. These include metamorphism, major periods of erosion and deposition, and major Earth movements causing thrusting. At first, you may think it very strange that highly metamorphosed rocks of the Moine lie on top of unmetamorphosed Cambrian and Ordovician sediments, and that the Moine rocks are older than the unaltered sedimentary rocks. The key to the apparent paradox is that the boundary between them is a thrust (see Figure 2.31, page 79).

You should have identified the six events described in Table 4.1, but not in as much detail.

Table 4.1 North-west Scotland: key events

Key event	Rock unit	Age in millions of years	Geological activity
6	–	480	Moine metamorphic rocks were transported at least 60 km westwards along the Moine thrust as the Iapetus closed, coming to rest on the Cambrian and Ordovician sedimentary rocks. The tilting of the sedimentary rocks probably occurred at about the same time as the thrusting
5	Cambrian and Ordovician	570–470	Deposition of shallow-water sandstones and limestones. To the east, sediments of the Moine were deeply buried and metamorphosed
4	–	800–600	Major uplift and erosion. The sediments that were to become the Moine unit were deposited tens of kilometres to the east
3	Torridonian	1000–800	Deposition of river sediments from land to north-west of Scotland (now Greenland)
2	–	1850–1000	Major uplift and erosion
1	Lewisian	22 700–1850	Deposition of sediments that were later metamorphosed and intruded

(a)

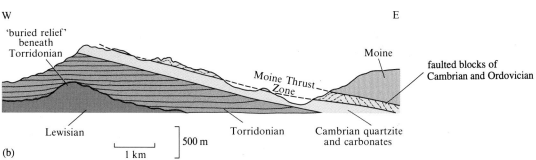

(b)

Figure 4.13 *The relationship between Basement and Caledonian rocks exposed in the west coast area of north-west Scotland. (a) Metamorphic rocks of the Moine series thrust over Cambrian strata. This photo shows the relationships displayed on the far right-hand side of the geological cross-section shown in (b); the Moine rocks occur in the upper part of the mountain side. The units are described below in order from west to east.*

Lewisian: metamorphic rocks with dykes of igneous rock, ranging in age from 2800 to 1300 million years.

Torridonian: red sandstones, conglomerates and shales deposited by rivers draining south-eastwards from mountains situated in the area which today is Greenland. These sediments are 1000–800 million years old.

Cambrian and Ordovician: shallow marine limestones overlain by sandstones also deposited in shallow water.

Moine: metamorphosed and folded sediments, originally mainly sandstones, that were probably deposited 800–600 million years ago, and metamorphosed 600 million years ago.

From this interpretation, it is clear that the Basement in north-west Scotland has only suffered uplift and some tilting over the past 1300 million years, with rocks caught up in the Caledonian mountain-building events being thrust over the top of it. This relationship, involving a lower relatively undeformed unit and an upper thrusted unit containing folded and metamorphosed rocks, is quite common along the edges of many mountain belts around the world.

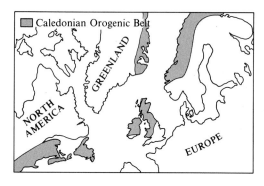

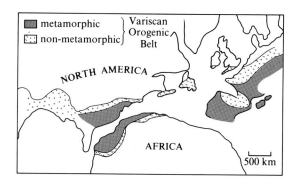

Figure 4.14
The distribution of the Caledonian and Variscan mountain belts on a map of the continents reassembled to the positions they occupied before the Atlantic ocean opened. Early protagonists of continental drift used reconstructions such as these as evidence in favour of the former unity of now widely separated areas of continental crust.

4.5 The birth and death of oceans

In this section, the geological record left by the opening of and closing of two oceans (the Iapetus and Rheic Oceans) and the opening of a third (the present-day Atlantic Ocean) is reviewed (see Figure 4.11 (a), (c) and (f)). Closing of the Iapetus and Rheic Oceans resulted in the formation of the Caledonian and Variscan mountain belts, the distribution of which is shown in Figure 4.14.

The Iapetus Ocean and the Caledonian mountains

In Section 4.3, the NE–SW 'grain' of the rocks of the Caledonian mountain belt visible on the geological map of Britain was noted. These Cambrian, Ordovician and Silurian rocks accumulated on the margins of the two continents that bordered the Iapetus Ocean, and, as it began to close, in ocean trenches and arcs of volcanic islands associated with destructive plate margins.

The Cambrian

During the Cambrian, the Iapetus Ocean was widening above a constructive plate boundary (Figure 4.15(a), page 144). Sediments accumulating on the margins of this new ocean record a major event in the evolution of life on Earth – the ability of organisms to develop hard shells which could easily be fossilized.

The sudden appearance of a large number of highly developed life forms in the Cambrian was a puzzle for many years. If life evolved gradually, then where were the forerunners of these creatures? We now know that life itself originated 3000 million years before this, in the depths of the Precambrian. Examples of Precambrian algae and bacteria are known from many places around the world. Soft-bodied animals rather like worms and jellyfish appear in sedimentary rocks about 600 million years old, and have been found in Britain in the Basement rocks in Charnwood Forest in Leicestershire and elsewhere in the world (Figure 4.16, page 143). The evolution of shells and skeletons at the beginning of the Cambrian 570 million years ago marked a turning point in the history of life. The rate of evolution became very rapid and a multitude of new life forms developed. Many of the animals which lived then have no descendants on Earth today. Natural selection killed off all but the most efficient and resilient of these new, experimental creatures. Those that remained showed a range of basic characteristics which are still seen in the animal kingdom today.

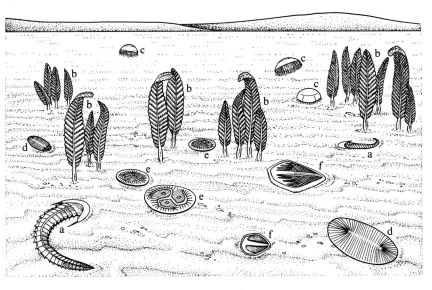

Figure 4.16 *Reconstruction of late Precambrian fossils found in the Ediacara sandstones of South Australia: a early arthropods, b sea pens; c jellyfish; d worms; e ancestral sea-urchins; f fossils of extinct groups. A conspicuous feature of the Ediacaran fauna is the absence of skeletons or shells.*

Cambrian rocks occur mainly in Scotland and Wales with a few outcrops in the Welsh Borders and the Midlands. In places Cambrian rocks lie on eroded Precambrian strata because as the sea level rose, large areas of low-lying coastal land on the north-western and south-eastern margins of the ocean were flooded to form extensive shallow seas. During this time, Britain lay about 30° south of the Equator and the climate was certainly tropical. Studies of Cambrian fossils, particularly trilobites (Figure 4.3), show that those found in Scotland are markedly different from those found elsewhere in England and Wales. This difference is consistent with the existence of an ocean between the two areas that was wide enough to prevent interbreeding and mixing of species.

The Ordovician

The Iapetus Ocean reached its greatest width early in the Ordovician and then began to narrow again. Limestones continued to accumulate in north-west Scotland and shallow-water muds, sands and limestones in the Welsh Borders and English Midlands. In between these two areas, enormous thicknesses of muddy sandstones were deposited on the margins of the ocean. Arcs of volcanic islands occurred as the ocean narrowed as one slab of oceanic crust plunged beneath another in what is today the Lake District and north Wales.

As in the Cambrian, most fossils found in the Ordovician rocks of Scotland are very different from those found in England and Wales. Clearly the shores of the ocean were still too far apart for the animals to migrate from one side to the other. However, by the end of the Ordovician, the Iapetus Ocean had closed sufficiently to allow free mixing of species.

Figure 4.15

The history of the Iapetus Ocean.

(a) During the Cambrian, the Iapetus Ocean was widening.

(b) In the Ordovician, the Iapetus Ocean started to close. Ocean floor melted as it was driven beneath continents, causing volcanic activity, and mountains began to form as the continental crust thickened.

(c) In the Silurian, the Iapetus Ocean had almost closed and a shallow sea separated the converging continents, where high mountains continued to form.

(d) The palaeogeography of the British Isles at the beginning of the Devonian, when continents that once planted the Iapetus Ocean had finally collided.

(a)

(b)

(c)

(d)

landmass; shoreline uncertain

Iapetus (width not to scale)

▲ volcanics

Old Red Sandstone

The Silurian

Silurian rocks indicate a gradual shallowing of the Iapetus Ocean as it closed (Figure 4.15(c)).

In the Midland Valley of Scotland the sea had shallowed and red mudstones were deposited, some of which bear mudcracks from being exposed above sea level. Today's Southern Uplands, Lake District and mid-Wales still lay beneath a deep sea in which thick muds and sands accumulated. In the shallower shelf sea of what was to become the present Welsh Borders, life abounded and the shells of marine animals accumulated on the sea floor, forming limestones (Plate 11). At times the water was clear enough to allow the growth of coral reefs. The fossils of the Silurian show none of the geographic differences noted in those of the Cambrian and Ordovician, for free movement and interbreeding had become possible between the animals on either side of the shrinking Iapetus Ocean.

Caledonian mountain building

At the end of the Silurian, a major period of mountain building resulted from collision of the two landmasses that had once been separated by the Iapetus Ocean. Earth movements had already affected sequences in the early and late Ordovician but these came to a climax at the end of the Silurian.

During this time, as well as being highly metamorphosed, the rocks of north-west Scotland were, as we saw earlier, thrust westward over the Basement. Crustal melting caused the formation of granite magma which rose and cooled to form the numerous intrusions that can be seen on the geological map in northern England and Scotland. The Shap granite examined in Chapters 1 and 3 is in fact a tiny part of a huge mass of granite underlying the Pennines and the Lake District.

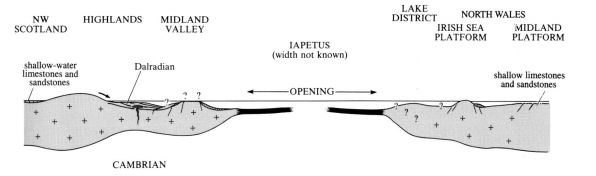

NW SCOTLAND   HIGHLANDS   MIDLAND VALLEY   IAPETUS (width not known)   LAKE DISTRICT   NORTH WALES   IRISH SEA PLATFORM   MIDLAND PLATFORM

shallow-water limestones and sandstones   Dalradian   ←—— OPENING ——→   shallow limestones and sandstones

CAMBRIAN

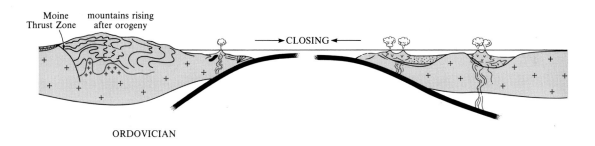

Moine Thrust Zone   mountains rising after orogeny   →— CLOSING —←

ORDOVICIAN

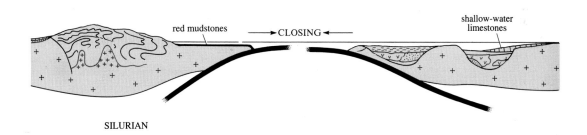

red mudstones   →— CLOSING —←   shallow-water limestones

SILURIAN

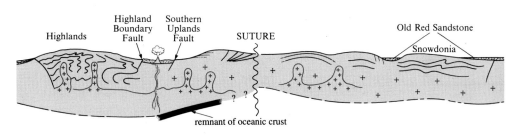

Highlands   Highland Boundary Fault   Southern Uplands Fault   SUTURE   Old Red Sandstone   Snowdonia

remnant of oceanic crust

EARLY DEVONIAN

145

South of the Southern Uplands of Scotland rocks of Cambrian, Ordovician and Silurian age were folded but not strongly metamorphosed. This produced a characteristic slaty cleavage which, in fine-grained rocks, makes good quality roofing slates, as can be seen in many quarries in north Wales and the Lake District. Figure 4.15(d) summarizes the palaeogeography and structure of the British Isles at the beginning of the Devonian, after the Caledonian mountains had formed.

The Rheic Ocean and the Variscan mountains

The demise of the Iapetus Ocean was accompanied by the birth of the Rheic Ocean to the south (Figure 4.17 (a)). Thus, by Devonian times, much of Britain was a mountainous area, bordered by the new ocean (Figure 4.17(b), Plate 7). The characteristic sedimentary deposit formed as a result of erosion of the Caledonian mountains is known as the Old Red Sandstone. It consists of sandstones, conglomerates and shales deposited by rivers draining south towards the Rheic Ocean and into intra-mountain basins in the Scottish area. The characteristic red colour is indicative of the arid nature of the climate, being the result of 'rusting' of the iron-rich minerals in the sediments.

Primitive land plants had just evolved, and the first insects appeared. In north-east Scotland, in the Orcadian basin (Figure 4.17(b)) a large lake formed in which primitive fish thrived. By the end of the Devonian, the first amphibians had evolved from these fish and emerged onto land. In swamps bordering this lake, early land plants flourished, and were exceptionally well preserved in the Rhynie Chert (Figure 1.14).

Along the shoreline of the Devonian sea to the south, marine muds and fossil-rich limestones (including reefs) were deposited in what is now Devon and Cornwall. The shales were converted to slates during later mountain building.

By Carboniferous times, the southern part of the Caledonian mountains had been eroded to near sea level, so that as global sea levels rose, the land was flooded by shallow tropical seas (Plate 8) in which the Carboniferous limestone was deposited, such as that studied in Chapter 3 at Tedbury Camp Quarry. During the later part of the Carboniferous, much of the British Isles was covered by deltas fed by rivers draining the remaining mountains in the north of Scotland. Swamps on top of these deltas accumulated think seams of peat (Plate 12), which became coal as they were buried beneath several kilometres of younger rocks. To the south, on the northern margin of the Rheic Ocean, thick sequences of deep-water sands and muds accumulated throughout the Carboniferous.

At the end of the Carboniferous, the Rheic Ocean closed, forming the Variscan mountain belt. Crustal thickening led to melting and the production of granite magma which rose and cooled to form a giant batholith postulated beneath Cornwall and Devon, the uppermost protuberances of which are exposed today (Figure 4.18, page 148). It is probable that the granites and the slightly metamorphosed rocks of the south-west peninsula were carried tens of kilometres northwards along thrusts comparable in scale to those associated with the Caledonian in Scotland (compare with Figure 4.13 on page 141).

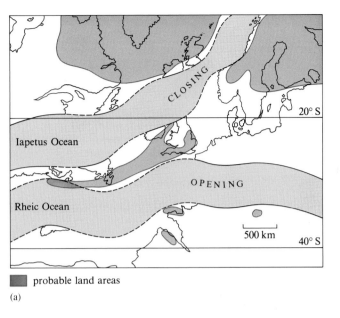

probable land areas

(a)

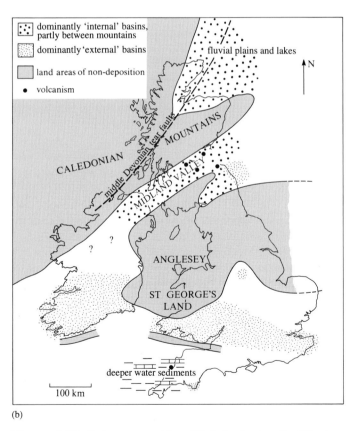

(b)

Figure 4.17 *Palaeogeography of Britain during the Silurian and Devonian. (a) The extent of the Iapetus and Rheic Oceans during the Silurian. (b) Britain during the Devonian.*

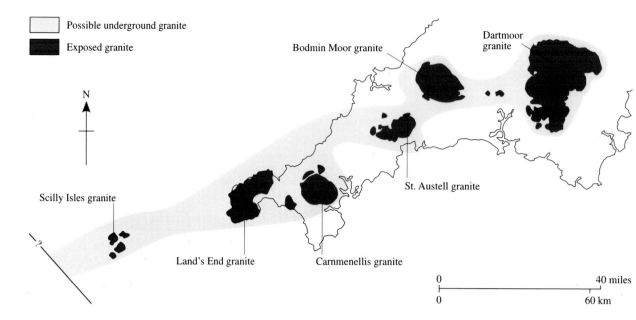

N

Dartmoor granite

Bodmin Moor granite

Scilly Isles granite

St. Austell granite

Land's End granite

Carnmenellis granite

0   40 miles

0   60 km

Figure 4.18 *The granite batholith of south-west England. The present-day exposures of granite (see also Plate 3) are the tops of relatively small protruberances above an extremely large mass of granite.*

The folded rocks of the Mendips (including those at Tedbury Camp Quarry) and south Wales mark the northern limit of the Variscan mountain belt. Further north, Devonian and Carboniferous rocks suffered only minor folding associated with mountain building, and comprise the Older Cover.

The Younger Cover and Atlantic opening

Since the formation of the Variscan mountains, the area of the British Isles has not experienced any major Earth movements associated with destructive plate boundaries, but the formation of Permian to Tertiary rocks of the Younger Cover was influenced by the opening and closing of the Tethys Ocean to the south-east (Figure 4.11 (d)–(f)) and the opening of the Atlantic Ocean to the west. The closure of the Rheic Ocean was the final stage in the assemblage of one supercontinent called Pangaea (Figure 4.11(d)). As this huge continent broke up during the Mesozoic (Figure 4.11(e) and (f)), extension of the continental crust in many places produced broad zones where the crust subsided over long periods. The resulting depressions were filled with thick accumulations of sediment to form sedimentary basins, such as in the North Sea. Here, over six kilometres of sediment were deposited; some of these layers were organically rich and when buried (and hence heated or 'cooked') have generated oil. Within the North Sea basin there are many porous sandstones that are potential reservoir rocks, and in certain areas, structures exist which have trapped the oil in huge quantities.

Closure of the Tethys Ocean resulted in the formation of the Alps. During this mountain-building episode, the crust over much of Europe was under compression, resulting in the development of the broad synclines and anticlines that can be seen on the geological map in south-east England (Plate 3, Figure 4.9) and smaller-scale folds such as those on the Dorset coast (Figure 2.32).

The Atlantic Ocean between the British Isles and Greenland began to open during the early part of the Tertiary, some 60 million years ago. The volcanic rocks of Northern Ireland and along the coast of north-west Scotland shown on the geological map record a major period of igneous activity that heralded the Atlantic opening. Not surprisingly, igneous rocks of the same age occur on the opposite side of the Atlantic on the east coast of Greenland. As well as piles of lava flows up to two kilometres thick exposed today at the Giant's Causeway and Fingal's Cave, large volcanoes built up over Arran, Mull and the Cuillin Hills of Skye.

4.6 Britain's northward drift

The previous section showed how the changing plate tectonic settings of the British Isles can be determined from the type of rocks and structures characteristic of different periods of geological time. It is also possible to interpret the nature of past climates from the features of the sedimentary rocks and any fossils they contain. And, as climate changes with latitude, it is possible to determine how the British area has changed its latitudinal position through time. This is indicated on Figure 4.11 (page 138), which shows that:

◆ between the Cambrian and Devonian, Britain was at about latitude 30 ˚S;

◆ during the Carboniferous, it was near the Equator;

◆ during the Permian and Triassic, it was at about 15–20 ˚N, after which it migrated steadily northwards to its present latitude of about 50 ˚N.

In fact, the latitudinal determinations used on Figure 4.11 were made by magnetic measurements of rocks of different ages. Such measurements enable magnetic minerals within rocks to be used as a kind of 'fossil compass'. This is based on the fact that if a compass needle is orientated vertically instead of horizontally, it will be near vertical at the Poles and near horizontal at the Equator; in other words its orientation approximates to its latitudal position. Using this relationship, the magnetic properties of rocks can be used to determine palaeolatitudes.

Before palaeomagnetic techniques were developed in the 1950s, it was difficult to explain why rocks characteristic of deserts or equatorial forests could be found in Britain. Had global climate changed radically, or had Britain moved across different climatic belts, as shown in Figure 4.11? We now believe the latter idea to be correct. Britain's northward drift has left key 'climatic signals' in the sedimentary record, as summarized in Table 4.2.

Table 4.2 Changes in climate and latitude

Millions of years ago	Period of geological time	Climatic signal	Latitude
205–present	Jurassic to present	Most sediments and fossil flora and fauna indicate subtropical conditions	Northward drift to present position: 50 ˚N
290–205	Permian, Triassic	Desert sands and lake deposits; evaporating inland sea (Plate 9)	20–30 ˚N
355–290	Carboniferous	Coal formed from peat that accumulated in equatorial forests (Plate 12)	10 ˚S–10 ˚N
410–355	Devonian	River deposits formed in desert climates (Plate 7)	25 ˚S
570–410	Cambrian, Ordovician, Silurian	Limestones with corals indicate deposition in tropical or subtropical climates (Plate 11)	30 ˚S
600	Very late Precambrian	Fossil boulder clays (tillites) in northern Scotland	80–90˚ S

This northward drift is of crucial economic significance to Britain for the following reasons (Plate 13):

◆ Coal formed from organic matter that accumulated in equatorial forests during the late Carboniferous. Coal of this age beneath the southern North Sea is the source of the natural gas found there.

◆ As the North Sea moved north into desert latitudes comparable to the Sahara today, wind-blown sands were deposited in what is known as the Rotliegend formation (German for 'red layers') that later became the reservoirs for natural gas.

◆ Natural gas would not have been trapped in the desert sandstone reservoirs unless they had been sealed by thick deposits of minerals such as halite (sodium chloride) through which gas under pressure cannot pass. These minerals formed by evaporation of an inland sea, called the Zechstein Sea, formed when the desert depression was flooded.

4.7 The Quaternary ice age

Introduction

In geological terms, the Quaternary is a very short period, lasting so far (it has not finished yet!) only about 2 million years, whereas the Tertiary had a duration of about 63 million years and the Carboniferous about 65 million years. Nevertheless, the Quaternary does stand out distinctly in the geological record because it marks a period of considerable global climatic instability, quite different from conditions during the Jurassic, Cretaceous or Tertiary. Evidence both from fossil faunas and floras and from estimates of ocean water temperatures suggest that during the Mesozoic and Tertiary, climates changed relatively slowly, episodes of abrupt change being rare. On the other hand, the Quaternary has been characterized by repeated cycles of rapid climatic change.

Continuous sedimentary records through the Tertiary and Quaternary only exist on the floors of the deep seas and oceans and perhaps in a few very ancient African lakes. Cores of ocean sediments, such as those recovered during deep-sea drilling, frequently contain abundant assemblages of microfossils, particularly the tiny calcareous skeletons of planktonic single-celled organisms – foraminifera – that floated near the surface of oceans. Many of the species concerned can still be found living today, and from knowledge of their present-day ecology it is possible to estimate the temperatures of the surface waters in which different fossil assemblages of these foraminifera from different depths in the cores were living. This kind of evidence shows that towards the end of the Teritary there developed on a global scale repeated periods of alternately warmer and cooler climate lasting about 100 000 years; they are known as *glacial–interglacial cycles* (Figure 4.19). These cycles became very much more pronounced about 2 million years ago, and during the colder intervals, expansions occurred of glacier ice on land and also of floating pack ice on the oceans, especially in the northern hemisphere. Seventeen cycles occurred during the last 1.8 million years, and they affected not only temperate latitudes, but also tropical and subtropical regions, where changes in temperature and especially rainfall took place.

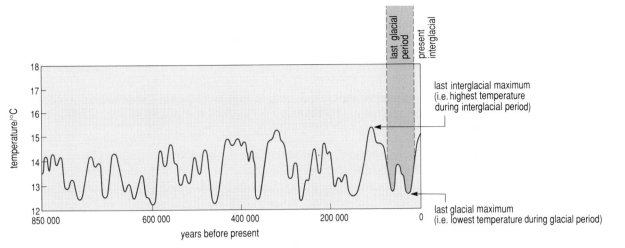

Figure 4.19
Changes in the average global surface temperature of the Earth during the past 850 000 years.

The onset of glacial conditions

Ice cover around the poles seems to develop when the polar areas become partly isolated from the main paths of the Earth's atmospheric and oceanic circulation. Thus the Antarctic is isolated by the circum-Antarctic wind and ocean current systems. Ice cover was established there as long ago as the Oligocene, when these current systems were established following the final separation from Antarctica of Australia and of South America, which had originally formed part of a single large continental plate, Gondwanaland.

However, the kind of climatic pattern that we refer to as an ice age (which involves an unstable climate and extension of ice sheets into temperate latitudes) was only established much later, towards the end of the Tertiary, when plate movements also led to the partial isolation of the Arctic Ocean. Important factors were probably:

◆ the closure of the strait between North and South America, which initiated a totally new ocean current system in the Atlantic, including the development of the Gulf Stream;

◆ the shallowness of the Bering Strait between Asia and North America which limits (or cuts off entirely during sea level lows of glacial periods) the flow of water from the Pacific into the Arctic Ocean.

The resulting deterioration of climate in the northern hemisphere is shown by the first development of glacial deposits in Iceland at about 3.5 million years ago. In the Atlantic Ocean off Britain, sea surface temperatures were some 10 °C lower than they are today. Probably the first major continental glaciation of Europe took place at about 2.3 million years ago, for palaeobotanical studies show that many temperate tree genera became extinct at this time. It is uncertain when the highlands of Britain were first glaciated during the Quaternary, but this probably occurred over a million years before the first surviving tills were deposited in lowland Britain about 0.5 million years ago. The size of glacial erosional land forms such as cirques and glacial troughs cut by valley glaciers suggest that an enormous amount of glacial and glaciofluvial erosion must have taken place since the end of the Tertiary, thus implying long periods of ice cover.

151

The glaciations of Britain

Although the most spectacular evidence for glaciation in Britain comes from mountain areas, the history of repeated glaciation can best be worked out in the lowlands. Extensive areas of Britain are still covered by till and glacial gravel deposits (Figure 4.20). The distribution of these deposits gives a rough impression of the maximum area of ice cover in Britain during the Quaternary. Considerable erosion and removal of till deposits has occurred locally; also not all areas were glaciated during the same ice advances.

At least three major, and several minor, ice advances have taken place in lowland Britain during the last half million years. The oldest of these penetrated deep into southern East Anglia, reaching the Chilterns, the north of London and the edge of the present Thames Valley. It was this advance recorded in Moor Mill quarry (Figure 1.6) that diverted the Thames from an older course that ran across East Anglia to join the sea on the Essex Coast, possibly near Clacton. The latest glacial stage of the Quaternary lasted from about 80 000 to 10 000 years ago, but the main period of actual ice advance took place only 25 000–15 000 years ago. The extent of this glaciation in Britain was less than during the previous major glacial episodes, for ice barely reached the Midlands or East Anglia.

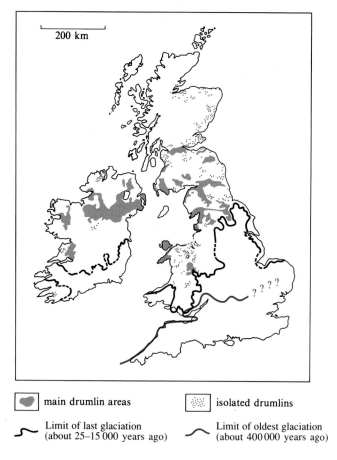

200 km

main drumlin areas   isolated drumlins

Limit of last glaciation (about 25–15 000 years ago)   Limit of oldest glaciation (about 400 000 years ago)

Figure 4.20 *The extent of glacial deposits in the British Isles. Drumlins are illustrated in Figure 2.21.*

We shall not discuss here the stratigraphic evidence for these ice advances, but you should note that they were separated not only by short interglacial episodes of temperate climate and vegetation, lasting 10–20 000 years, but also by even longer unglaciated but nevertheless intensely cold periods, during which periglacial processes such as seasonal freezing and thawing of the ground were sometimes very active. The deep-sea sedimentary record demonstrates clearly that, for most of the Quaternary, climatic conditions have been much colder than they are today, not only in Britain, but in virtually all the present temperate areas of the world.

The study of landforms, particularly those formed by glacial deposition such as drumlins, eskers, kettleholes and moraines (Figures 2.21 and 2.22), is extremely important in our understanding of the recent Quaternary history of Britain. Often these landforms can be used to reconstruct quite detailed local patterns of ice advance and retreat, since, unlike erosional landforms, they relate to particular stages in the Quaternary and even to particular local geological events.

Drumlins only occur within the margins of the last ice advance, because when a glacier invades an area it tends to destroy and rework the unconsolidated deposits over which it passes, such as the tills of older glaciations. This ice advance has left behind a landscape characterized by fresh depositional features – not only drumlins but also moraines, eskers, kames and kettleholes. Their distribution makes it possible to map fairly accurately the maximum limits of the last major ice advance.

You can see from Figure 4.20 that to the south and east of the margin of the last glaciation is an area glaciated by the previous ice advances; this still possesses widespread patches of till and glacifluvial deposits. However, although these deposits have not been reworked by ice, other processes of erosion have destroyed virtually all the glacial landforms of these deposits.

The latest episode in the glacial history of Britain took place relatively recently. The main ice sheet of the last glaciation melted very rapidly, and by 13 000 years ago summer temperatures at least were as warm as at the present day. Suddenly, however, the climate deteriorated again, and it is a measure of how erratic and how rapid Quaternary climatic changes can be, that during a very short interval (about 11 000–10 000 years ago) known as the *Loch Lomond Readvance*, an ice cap was re-established in the western highlands of Scotland, as were cirque (corrie) glaciers in the mountains of Wales and the Lake District. By 10 000 years ago, these glaciers had melted as rapidly as they had appeared. In the Scottish highlands, and elsewhere at high altitude, they left behind the freshest and best preserved hummocky glacial landscapes, moraines and glacifluvial deposits to be found anywhere in Britain. They also left a reminder that climatic change on this scale could certainly be repeated.

Beyond the glaciations

During long cold periods, the amount of water locked up in ice caps grew so that the sea level fell, resulting in Britain being joined to the continental mainland of Europe. The vegetation was dominantly of a tundra type, consisting of bog and open ground with a discontinuous cover of Arctic herbs, grasses and dwarf shrubs. There was a mammal fauna of mammoth, reindeer, woolly rhino and musk ox, or perhaps horse and bison when conditions became slightly milder. Only in the short interglacial periods did a warmer climate permit the growth, first of coniferous forest, such as is now found in Scandinavia, then of deciduous forest with oak, elm and ash, such as we have in Britain today. The interglacial fauna consisted not only of familiar animals such as deer, badger and fox, but also of exotic species, such as straight-tusked elephant, hippopotamus, lion and hyaena, which are now extinct or confined to tropical regions.

Humans also first appeared in Britain during an interglacial period about 700 000 years ago, and they eventually mastered the environments near the icesheets as hunters of mammoth, bison and reindeer. Stone tools are found in Quaternary lake sediments, in river gravels and (rarely) in tills. Only in postglacial times did humans develop the skills of crop and animal husbandry that ultimately permitted the development of urban civilizations. These skills were first developed in the Near East, but reached Britain with the first Neolithic peoples about 5500 years ago. With the development of modern civilizations, humans have largely imposed their own ecosystems on our landscapes, and their activities are now both changing those landscapes and modifying many of the geological processes that sculpture them.

◆ PART 3 ◆

CONSERVATION IN ACTION

Study comment

Before studying Part 3, please read or reread Chapter 1, Section 1.5 'Some basics of Earth heritage conservation', as this summarizes the justification for site conservation, including the usage of sites by various categories of visitor. Chapter 5 extends the discussion of Earth heritage conservation (EHC) and introduces strategies that can be used to promote it both generally and in terms of individual sites.

The next four chapters review the 'nuts and bolts' of practical conservation. Chapter 6 discusses the conservation classification of sites. When you have finished studying it you should be able to apply the classification in order to decide on the broad nature of conservation methods that need to be used for particular sites. Chapter 7 explores in more detail the practical methods that can be used to conserve sites, and where possible to reconcile these with other interests. Chapter 8 examines the role of partnerships of people and organizations in practical conservation work, and in Chapter 9 the important role that RIGS (Regionally Important Geological/geomorphological Site) schemes play in bringing a wide range of groups together is explored.

Finally, Chapter 10 considers practical methods by which public awareness of geological and geomorphological sites can be enhanced, and how individuals can become involved in such activities.

Allow 10 hours to study Part 3.

Chapter 5

EARTH HERITAGE CONSERVATION – AN OVERVIEW

Study comment

This chapter builds on Chapter 1, Section 1.5 by:

◆ briefly reviewing the extractive and cultural resources of the Earth;

◆ comparing the concept of Earth heritage conservation (EHC) with that for wildlife conservation;

◆ elaborating the justification of EHC introduced in Chapter 1;

◆ introducing strategies (developed in later chapters) which are used both to promote the need for EHC and to conserve individual sites.

5.1 Extractive and cultural physical resources of the Earth

What is a resource? The word has a variety of meanings in everyday speech, and it is often used in the plural. It is probably most often applied to a source of economic wealth, especially of a country (for example its mineral resources), or to a business enterprise (for example its capital resources, equipment resources, personnel resources). A resource is often seen as the means of doing something, especially in time of need, such as being able to supply shelter, food and medicines after an earthquake, or being able to save people and animals from a major flood. 'Human resources' usually refers to the total of a group of people's intellectual and physical capabilities. Individuals are often said to draw on resources such as stamina or strength. All meanings of 'resource' have in common the notion of something that is useful or of value to humans.

The Earth provides us with physical and biological resources that sustain the activities of society. (Physical resources comprise the inorganic material available for extraction from the Earth.) We exploit these resources to provide ourselves with food, water, heat, shelter and transport. But we also value the planet's physical resources in a cultural sense. This is because we wish to continue to seek the means to advance our knowledge of processes both in the past and at the present time. Equally importantly, we value the beauty of the physical world as an inspirational and aesthetic resource. Thus we have two value sets which sometimes conflict with each other. One is concerned with the exploitation and conservation of physical resources as commodities and the other with conserving them as 'heritage'. The latter set of 'heritage values' is inextricably linked to our own history as a species, because not only do we find beauty in unspoilt wilderness and landscapes, but we also value landscapes – both rural and urban – which we have created.

Figure 5.1 summarizes the distinction between the extractive and cultural physical resources of the Earth; a similar diagram could be drawn for biological resources. There is now much debate about physical resources conservation in the context of sustainable development, which is development that meets the needs of the present without compromising the ability of future generations to meet their own needs. This debate is not the concern of this text, but sustainable use of Earth heritage resources certainly is. Therefore Earth heritage conservation can be defined as being *concerned with sustaining the part of the physical resources of the Earth that represents our cultural heritage, including our geological and geomorphological understanding, and the inspirational and aesthetic response to the resource.*

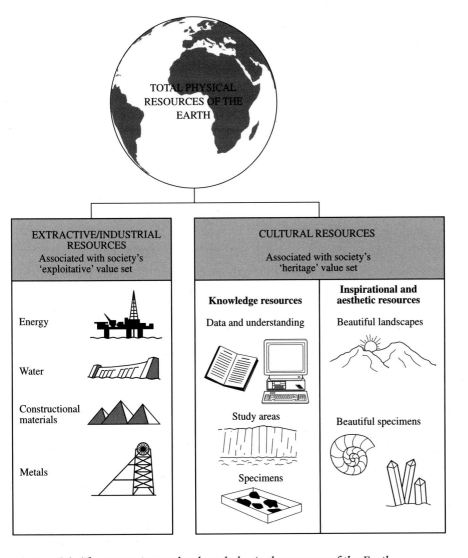

Figure 5.1 *The extractive and cultural physical resources of the Earth.*

5.2 Why Earth heritage conservation?

Most people are aware of the need or justification for the conservation of living things and of natural habitats; this is 'biological heritage conservation' – a concept familiar to and accepted by the public, although not with the 'heritage' label. The concept of diminishing habitats (such as the tropical rain forests) and the idea of endangered species (such as the elephant) has broadened people's perception of the need for the protection of the natural environment.

Consider the following, paraphrased from the leaflet *Why Conserve Wildlife?* published by the former Nature Conservancy Council:

> The natural world is the basis of life itself – the fabric upon which we all depend for survival. Together all organisms resemble a living body with each part dependent upon others. Many of these cannot be necessarily essential for the continuation of life. But we do not know for certain what the effects of losing a particular species could be. Nor do we know which ones could prove most valuable in the future. Who would have guessed that a mould like *Penicillin* would save so many lives? The natural world can also help us to understand the environment in which we live. Finally, the natural world offers us all a source of wonder and refreshment amidst the complexities of modern life.

This leaflet was written with the conservation of wildlife in mind. Many of the arguments seem familiar, and most people would agree that protection of species and habitats is important:

◆ for their own sake;

◆ for their potential value and use to people;

◆ as an attractive natural park.

We can regard these as the key justifications for wildlife conservation.

But why should Earth science features need conserving, and what is the justification for doing so? Surely rocks and landforms can look after themselves; after all, they are hard and durable in most cases. We have seen in Chapter 4 that the record of the rocks has been built over a great many millions of years. Isn't it true that they are likely to remain the same in the future?

These questions are explored in Activity 5.1.

ACTIVITY 5.1

THE JUSTIFICATION FOR CONSERVING EARTH HERITAGE SITES – AND POSSIBLE THREATS TO THEM

In the light of the justification for wildlife conservation, and with the questions posed above in mind, consider the three photographs in Figure 5.2. They show three major Earth heritage sites in Britain. You studied them in Chapter 1 and we shall visit them again later in the text. The first is the exposure of the major unconformity between the Jurassic and Carboniferous at Tedbury Camp Quarry which was examined in detail in Chapter 3. The second is a series of natural clay cliffs exposed at the coast at Barton in Hampshire. The sedimentary rocks forming these cliffs were deposited during the Tertiary, and are rich in fossils indicating a warm sea teeming with life. The third site is a natural river system

Figure 5.2 *Three important Earth heritage conservation sites. (a) Tedbury Camp Quarry, Somerset. (b) Barton Cliffs, Hampshire. (c) River Feshie, Highland Region.*

(a)

(b)

(c)

in northern Scotland, the River Feshie. This system is actively changing its course and moving its bedload of gravel, as it has done since the ice age.

First, consider the three sites in the light of the three key justifications for wildlife conservation given above. Try and apply these justifications to the sites, and give your reasons. Don't worry if you can't apply all three to each site. Do this before reading on.

Second, consider what possible threats there could be to these sites. Conservation implies that protection from some threatened damage is needed. What form could this damage take? Do this in the light of the questions raised above.

Write down your answers before reading on.

◆ ◆ ◆

Tedbury Camp Quarry

Key justification

Tedbury Camp Quarry is important for three reasons.

◆ *For its own sake.* The quarry provides a three-dimensional exposure of a major unconformity, revealing successive episodes in the geological history of south-west England.

◆ *For its potential value and use to people.* Tedbury Camp Quarry is recognized as an important educational site. It provides safe access to rock faces, and demonstrates a superb 'textbook' example of an unconformity for study.

◆ *As an attractive natural park.* The exposures of rock and the overgrown parts of the quarry provide natural features of interest which can be visited by the public using the local network of footpaths.

Potential threats

As described in Chapters 1 and 3, after quarrying ceased Tedbury Camp Quarry was used as a site for tipping hardcore. Later, with the co-operation of the owners, it was cleared, and the lower face of the Carboniferous Limestone was made accessible by building a bank of hardcore against all but the top few metres. Collaboration between conservationists and the owners not only removed the major threat to the site, but also improved it by clearing faces and the unconformity surface, and making access to exposures safer. The only remaining threats are that vegetation will obscure the site, and that weathering and hammering will degrade the Jurassic limestone faces. Periodic clearance of shrubs and rock debris easily counters this threat.

Fortunately, collaboration between conservationists and site owners can often result in a creative solution such as that reached in the case of Tedbury Camp Quarry. But sometimes conservation and other interests are irreconcilable, and compromise solutions may have to be reached through adjudication at a public inquiry, as was the case at Barton Cliffs.

Barton Cliffs

Key justification

Barton Cliffs can be considered important for three reasons.

◆ *For their own sake.* The cliffs illustrate how natural processes sculpture a particular landform, and so they are attractive in their own right.

◆ *For their potential value and use to people.* Barton Cliffs are an important site for stratigraphers. Because they expose a sequence of strata that provides a reference section for the Bartonian Stage (spanning the period between 41 and 45 million years ago) they are of worldwide importance to science. The cliffs have been an important training ground for countless geologists, some of whom have contributed to the nation's wealth through exploration for oil and gas and other minerals. The cliffs are a relatively safe educational resource for schoolchildren; the abundant fossils help them to understand the concepts of evolution and changing environments. The cliffs may be studied for a greater understanding of coastal erosion processes.

- *As an attractive natural park.* Barton Cliffs are natural features which contribute to the beauty of the Hampshire coastline.

Potential threats

Barton Cliffs are being eroded by coastal processes such as wave attack. This is a natural process which replenishes the exposure of clay; the major threat lies with interference in this process through the building of coastal protection such as sea walls and promenades. Many of our most important coastal sites are under threat in this way. Building a concrete sea wall destroys the natural beauty and educational and scientific research value of cliffs by covering them up forever.

It is clear that the need to conserve Barton Cliffs is based upon the same three key justifications that we identified in the conservation of wildlife sites. Barton Cliffs are not durable: they are made from clay, but left untouched they contribute to the natural system of sediments which are distributed around our coastline and which help build up our beaches; these are natural defences against wave attack. Unfortunately, the cliffs are under constant threat, not from these natural processes but from people's desire to arrest the erosional effects of the sea and to build concrete or other hard coastal defences. Especially common where eroding cliffs are close to an area of habitation, coast protection ultimately destroys the natural beauty of such cliffs, and through covering them or allowing them to grow over destroys their research and educational value.

As described on page 24, a public inquiry in 1991 reached a compromise between conservation and coastal protection interests by allowing one instead of three drains to be dug into the cliffs.

River Feshie

Key justifications

The River Feshie may also be considered important for three reasons.
- *For its own sake.* The Feshie is an attractive natural river system which contributes to the beauty of the Cairngorm Mountains.
- *For its potential value and use to people.* The Feshie is an actively developing river system. It is of value because study of the processes involved will allow people to understand better how rivers develop, flood and move sediment, and therefore modify these actions where they are a problem elsewhere in the world. The River Feshie provides a training ground for geomorphologists who contribute to the economy of Britain through their understanding of the effects of natural processes on the landscape.
- *As an attractive natural park.* The Feshie is an integral feature of one of Britain's most attractive natural areas.

Potential threats

The Feshie is a naturally and rapidly evolving river system and so it is apt to flood adjacent areas. Such flooding is damaging to agriculture as presently practised on the site. Therefore a major threat would be an attempt to stop these natural processes through interference with the course of the river (artificial channelling), which would destroy not only its natural beauty but also its value for scientific study.

The course of the River Feshie is neither hard nor durable; although it has existed for many thousands of years it is constantly changing and ephemeral. It has both natural beauty and scientific value, but the natural processes which give the river its value are seen by some as damaging. The threat here is once again human interference, which, as with Barton cliffs, would reduce the amenity and study potential of a natural system.

From Activity 1 it should be clear that the conservation of wildlife and natural habitats and the conservation of Earth heritage sites share the same aims. All of the natural world, including what may be termed the biosphere (wildlife and habitats) and geosphere (geological and geomorphological features and landforms) is fragile and subject to drastic change by human activities. Both wildlife and Earth heritage sites earn the right to conservation for the three key reasons given above. Both wildlife and Earth heritage sites are susceptible to interference and are not durable or permanent. In summary, the need for conservation of Earth heritage sites should be as prevalent in our awareness as the need for conservation of wildlife and habitats. Box 5.1 gives a fuller justification for the conservation of Earth heritage sites.

Box 5.1 The justification for Earth heritage conservation

The justification for the conservation of Earth heritage sites lies primarily in:

◆ a commitment to the conservation of our natural heritage, whether it be wildlife, habitat, landform or geological feature;

◆ a need to allow research for the advancement of science, industry and the understanding of natural processes and their effects on people;

◆ a need for naturally occurring Earth heritage sites to train Earth scientists and to provide teaching facilities for schools;

◆ a need to maintain naturally occurring Earth heritage sites as part of our natural landscape, and in so doing aid greater awareness of natural beauty and natural systems.

5.3 Earth heritage conservation in Great Britain – a strategy

Despite the obvious need for the conservation of geological and geomorphological sites, Earth heritage conservation is a relatively new concept. Wildlife conservation groups have existed since the middle of the 19th century and their influence has lead to the widespread acceptance of the need for wildlife conservation in Britain. The impetus for conservation in the Earth sciences did not develop until much later.

Although there were some early practical achievements, systematic Earth heritage conservation began only in 1949 when the Nature Conservancy (later to become the Nature Conservancy Council, NCC) was first set up. Its role was to advise on conservation in all fields, including Earth sciences, and to designate areas as Sites of Special Scientific Interest (SSSIs) 'by reason of [their] flora, fauna or geological or physiographical features'. This provided protection for many of Britain's most important and cherished Earth heritage sites, and this protection continues to this day with the new national conservation agencies (NCAs) in England, Scotland and Wales, which are successors to the NCC. Although the conservation agencies are official bodies, they rely on the help of amateurs and professionals alike in carrying forward the task. The NCC and its successors have also helped in the setting-up of another network of sites, the Regionally Important Geological/ geomorphological Sites (RIGS). SSSIs and RIGS will be explored in Chapters 8 and 9.

One of the last major achievements of the Nature Conservancy Council before it was broken up was the publication in 1990 of the document *Earth Science Conservation in Great Britain – A Strategy*. The main aim of the document was to provide a strategy to help direct the efforts and enthusiasm of interested people towards active conservation in the Earth sciences. This valuable publication set out in a clear and detailed way the need for what in this text is referred to as Earth heritage conservation by presenting a consensus of views from people who use, research, own and develop Earth heritage sites in Britain. It is the basis for conservation in the Earth sciences, and the rest of this book draws heavily on its wisdom.

The strategy provides a clear overview of the need for Earth heritage conservation, the means by which it can be effected, and the bodies most able to take an active role. Not all sites of scientific importance or of educational value can be protected by law. Therefore the document presents a scheme for fostering the effectiveness of local groups in providing the initiative for conservation of sites not afforded legal protection.

Figure 5.3
The strategy document and its appendices.

The strategy has six main themes, outlined below and in Box 5.2 on page 164:

◆ maintaining the SSSI network;

◆ extending the RIGS network;

◆ developing new conservation techniques;

◆ improving the documentation of sites;

◆ increasing public awareness;

◆ developing international links.

In addition to setting these clear goals for conservation through its themes, the strategy makes a major contribution to practical site conservation by presenting a detailed guide to solving the technical problems often facing conservationists in Earth sciences. This guide is in the form of a series of appendices which provide a catalogue of techniques and other information of direct relevance in practical conservation.

Box 5.2 The themes of the strategy document

The document *Earth Science Conservation in Great Britain – A Strategy* provides very clear guidelines for people involved or about to be involved with the conservation of Earth heritage sites, whether professional or amateur. It does so in a series of themes which set clear objectives for conservationists.

1   That the statutory SSSI system, selected on pure research criteria, should be defended and updated where necessary. The SSSI system is based on mutually supportive networks of sites so that loss or damage of sites in these would render these networks incomplete (see Chapter 8).

2   That the network of non-statutory RIGS sites should be expanded. These sites complement the SSSI networks and are important in their own right. They are selected regionally by a variety of criteria, including research value but also taking into account educational and wider landscape use not covered in the SSSI network. The RIGS sites are selected and actively protected by groups including local amateur and professional Earth scientists, planners and museum groups (see Chapter 9).

3   That new conservation techniques should be devised. Through NCC experience it is clear that the most effective way of countering major threats to Earth heritage sites is to suggest alternative, practical ways in which developers may plan their development to be conservation-friendly. Many of the site types, whether SSSIs, RIGS or other sites, have quite specific types of threat associated with them; but by focusing attention, ideas and research on these threats many could be countered (see Chapter 7).

4   That documentation of sites and collection of specimens from them should be improved. Armed with specific information on the distribution of the most important features of a site, and the knowledge of how a site fits into a network, or why it displays better or worse features than others in the same area, a conservationist can assess and counter potential damage to sites. Greater involvement in documentation schemes such as the National Scheme for Geological Site Documentation (NSGSD) (see Chapter 8) or the RIGS initiative will help fulfil the aims of this theme. Information on sites and specimens from them are an important facet of Earth heritage conservation.

5   That public awareness should be increased. Countless media references help reinforce people's awareness of the need for conservation of wildlife, aided by major conservation organizations like the Royal Society for Nature Conservation, Royal Society for the Protection of Birds, World Wide Fund for Nature, etc. With similar coverage the needs and aims of Earth heritage conservation would be widely known, increasing its standing, and really involving people in the process of conservation (see Chapter 10).

6   That international links should be developed. Wildlife conservation is truly international, and it is clear that involvement in worldwide Earth heritage conservation issues will create a similar international involvement. The precedent is set: the important Grube Messel vertebrate site in Germany, yielding rare fossils of bats and rodents, was saved from landfill by international pressure, albeit from a professional minority (see Chapter 10, Section 10.5).

Chapter 6

THE NATURE OF EARTH HERITAGE SITES

Study comment

This section examines the variety of Earth heritage sites, and explains how they are classified in order to guide plans for their practical conservation. At the end of this chapter you should be able to identify the type and nature of the features to be conserved, and therefore be in a position to decide on the course of action to be taken to conserve them.

6.1 Approaches to Earth heritage conservation

As with any subject, it is best to approach conservation in a systematic manner. An ancient woodland or the nesting site of a golden eagle will require different approaches. In these examples it is clear that in the first instance we are trying to conserve the trees themselves, and in the second to prevent the disturbance of the eyrie of the eagle. Clearly, we have first:

◆ to identify the type of feature to be conserved;

and then:

◆ to decide on a course of action to conserve it.

This approach is applicable to all fields of conservation, including Earth heritage.

As you have seen in Part 2, Earth heritage covers a range of interconnected but nevertheless quite distinct subdisciplines which together help to explain how the Earth formed and changed through time, both at depth and at the surface. Earth heritage features to be conserved are correspondingly varied. All geologists and geomorphologists use the information available to them at the surface to help to build up this picture. They usually collect this information from discrete areas of geological or geomorphological interest which can be referred to as 'sites'. From now on we will use the term *site* to cover the area and feature which we will attempt to conserve. This might apply to an exposure or outcrop of rock (which to a geologist includes both hard and soft materials, such as granite and clay for instance), or to a landform.

The following exercise may help you to realise the variety of sites to be conserved.

ACTIVITY 6.1
THE VARIETY OF SITES

From what you know about geology and geomorphology, developed from your own experience and what you have learned from Part 2 and your preliminary study of sites in Chapter 1, make a list of as many types of Earth heritage sites that you can think of. Include different types of landforms and geological exposures. Do this before reading on.

It is best to approach this as a 'brainstorming' exercise, writing down ideas as they come to you, without bias or order, and rearranging them in your final list.

Can you identify major groupings of sites?

The different types of sites, defined from a conservation point of view, are explored later in this chapter.

◆ ◆ ◆

You may have realized that rocks, both hard and soft, may be *naturally* exposed by the processes of wind and water erosion, or they may be exposed *by human activity*, in quarries, pits and mines. On the other hand, landforms are inherently created by natural processes, although people can have a direct influence on their development. Thus sites may be described as:

◆ *static,* created by processes acting in the geological past; or

◆ *active,* forming and evolving on a human timescale.

From this brief exercise you can perhaps appreciate how varied the sites are that Earth heritage conservationists protect. We have gone some way in our approach to conservation in *identifying the type of site*, before *deciding on a course of action*. In your list, you may have written down 'quarry' and 'mountain'. Clearly, these will require different courses of action in order to conserve them. Is the quarry disused or active? Is the deposit exposed in the quarry limited in extent? Does the mountain itself need conserving as a particular landform type, or does the mountain side expose a number of important rock outcrops? Answers to questions like these will ultimately lead to appropriate methods of conservation. Therefore, we need to go further in classifying sites in order to identify appropriate courses of action.

6.2 Exposure and integrity sites

All Earth heritage sites fall into one of two contrasting major types: *exposure* (E) and *integrity* (I) sites (Figure 6.1). The importance of distinguishing these two categories is that *their conservation employs fundamentally contrasting approaches*. This section defines these two terms so that you can be thinking about the sites in your local area in this way.

Exposure sites

Exposure sites usually provide *access* to geological deposits which are extensive and plentiful underground. Without this access or exposure such deposits could not be seen and studied. However, if the material comprising a cliff or quarry face were destroyed by erosion or quarrying, new faces would be created (Figure 6.1(a)). So the site would still have the equivalent value in conservation terms if either access was maintained to the face of the quarry, i.e. to the exposure, or the quarry was infilled, but a new face was cut elsewhere.

(a)

(b)

Figure 6.1 *Exposure and integrity sites.*
(a) Cliffs at Hunstanton, Norfolk exposing normal white Chalk overlying red Chalk and dark coloured sandstones. Debris along the foot of the cliff indicates rapid erosion, ensuring that the rock sequence is always well exposed. As there is no chance of erosion completely removing the rock sequence (it extends way back beyond the cliffs), it is classed as an exposure site.
(b) Coastal sand dunes at Morfa Harlech, Gwynedd. These landforms would be destroyed by erosion or commercial extraction of sand. They therefore need conserving in their existing state and so are an example of an integrity site.

Integrity sites

Integrity sites either contain or display deposits which are limited in extent and are therefore a finite resource, or are landforms which could not be recreated if they were to be destroyed (Figure 6.1(b)). Glacial landforms and unique mineral or fossil deposits are typically integrity sites; a good example is the Rhynie Chert (page 34). This is an internationally important and world-famous deposit for early fossil plants formed under exceptional conditions, and is limited in extent. Any quarrying would quickly remove the whole deposit and destroy the scientific value of the site.

Box 6.1 Checklist for recognition of integrity and exposure sites

Geological sites

◆ Is the potential outcrop of the deposit exposed large (in whatever form)? In other words, does the information available (maps, published data, SSSI, RIGS or National Scheme for Geological Site Documentation (NSGSD) data sources), indicate that the deposit continues for some distance underground? If 'yes', it is usually an *exposure site*.

◆ Does the deposit contain limited accumulations of unique minerals or fossils, which are of significant research importance? If 'yes', it is usually an *integrity site*.

◆ If the site is a mine, does it have dumps of mining spoil with unique mineral or fossil assemblages? If 'yes', it is an *integrity site*.

Landform/geomorphological sites

◆ Almost all landforms worthy of conservation are *integrity sites*. Conservation relies upon whether they are *static* sites (such as the esker shown in Figure 2.2(a)) or *active process* sites (such as the River Feshie, Figure 5.2(c)).

6.3 *The Earth Heritage Conservation Classification (EHCC)*

The Earth Heritage Conservation Classification (EHCC) was developed by the Nature Conservancy Council in order to rationalize the practical approach to conservation of the various types of sites, some of which you will have listed when doing Activity 6.1. The classification has two main elements which form the horizontal and vertical axes of a grid or *matrix* within which individual sites can be placed; these elements are *site type* and *site use*. The value of this type of 'pigeonholing' exercise is that it helps to characterize the nature of a site and to decide upon an appropriate course of action to conserve it. This enables a *conservation profile* to be drawn up, which provides guidelines for the conservation of the specific site types in the classification. A set of conservation profiles is provided as an appendix to the strategy document described in Chapter 5, and an example is given in Box 6.2. The profile helps to provide would-be conservationists with a series of principles by which they can counter proposed new operations or developments which could damage or destroy sites.

The classification has as its basis the division into integrity and exposure sites. Once you have decided on this basic subdivision, it is possible to classify the site according to its type and use, and thereby find it a place within the EHCC matrix.

Category: Exposure site

Profile of possible threatening developments and methods of site enhancement

Coast protection

Engineering schemes which involve loss of geological exposure or prevent the continued erosion which maintains exposure are generally incompatible with effective site conservation.

Developments above cliffs

New developments proposed adjacent to eroding sea or river cliffs are not themselves directly damaging, but they may lead to a requirement for coast protection or river bank works at some time in the future.

Chalet/beach hut development

Developments which are sited at a distance of at least 5 metres from the cliff foot are normally compatible with effective site conservation, but may lead to a long-term requirement to stabilize cliffs, to the detriment of the *in situ* exposure.

Recreational development

In general, recreational developments are compatible with conservation. Exceptions to this are any reprofiling of faces, leading to loss of exposure, and activities that unreasonably impede access to the cliffs or cause damage to rock exposures.

Signs, paths and fencing

Provision of 'amenity' developments is compatible with effective site conservation provided that they do not obscure outcrops or prevent access to the site.

Tree and scrub clearance

Clearance of scrub from coastal or river cliffs is normally beneficial, but there is a risk that some exposures may be damaged by vehicle tracks.

Dumping at cliff foot

Dumping is normally incompatible with conservation.

On-site interpretation

Coastal cliffs provide excellent opportunities for interpretation.

6.4 Site type – the vertical axis of the EHCC matrix

As we have seen, the basis for the identification of different types of site is the distinction between exposure and integrity sites. A further subdivision can be made according to the nature of the exposure (such as a quarry or a coastal cliff) or the special features of the deposit or landform (Table 6.1, overleaf). Some of these you will already have recognized when completing Activity 6.1. The classification employs a shorthand way of describing the site type, and consists of a first letter denoting Exposure or Integrity site, and a second letter denoting the nature of exposure, or special feature (for example Exposure, Disused quarry, site type ED, or Integrity, Mineral or fossil deposit, site type IM). This shorthand notation will be introduced as we go through the various site types.

Table 6.1 The vertical axis of the EHCC matrix

	Category codes
Integrity sites	
Static (fossil) geomorphological sites	IS
Active process geomorphological sites	IA
Caves and karst (distinctive limestone features such as pavements and swallow holes)	IC
Unique mineral, fossil or other geological sites	IM
Mine dumps (continuum with specimen collections)	ID
Exposure sites	
Disused quarries, pits and cuttings	ED
Active quarries and pits	EA
Coastal and river cliffs	EC
Foreshore exposures	EF
Inland outcrops and stream sections	EO
Mines and tunnels	EM

Each site type will have specific threats associated with it, as discussed in the examples in Chapter 1 and Chapter 5. Barton Cliffs, an exposure site, are threatened by coastal protection works, while the River Feshie, an integrity site, is threatened by artificial channelling works. It is the experience of Earth heritage conservationists that threats to the wellbeing of sites are dominated by one or two major problems with many smaller, related ones. As we go through the types of site in this chapter we shall examine the typical threats they face. Quite often the distinction of site type can be blurred: sometimes unique mineral or fossil deposits fall within a larger exposure site, in a quarry for example, or within a large coastal site. In this case it may be that both distinctions apply, with the usually smaller integrity sites as a subdivision of the larger exposure site, each with its own specific threats.

ACTIVITY 6.2

THREATS TO SITES

As each of the major site types given below is introduced, prepare a list of threats which might affect its wellbeing. An example of a typical threat might be the loss of geological exposure by filling a quarry with domestic waste.

Prepare these lists using the brainstorming procedure, and then order the threats according to their relative importance. Compare your lists with the discussion of threats given. Take particular note of threats that you might have given particular emphasis to, but that have not been ranked as particularly important in the discussion.

A reminder about this exercise is given after the introduction to each site.

◆ ◆ ◆

6.5 Quarries, pits and cuttings

As the example in Figure 6.2 shows, quarries and pits are exposure sites created by human activity, although in some cases they may also be or contain integrity sites (for example a gravel pit cut in a landform; a unique mineral deposit in a quarry). A distinction is usually made between workings extracting relatively hard rock, such as granite and limestone (quarries), and those extracting softer materials, such as clays, sand and gravel (pits). Quarries and pits are usually originally cut for the extraction of the raw materials for brickmaking, for building stone and for aggregates. They often represent the biggest geological exposures away from coastal cliffs. Quarries and pits can be further subdivided into *disused* (ED) and *active* (EA) examples.

ACTIVITY 6.2
THREATS TO SITES (CONTINUED)

What are the threats to disused quarries and pits? Make a list and compare it with the one below. Is the order of your list the same as that given here? Are there are any threats you have given that are not listed? Consider why.

───────────────── ◆ ◆ ◆ ─────────────────

Disused quarries (ED) are obvious targets for the disposal of waste materials (Figure 6.2). Such large 'holes in the ground' are the most obvious receptacles for domestic and industrial waste, and their filling by waste disposal companies is a

Figure 6.2 *A disused quarry in Devonian Old Red Sandstone in the Forest of Dean, Gloucestershire. This exposure site is threatened not only by 'flytipping', but by degradation of the quarry faces by weathering and the growth of vegetation.*

profitable business. In some cases the quarry is seen as a scar on the landscape, and filling with waste products is a way of restoring the landscape. Obviously, in areas of large conurbations few quarries will escape the attentions of the waste disposal industry. Such landfill, as it is called, buries the exposure and thus removes the geological interest. Sections of rock face can be maintained by properly designed partial infill of a quarry, but this has its own problems. Other alternatives include the cutting of a completely new geological exposure in the same vicinity. These and other approaches are discussed in Chapter 7.

The next most common threat after waste disposal is building development: disused quarries often make prime sites for 'out of town' industrial or retail units or caravan sites. Without careful planning, badly placed buildings can obscure geological faces.

Finally, the natural processes of rock fall, slumping, general degradation of quarry faces and growth of vegetation lead to the geological features being obscured. With careful management, such degradation can be minimized or controlled.

ACTIVITY 6.2
THREATS TO SITES (CONTINUED)

What are the threats to active quarries? Make a list and compare it with the one below. Is the order of your list the same as that given here? Are there any threats you have given that are not listed? Consider why.

Active quarries (EA) provide exciting new exposures, and usually extension of the quarrying activity is a welcome source of new and fresh exposure, especially where the geological material concerned is prone to weathering. Perhaps surprisingly, then, quarrying is normally not a threat to Earth heritage interests. The exception is where there is an integrity deposit incorporated within the exposure site. This highlights the similarities between Earth heritage conservation integrity sites and wildlife sites.

Threats to active quarries are few, the main one occurring in the proposed after-use of the quarry, usually in one of the ways discussed above. Where the quarry owner does not have a legal requirement to restore the landscape to its former pattern, faces are often left in a poor condition, especially in hard materials where near-vertical faces, unstable from blasting, can be left, posing a threat to the safety of visitors. Careful planning and improved blasting techniques can avoid this.

An important point to remember is that active quarries are exceptionally dangerous places to work in and study, and it is always essential to gain co-operation from operators for access.

So far, the discussion has concentrated on quarries and pits from which material is extracted because it has a commercial value. Road cuttings also provide important exposures of rocks and geological structures. In this case the principal threat is from the designers of road schemes, who usually prefer to landscape cuttings by covering rock exposures with soil and subsequently seeding them with grass and planting shrubs and trees. This fetish is not always justified. Landscaping can be

(a)

(b)

Figure 6.3 *Road cuttings excavated by smooth blasting techniques.*
(a) A cutting through Lewisian metamorphic rocks near Laxford Bridge, north-west Scotland. The closely spaced vertical shot holes resulted in a sheer stable rock face with very little shattering due to blasting, leaving a stable cutting providing a beautiful exposure.
(b) A new road cutting at Farley Dingle, Shropshire, showing a stable high angle face which required less rock material to be removed than would have been the case if a lower angle soil-covered face had been designed. The step in the face adds to stability and safety, and will enable vegetation to be established to 'soften' the appearance of the cutting.

designed sympathetically with Earth heritage conservation interests in mind. Moreover, smooth blasting techniques not only enable 'clean' and safe faces to be left after excavation, but can cut costs by enabling steeper faces to be designed, thus reducing the amount of rock material that has to be removed (Figure 6.3).

6.6 Coastal cliffs and foreshores

Coastal cliffs (EC) and foreshores (EF) are naturally occurring exposure sites, and often provide the biggest and best opportunities to study geology. They are also geomorphological features in their own right, and so may also be integrity sites in some cases (see below). Coastal areas with 'hard' coastlines (in igneous, metamorphic or durable sedimentary rocks) often have magnificent exposure, usually with a rocky foreshore platform left by the retreating rock face. Areas with 'soft' coastlines, mostly in the geologically younger sedimentary rocks of the eastern and southern England, rely on the washing action of the sea to prevent the degradation of the cliff line into deeply weathered clays and grassy slopes.

ACTIVITY 6.2
THREATS TO SITES (CONTINUED)

What are the threats to coastal cliffs and foreshores? Some examples are shown in Figure 6.4 overleaf. Make a list and compare it with the one below. Is the order of your list the same as that given here? Are there any threats you have given that are not listed? Consider why.

◆ ◆ ◆

Figure 6.4 *Examples of coast protection works. (a) Part of the sea front at Bournemouth, Hampshire: a sea wall, capped by a road, has been built, and the cliff graded to prevent rock material tumbling on to the beach huts and the road. (b) Penarth Coast SSSI, Glamorgan: a cliff-foot wall has been built in an attempt to prevent wave erosion at the foot of the cliff. Build-up of scree material behind the wall is beginning to obscure the exposure. (c) Whitesand Bay SSSI, Isle of Wight: wire netting boxes filled with rocks (gabions) have been laid against the cliff to prevent coast erosion, and now obscure the original exposure. (d) West Runton Cliffs SSSI, Norfolk, exposing glacial deposits. The revetment has reduced wave attack at the cliff foot, helping to prevent sediment thrown up by storm waves from being washed back into the sea (note that the beach level is higher behind the revetment).*

Overwhelmingly, the biggest threat to coastal exposure is that of coast protection works, particularly massive concrete structures and the dumping of large blocks of durable material (often referred to as 'rock armour' or 'armour stone') at the base of the cliffs. These works have the effect of both directly obscuring the geological exposure and preventing the slow erosion necessary to preserve exposure of softer materials. All too often individual maritime councils have not worked in conjunction with their neighbours in planning strategies for the protection of their stretch of coastline. This has led to the unfortunate and all too common circumstance that construction of coast defences, or the building of features designed to contain the beach on a stretch of coast (groynes), has merely deflected the problem along the coast, usually with serious consequences. A good example of this is Barton Cliffs (see Chapters 1 and 7).

6.7 Mines and their dumps

The underground workings left after mineral extraction reveal valuable information about how minerals and rocks were formed or deposited, and are valuable sources of exposure (EM). A by-product of mines is their dumps, which often contain rare and interesting minerals mined with the metal ore or other commercial raw material, but dumped as a waste product. Mine dumps, although produced by human activity, represent a limited resource in abandoned sites, and as such are integrity sites (ID).

ACTIVITY 6.2
THREATS TO SITES (CONTINUED)

What are the threats to mines and their dumps? Make a separate list for each and compare it with the one below. Is the order of your lists the same as those given here? Are there any threats you have given that are not listed? Consider why.

◆ ◆ ◆

Mines, and in some cases tunnels, created by human activity are dangerous. Key threats are instability and flooding as the workings increase in age, and often thoughtless dumping of waste materials, solid or liquid, making access difficult or impossible.

Mine dumps are frequently threatened by levelling, reprocessing, burial and afforestation, all with their attendant problems.

6.8 Landforms

By their very nature, landforms span a wide range of interests and types. What links them is their sensitivity to human activities, and as such they are usually integrity sites. An important difference between many landform sites and other site types is that they often extend over a much larger area. It is convenient to talk of two broad landform types, already introduced above: static and active landforms.

Static landforms (IS) include geomorphological features created by the passage of glaciers over most of Britain during the ice age, or the Quaternary. These features are not replaceable, having been created over the last million years by conditions now absent from this country. Glacial features include many landforms created from material swept up by the movement of the glacier and later deposited during melting. These features may be linear, following the line of the glacier or ice sheet, such as an esker (Figure 2.22(a)), or they may be individually limited but grouped together, such as drumlins (Figure 2.21(a)).

What are the threats to static landforms? Make a list and compare it with the one below. Is the order of your list the same as that given here? Are there any threats you have given that are not listed? Consider why.

Many of these landforms are rich in aggregate materials, i.e. sand and gravels, and as such are obvious targets for extraction companies. The aggregate resource is finite, so much so that unchecked removal will effectively result in the loss of the whole landform. On the other hand, small-scale aggregate extraction can aid in interpreting the mode of formation of the glacial feature.

Another major threat is from forestry. A lot of static landforms are in upland areas – prime areas for afforestation. Dense coniferous forests will effectively prevent the overall pattern and wider understanding of the landform from being seen, enjoyed or investigated.

Active landforms (IA) are typically rivers, cliffs, coastal features, slopes and so on, which are continually evolving through natural processes of change.

ACTIVITY 6.2

THREATS TO SITES (CONTINUED)

What are the threats to active landforms? Make a list and compare it with the one below. Is the order of your list the same as that given here? Are there any threats you have given that are not listed? Consider why.

In thinking about threats to active landforms, consider the development of a coastal landform such as Chesil Beach in Dorset (Figure 6.5). This classic example of a shingle beach and ridge is maintained through the natural and continuing processes of beach sediment transport. Interference with this movement of materials or unchecked removal of pebbles for aggregate could interrupt the natural system and lead to severe erosion of the beach. Consider also the processes involved in the development of a river course, like the River Feshie. Attempts to protect river banks from erosion, or to straighten the river course, would greatly affect the natural system, and the original geomorphological configuration would be severely altered. Active process sites are therefore sensitive to any human interference.

6.9 Caves and limestone scenery

Caves are usually associated with major areas of limestone in Britain. This is because caves have generally developed by the action of solution, from slightly acid percolating groundwaters dissolving away the calcium carbonate of the limestone. Caves exist as natural systems, rather similar to active process landforms, and are also sensitive integrity sites (IC). Although caves are

Figure 6.5 *Chesil Beach, a shingle ridge connecting an island (the Isle of Portland) to the mainland. Such a ridge is termed a* tombolo.

continually being dissolved away, there is also deposition within them. Muds and other sediments are deposited from water flowing through the system (cave sediments), and features are produced by gradual precipitation of limestone from lime-rich waters (referred to as *speleothems*, examples being stalactites and stalagmites). Some caves also contain the remains of former occupants, most notably the cave bear, living in Britain during the last ice age.

ACTIVITY 6.2

THREATS TO SITES (CONTINUED)

What are the threats to caves? Make a list and compare it with the one below. Is the order of your list the same as that given here? Are there any threats you have given that are not listed? Consider why.

◆ ◆ ◆

One of the most significant threats to caves is recreational visitors who unwittingly damage the delicate cave formations or speleothems, no matter how careful they are. Quarrying will obviously destroy cave systems and limestone pavements commonly associated with areas of cave development (Figure 6.6, overleaf). Finally, waste disposal pollutes the underground water and has significant effects on development of deposits within caves like stalagmites and stalactites.

Figure 6.6 *An area of limestone pavement beneath Ingleborough in the Pennines. Water percolating through joints in the Carboniferous Limestone has produced deep clefts. Weathered blocks like these are valued in rockeries, but areas such as this are afforded some statutory protection by limestone pavement orders.*

6.10 Unique deposits

Unique mineral and fossil deposits (IM) often form a small part of a larger geological picture, and are among the smallest integrity sites. Often their importance is disproportionate to their size. Usually they are limited in extent. Examples are unusual minerals formed under a specific set of conditions not occurring commonly, and fossils not normally preserved, such as insects or mammals.

A good example of the main threats to unique deposits is represented by the Rhynie Chert introduced in Chapter 1.

ACTIVITY 6.2
THREATS TO SITES (CONTINUED)

What are the threats to unique deposits? Make a list and compare it with those given below. Is the order of your list the same as that given? Are there any threats you have given that are not listed? Consider why.

◆ ◆ ◆

The Rhynie Chert contains fossils of some of the oldest known land plants. It is extremely limited in extent; losses of the deposit to any form of development (construction, etc.) or removal (quarrying or unlimited collecting) would be serious. The principal justification for conserving these types of deposit is to provide material for future scientific study.

Box 6.3 Summary of steps in identifying site type

- ◆ Is the site an exposure of an otherwise widespread deposit (exposure site, E); or is it a finite resource or landform (integrity site, I)?
- ◆ If it is an exposure site, consider whether it is the result of extractive activity (quarry, active, EA and disused, ED; mine, EM) or naturally occurring (coastal cliff, EC, and foreshore, EF; inland exposure or valley section, EO).
- ◆ If it is an integrity site, consider whether it is a landform or a deposit. If it is a landform, is it static (IS), actively forming (IA) or a cave (IC)? If it is a deposit, is it a mine dump (ID) or a naturally occurring unique mineral or fossil site (IM)?

6.11 Site use – the horizontal axis of the EHCC matrix

In order to complete the EHCC matrix we now need to consider the horizontal divisions shown in Table 6.2. Here we can employ the use to which a site is put and its status as a practical guide to the methods of conservation to be used.

To date the motivation for the conservation of statutory Earth heritage sites (that is, Earth heritage SSSIs) has largely been based on the idea of value attached to *primary research worth*. In other words, the SSSIs are selected as part of the Geological Conservation Review (GCR) process described in Chapter 8. This is based primarily on the criterion of international or national importance to particular fields of scientific research. Usually, no criterion of educational or aesthetic value is applied.

In promoting the idea of RIGS and in supporting the documentation and recognition of smaller sites under the NSGSD scheme (Chapter 8), a wider range of criteria, discussed below, was advocated. These may include research importance, which may also be high in a regional rather than a national context, but will also place importance on such features as setting and educational value.

Therefore a division between SSSIs and RIGS or other sites could be considered to be the difference between research importance and educational importance, and this in effect is the major division on the horizontal axis of the classification. For example, a prime educational site might have a number of characteristics, such as clear exposure and safe environment, which would influence the selection of the site as part of a network, and the conservation principles to be applied at the site, which may be to maintain access and provide interpretational information. A prime research site may be important despite having no clear value to educationalists; here conservation would be geared towards maintaining exposure for future research: the conservation principles are quite different. Put together with the site type in the matrix of the EHCC, conservation profiles for each of the pigeonholes can be constructed and conservation principles applied.

In this way, the horizontal axis of the EHCC matrix has four divisions based primarily on the ideas of research and educational importance, as shown in Table 6.2.

Table 6.2 The horizontal axis of the EHCC matrix

Research importance			
Nationally/ internationally important	Regionally important	High educational or other importance	Other sites
1	2	3	4

Clearly, the Nature Conservancy Council and national conservation agncies have identified the majority of sites of high research importance; these form the Earth heritage SSSI network. Sites which are regionally important, and/or which are valuable educational sites, qualify as RIGS. Other sites worthy of conservation on a local level are usually small sites documented in the NSGSD survey.

The full Earth Heritage Conservation Classification matrix is shown in Table 6.3.

Table 6.3 The complete EHCC matrix

	SSSI	RIGS (research)	RIGS (education)	NSGSD site
Exposure sites				
Discused quarries, pits and cuttings	ED1	ED2	ED3	ED4
Active quarries and pits	EA1	EA2	EA3	EA4
Coastal and river cliffs	EC1	EC2	EC3	EC4
Foreshore exposures	EF1	EF2	EF3	EF4
Inland outcrops and stream sections	EO1	EO2	EO3	EO4
Mines and tunnels	EM1	EM2	EM3	EM4
Integrity sites				
Static (fossil) geomorphological sites	IS1	IS2	IS3	IS4
Active process geomorphological sites	IA1	IA2	IA3	IA4
Caves and karst	IC1	IC2	IC3	IC4
Unique mineral, fossil or other geological sites	IM1	IM2	IM3	IM4
Mine dumps (continuum with specimen collections)	ID1	ID2	ID3	ID4

Box 6.4 Summary of steps in identifying site use

◆ Is the site nationally or internationally important for Earth heritage research (Type 1)? This can be determined through literature and library searches and consultation. These sites make up the SSSI network. Educational value is not considered, although it may be variable.

◆ Is the site of regional importance to Earth heritage research, that is, does it illustrate a geological exposure or geomorphological feature peculiar to a region but not important nationally (Type 2)? Educational value and other significant features are considered separately from research importance for the purposes of the EHCC matrix. This type of site is appropriate as part of a RIGS network.

◆ Is the site of high educational importance, but no great research importance (Type 3)? Other significant features, such as setting in the landscape or historical importance may also be important. This type of site is appropriate as part of a RIGS network.

◆ Is the site of no great research or educational significance, but of local interest (Type 4)? This type of site may be incorporated in the NSGSD database.

6.12 Delimiting sites

We have seen that geological exposures and geomorphological features and landforms can be considered as discrete 'sites', and that these sites may be classified by site type and site use. The approach to conservation is defined by these parameters, as we will see later.

However, one final act is needed before practical conservation of the site can be undertaken. We need to clearly *delimit* the site. In most cases a clear boundary or line can be drawn on a map to delimit the boundaries of the site, and this is usually the limit of the important exposure or landform. A good example would be a disused quarry. A quarry is cut into the earth and exposes rock which would not otherwise be exposed in the landscape. Delimiting the site is often a case of drawing the boundary to include all the features exposed in the quarry, and would usually not include the surrounding fields which are barren of rock exposure. Quite often this would simply mean drawing a line on a map around the actual quarry workings. Delimiting an active quarry, on the other hand, would entail drawing a line around the proposed limit of workings, otherwise eventually the faces to be conserved would be outside the boundary.

Delimitation is important because it helps conservationists express to other people, perhaps potential developers, just where the features of interest are to be found, and makes it clear exactly what is important and what is not. As developers almost always want to avoid conflict on conservation matters, making it absolutely clear where important features lie prevents ambiguity and mistakes when planning permissions are sought. But what about scattered exposures in a mountainous area, or where the track of an ancient glacier has left a variety of deposits as a series of distinct landforms? In such a case it is not easy to delimit a clearly defined 'site'. It would be just too large, and it would be impractical to suggest that every small portion of a large mountain side or valley, for example, is of the same importance. In these examples an alternative method of delimitation would involve the concept of *zoning*. For example, in large upland areas with exposures of rock or geomorphological features, 'contours' could be drawn of relative high to low interest to help integrate conservation with other land use, perhaps with forestry, for example. Thus in the example of a drumlin field (Figure 6.7(b)), the drumlins themselves are clearly identified, with the crestal parts being the most important (1), the surrounding zone slightly less important (2), and the areas between them the least important (3). Clearly, afforestation of the crestal zones would obscure the topography of the drumlins, whereas some tree growth in the inter-drumlin areas would do little damage to the appearance of the site. So it can be seen that zoning sites allows active management strategies to be drawn up in conjunction with potential developers, in this case the forestry agencies. In some instances, within large 'super-quarries', the zoning principle could be used where particular research or other interests are relatively concentrated into one face or area.

The idea of zoning is a new one in the field of Earth heritage conservation, and is an answer to the problem of larger, more scattered site areas. Although not employed in the delimitation of current SSSIs, it has its greatest potential in the conservation of the major upland areas of Britain, such as in Scotland, northern England or north Wales.

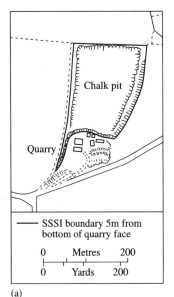

SSSI boundary 5m from bottom of quarry face

```
0        Metres      200
0         Yards      200
```

(a)

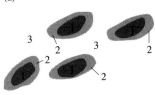

$1 \rightarrow 3$ = zones of decreasing importance

(b)

Figure 6.7 *Delimiting sites. (a) Example of site delimitation around a disused quarry (Charnage Chalk Pit SSSI, Salisbury Plain). (b) Idealized zonation of a drumlin site (compare with Figure 2.21).*

Box 6.5 Steps in delimiting site boundaries

1 In order to be able to delimit the boundaries of a site to be conserved, the nature of the features present in the site should be identified and documented in the manner described above. This will give a full picture of the disposition of features of geological interest within the site.

2 If the site is composed of dispersed exposures or landforms, consider the importance of individual areas relative to one another. If a pattern emerges of important features or exposures set within a larger area without exposure or landform interest, consider zoning the area using contours of greater and lesser importance.

3 Delimit the boundary of the site on large-scale topographic maps (1:25 000 scale at least). For quarries, the extent of the quarry workings is usually the boundary. In notifying SSSIs, the national conservation agencies take into consideration future working of active quarries by drawing the boundary coincident with the proposed extent of the quarry at the end of quarrying. For eroding coastlines, allow some leeway for erosion.

4 Produce an annotated map of the geological and geomorphological features to be found within the boundary of the site. This kind of specific information always aids in practical conservation.

6.13 Summary

In this chapter the nature of Earth heritage sites was considered. The term 'site' can apply to a wide range of features which illustrate the development of the Earth. There are two major site types, integrity and exposure sites, for which different principles apply. In addition, all sites may be placed within the matrix of the Earth heritage conservation classification, utilizing site type as the vertical axis, and site use as the horizontal. In so doing, prescriptive conservation profiles may be drawn up for each cell of the matrix to provide practical guidelines when approaching site conservation. The means by which the limits or boundaries of individual sites can be defined was described, so that it is clear when countering threats just where significant areas are; this might entail the use of site zoning.

Chapter 7

PROTECTING EARTH HERITAGE SITES

Study comment

Chapter 6 introduced the concept of classifying sites in order to decide on an approach to conservation. In this chapter we examine the practical aspects of countering threats to Earth heritage sites, starting with the pressures that threaten sites; and methods of conserving them, both in general terms and in more detail through individual case studies.

7.1 Pressure on Earth heritage sites

We are all familiar with the current pressures on habitats and wildlife: it is a constant subject of discussion in the media. Areas of truly natural habitats are dwindling, especially in southern Britain, where they are closest to the largest areas of human habitation.

But what about pressures on Earth heritage sites? We have seen that the aims and objectives of wildlife conservation and Earth heritage conservation are broadly similar. There are similarities in the threats faced by wildlife and Earth heritage sites. Many have faced, or will face, proposals to develop, infill, remove and destroy them.

Consider the following quotation, from an article entitled 'Conservation, compromise and the Chalk' which appeared in the journal *Earth Science Conservation*.

> In a BBC Panorama interview earlier this year, Dr Andy Gale ... a leading Chalk stratigrapher, expressed his fears that coastal protection and development schemes would lead to the eventual degradation and vegetation of the Chalk cliffs of south east England. [In addition] there is mounting pressure on inland Chalk sites, such as quarries and pits, from increasing landfill operations.

(*Earth Science Conservation*, No. 28, 1990, p.18.)

Clearly, there is exceptional pressure on even just this one geological stratum, within sites close to the concentration of conurbations in the South East, particularly, of course, those near London. Although Chalk is a familiar rock to anyone living in the South East, many Chalk sites in the region are threatened with major damage from coast protection (as in the resort area of Thanet, with much of its coastline made of eroding Chalk cliffs) and landfill (as at Southerham Grey Pit, Sussex, an important quarry in the Lower Chalk (see Chapter 1, Section 1.4)). Obviously, with such pressure sites will be lost, and the opportunities to study, research and enjoy Chalk outcrops will disappear.

7.2 Approaches to practical conservation

One of the most significant benefits of the Earth Heritage Conservation Classification is that it allows us to standardize our approach to conservation. This is of immense use in practical conservation.

Stripping away the detail of the classification, perhaps the two most important decisions to be made are:

◆ Site type: integrity or exposure?

◆ Site use: research or educational?

The answers to these questions will help shape our approach to practical conservation of a site, through the definition of conservation principles:

Integrity or exposure?

Site type	Conservation principle
Integrity	Preserve resource
Exposure	Maintain exposure

Research or educational?

Site use	Conservation principle
Research	Maintain the research value
Educational	Maintain the educational value

The approaches used in the various site types are usually markedly different. Faced with the possibility of damaging operations at a site, we can regard these as the basic principles by which we can conserve a particular site.

But how does this work in practice? Let us look at two examples – the Rhynie Chert SSSI and the Tedbury Camp Quarry RIGS – to illustrate the point.

Rhynie Chert SSSI

Site type: Integrity (unique deposit, IM)

Site use: Research (deposit currently under pasture)

The Rhynie Chert (Chapter 1, pages 34–36) is an integrity deposit, very limited spatially, and enormously important for scientific research; in fact burial is the best possible way of protecting the integrity of this deposit. This site has next to no practical educational value in its present state. Buried under pasture, it cannot be studied by a hands-on approach, and signboarding would serve only as an indicator that the observer is standing on or near to an internationally important geological deposit.

The key conservation principle is conservation of the research interest of the site through protection of the integrity of the deposit. Individuals or small groups of scientists are allowed small-scale excavation for research purposes, if they submit rigorous proposals.

Tedbury Camp Quarry RIGS

Site type: Exposure (disused quarry, ED)

Site use: Primarily educational

This site has some importance for research, exhibiting good exposure and opportunity for study. You have already studied it in some detail in Chapters 1 and 3. The quarry floor exposes an unconformity surface, which is very important for teaching the concept of breaks in the stratigraphical record. It has a lot of well-preserved fossils, showing how they were actually colonizing and living on what was once a rocky seashore. Because of these features, the site is superb for teaching geology and is a site of key importance to Earth science education. The deposit is an exposure deposit, extensive underground, and with other nearby sites demonstrating similar features. The nature and extent of exposure and the safety and stability of the faces are the critical features of conservation interest at this site.

The key conservation principle is conservation of the educational interest through maintenance of access, safety of the faces, and exposure.

ACTIVITY 7.1
APPLYING CONSERVATION PRINCIPLES TO A LOCAL SITE

Using a local site for which you have some information, or for which information is available, document the key conservation principle to be applied, as in the two examples above.

◆ ◆ ◆

Firstly, decide whether the site is an exposure or an integrity site. This is obviously important for the way we conserve it for its research interest. Decide whether the site is primarily of educational or research importance; it may be both, like Tedbury Camp Quarry. This will also help identify the conservation principles.

If you do not have access to a local site, do the same exercise using the information provided for Shap Quarry in Chapter 3, Section 3.4.

The conservation principles of preserving resource or maintaining exposure apply to all subdivisions of the EHCC classification. They are overriding principles applicable to site types as different as coastal cliffs and disused quarries.

Obviously, the way we *apply* these principles will vary according to the type of site and type of threat. Quarries are commonly threatened by landfill, so maintenance of the exposure is the conservation principle. It can be applied through only partially filling the quarry and leaving an important face clear.

7.3 Threats to sites

In the exercises in Chapter 6, you recognized many threats peculiar to individual site types in the EHCC, such as landfill in quarries and coastal protection in coastal areas. In fact, there are only a few types of threat that are commonly encountered, and so the choice of the tactics used to conserve sites is not very difficult in practice.

ACTIVITY 7.2
DEFINING MAJOR THREATS TO SITES

Refer again to the EHCC matrix in Chapter 6 (page 180), and the lists of threats affecting the wellbeing of Earth heritage sites which you drew up.

Consider whether the major threats can be summarized in a relatively short list. For instance, you may be able to recognize smaller variants of the same types of threat.

From your knowledge gained so far, try and draw up a list of only six or seven major threats which affect Earth heritage sites.

Using the classification notation (for example, ED for Exposure site, Disused quarry), list the types of site affected by these threats.

Do this before reading on.

The commonest recurrent threats are summarized in Table 7.1, along with the main site types of the EHCC affected.

Table 7.1 The main threats to Earth heritage sites

Major threats	Main sites threatened
Coastal protection	Coastal cliffs (EC) and foreshores (EF)
	Active coastal landforms (IA)
Landfill and effluent disposal	Disused quarries (ED) and mines (EM)
	Caves (IC)
Degradation and unstable faces	Disused quarries (ED) and mines (EM)
	Inland outcrops (EO)
Industrial development and roads	Occasionally, disused quarries (ED) and active quarries (EA)
	Occasionally, inland outcrops (EO)
	Integrity sites (IA, IS, IC, IM, ID)
Mineral/aggregate extraction	Occasionally, disused quarries (ED)
	Integrity sites (IA, IS, IC, IM, ID)
Afforestation	Upland outcrops (EO)
	Static (IS) and active (IA) landforms
We could also add:	
Large-scale collecting	Unique deposits (IM) and mine dumps (ID)
	Caves and karst (IC)

Many people are surprised by the fact that normal collecting, not involving mass removal of specimens, is not perceived as a major threat to almost all sites apart from sensitive cave deposits (such as removal of stalactites and stalagmites) and unique deposits (large-scale removal of rare fossils and minerals) exposed at integrity sites. Why is this? This question is explored in Activity 7.3.

ACTIVITY 7.3
FOSSIL COLLECTING AT BARTON CLIFFS

Here fossils are wonderfully abundant and beautifully preserved. The Geological Museum (now part of the Natural History Museum) guide *British Fossils* by John Thackray (HMSO, 1984) includes this site as one of nine classic British fossil localities, illustrating the great variety of fossils to be found. The cliffs at Barton expose a series of clays that were deposited extensively within the Hampshire area during the Eocene, a subdivision of the Tertiary. Similar beds are found throughout Hampshire and the Isle of Wight, but nowhere are they as rich in fossils as they are at Barton. The cliffs themselves are under continual attack by wave action, and are constantly retreating; the fossils are continually being weathered out and washed away.

◆ Using the information provided in Chapter 1, decide whether the Barton Cliffs site is an integrity or exposure site. Write a short justification of your decision. What designation should you give the site under the EHCC matrix? The site has been an SSSI since 1956.

◆ Prepare a 'pros' and 'cons' list for and against the idea of restriction of fossil collecting at Barton Cliffs. Try and marshal as many arguments as you can collecting of fossils from this site. Which side has the more arguments in its favour?

◆ ◆ ◆

The cliffs at Barton represent a coastal exposure site, and as an SSSI fall within the EHCC matrix classification as EC1. The fossils are extremely abundant, indicating the wide variety of sea life in this area during the Eocene. The cliffs are continually being eroded, and countless beautifully preserved fossils, many of them rare, are lost. In reality, no amount of fossil collecting would reduce the scientific value of this site. It is inconceivable that the fossil reserves could be significantly depleted; the Barton beds are laterally extensive in the Hampshire Basin. Because of this natural loss it is important that people collect what would otherwise be washed away and destroyed. Therefore, as collecting is not restricted at the site, it can also be classified as an educational site (EC3). Equally important is the maintenance of some form of erosion of these cliffs, as without this, the cliffs would very quickly degrade into grassy slopes which would be impossible to study in any significant way. It is, of course, bad practice for individuals, as well as field parties, to collect large amounts of material. Responsible geologists, whether professional or amateur, should always keep collecting to a minimum, and always follow the Geologists' Association *Code for Geological Fieldwork* and the English Nature guide *Fossils and Collection and Conservation*. (See 'Further reading, useful addresses and information' at the end of this book.)

Collecting is therefore only a threat where it is unrestrained, and the deposit is a finite source, as in unique deposit sites (IM, ID) and caves (IC). The main threat at this exposure site, as we have seen, is through proposals for major coastal protection works, which would cause degradation and loss of exposure at these classic cliffs.

But what effect would these threats have, and how do they compromise the key conservation principles? Basically, there are three major types of threat to sites, the effects of which are summarized in Box 7.1. It is these major effects on sites that Earth heritage conservationists are trying to counter. In the next section, we will look at how this might be achieved in a practical way.

Box 7.1 Major effects of threats to sites	
Major effects of threat	*Result in conservation terms*
Burial of exposure: (e.g. landfill, coast protection, degradation of faces)	Exposure not maintained
Denial of access: (e.g. afforestation, flooding)	Exposure not available
Removal of, or damage to, deposit/site (e.g. by extraction or development)	Integrity not preserved

7.4 Countering threats – practical conservation techniques

We have seen that there is considerable pressure on Earth heritage sites in the face of development. How can we hope to achieve conservation of Earth heritage features in the face of this? This section looks at what may be achieved in attaining the conservation principles discussed above.

It is the experience of conservationists that in many cases practical site conservation calls for some form of compromise which adequately protects important features, and yet allows some development of sites. Perhaps surprisingly, this does not have to be damaging. In fact, in some cases development can actually *aid* in the conservation of sites. Take, for example, thoughtful quarry floor developments. Sensibly placed away from rock faces, building and plant need not deny access to quarry faces; indeed, this can even be improved by providing parking. For the most part, the experience of the NCC and national conservation agencies is that it is usually possible to successfully conserve sites in this way.

But how do we actually combat threats to the wellbeing of sites, and how do we know what is an acceptable compromise?

One of the most important achievements of the Nature Conservancy Council was to commission a series of reports from expert consultant engineers to investigate the ways in which threats could be countered and yet provide the developers with an acceptable alternative scheme.

Take three of the most frequently occurring threats: coastal protection, landfill and effluent disposal, and degradation and unstable faces, all leading to burial of exposure. As a positive approach to conservation of sites facing these threats, the NCC commissioned the following reports:

♦ alternative methods of conservation-friendly coast protection schemes which maintain exposure;

♦ methods by which exposure of faces may be maintained in landfilled quarries;

♦ methods of making stable and preventing degradation of faces in disused quarries to prevent them from becoming obscured.

The value of these reports is that they present practical *alternative solutions* to problems. As an example, consider the threat of landfill in disused quarries (exposure sites, ED). The threat posed by landfill operations is clear. The *landfill operators* wish to maximize their revenue by complete infilling of the quarry. They argue that this will return the landscape to its former contouring, hiding what in their eyes, and those of the public, is often seen as an eyesore. The *conservationists* argue that maintenance of the exposure and access to the faces are important. How can a compromise be reached?

Consider the following, taken from an article entitled 'Of rocks and rubbish! – conserving rock faces in refuse sites', which appeared in the journal *Earth Science Conservation*.

> If geological SSSIs are to be conserved in landfill situations both the waste disposal industry and the planners must be convinced of the importance of the exposures. In order to achieve this aim imaginative, cost effective and safe solutions must be available ... the project [an investigation of landfill slope stability] has been designed to look specifically at the conservation of faces, [and] some of the techniques put forward should provide solutions to ... technically difficult situations.

> (*Earth Science Conservation*, No. 27, 1990, pp.9–11.)

Clearly, the importance of the site needs to be stressed to the developers and planners. Developers are usually willing to accommodate reasonable conservation proposals. They may be willing to leave a face exposed while allowing infill of the majority of the quarry. The report commissioned by the NCC offers practical solutions. It suggests the use of retaining walls, reinforced earth structures and designs for engineered soil slopes which operators can apply in solving their particular problems (Figure 7.1). By doing this it actively helps operators conserve sites by providing technical information and solutions, rather than just either finding their own solutions or claiming 'it can't be done'.

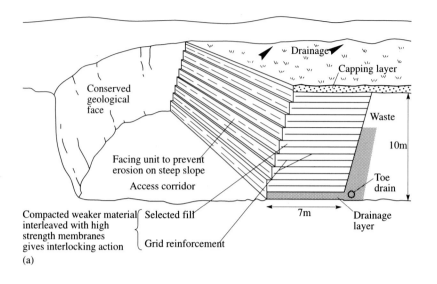

(a)

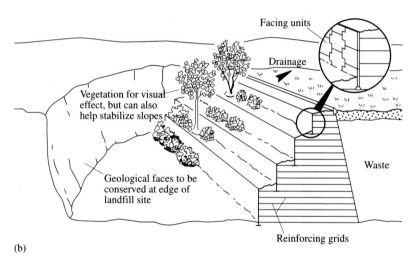

(b)

Figure 7.1 *Possible designs for reconciling the retention of accessible quarry faces with landfill operations. (a) Reinforced soil structure wih facing material such as 'geofabric netting'. (b) Idealized completed reinforced soil structure with planting to approve appearance. (c) Retaining walls (very expensive!).*

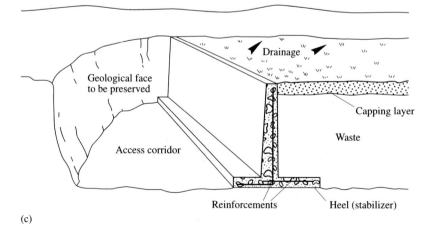

(c)

In this way conservationists can take a proactive role, and the experience of the success of this approach has lead directly to the production of the appendices to the NCC's strategy document. These provide a very detailed guide to the application of conservation techniques. The techniques are for the most part based on straightforward conservation principles that we have met already; some examples are discussed in the next section. Armed with these techniques, you will be able to counter threats to your own local sites.

7.5 Practical conservation in action

This section presents a series of case histories to illustrate conservation in action.

Firstly, here is a reminder of the principal threats to Earth heritage sites:

◆ coastal protection;

◆ landfill and effluent disposal;

◆ degradation and unstable faces;

◆ industrial development;

◆ mineral/aggregate extraction;

◆ afforestation.

Secondly, here is a reminder of the principal effects on sites if threats become a reality:

◆ burial of exposure; exposure not maintained;

◆ denial of access: exposure not available;

◆ removal of, or damage to, deposit/feature: integrity not preserved.

As a first approach to practical conservation, there are some basic principles to conserving sites, which depend upon our decisions:

◆ site type: integrity or exposure?

◆ site use: research or education?

Remember, these principles are of overriding importance in defining our approach.

Once the conservation principles have been decided upon (integrity or exposure, research or educational) any threats can be countered by first:

◆ convincing the developers/planners of the site's worth;

and, usually, second:

◆ seeking to divert the threat if damage is inevitable, or, when this is not possible, agreeing on a compromise acceptable to both parties by suggesting appropriate alternative solutions.

The best way to appreciate how this process works is by examining case histories of sites. The case studies are chosen to be representative of exposure and integrity sites, and the threats facing them; they do not illustrate all the site classifications or threats.

In these case studies, you will be asked to consider the conservation of the site through a series of questions that will be asked at appropriate points. Answer these before reading on.

Practical conservation of a coastal site: Barton Cliffs, site classification EC

Barton Cliffs in Hampshire is a classic coastal site introduced in Chapter 1. It is one of Britain's most cherished Earth heritage sites, at amateur, academic and professional levels. The cliffs are important to stratigraphy, giving the stratigraphical name 'Bartonian' to the world, and are of great importance for the range of fossils they yield, which are of both vertebrate and invertebrate animals and plants. As we have seen, constant marine erosion at this site continually provides fresh exposures.

From a local government point of view Barton Cliffs are a problem: they span two local authority boundaries. The soft clay cliffs are subject to constant wave attack, and the cliff profile is constantly changing. The sea attacks the base of the cliffs and promotes erosion and slumping. Water flowing along layers within the clay strata adds to the instability of the cliffs.

ACTIVITY 7.4

BARTON CLIFFS FROM THE COUNCIL'S POINT OF VIEW

List the potential benefits of protecting the coastline. Make a separate list of any benefits in leaving the coastline unprotected. Do this before reading on.

The council wished to prevent coastal erosion, to protect property behind the cliff edge. This includes a large holiday camp, and houses and flats further inland. Although they appreciated the scientific importance of their cliffline, they considered that it could not be left unprotected. They proposed that effective protection might be achieved by preventing wave attack, and by draining water from the clay in the cliffs to reduce landslipping.

Two schemes were suggested to protect the cliff. One entailed the dumping of large blocks of stone at the foot of the cliff; the other involved the construction of a stone block breakwater not in direct contact with the cliff foot, but directly parallel to it (Figure 1.9(a), page 25).

▼   Consider the key conservation principles at this exposure site, and the probable effects of the two schemes on conservation. Which one is the more damaging, and why?

▲   The stone blocks placed at the base of the cliff would directly obscure a significant part of the stratigraphical succession, and would prevent direct wave attack and erosion of the cliffs. This would not maintain exposure; it would *bury* part of the exposure, and *deny access* to the rest, through degradation of the slope. The offshore structure would drastically reduce direct wave attack, although allowing the sea to reach the cliffs. This scheme is an acceptable compromise; it would slow the rate of erosion enough to meet the council's aims, but allow enough to meet the conservationists' need to maintain exposure.

The offshore structure was suggested as an alternative scheme by the Nature Conservancy Council as a compromise solution. This scheme was accepted by the local council, but they also included a series of drains cut into the cliff, which could result in plant growth that would obscure the exposure. The NCC suggested an alternative scheme, with a drain behind the cliff line to intercept water flow. This would reduce the flow of water and maintain the exposure. The result of the public inquiry was a compromise – the council were allowed to build *one* drain cut into the cliff.

Summary

Coast protection is usually incompatible with conservation of Earth heritage sites, unless it:

◆ does not directly obscure the important exposure;

◆ does not lead to degradation and vegetation of cliffs through total prevention of erosion, although it may slow this process down.

These are the most important practical considerations, and a compromise may often be achieved using these principles. The offshore structure suggested by the NCC is an example of this at Barton Cliffs.

Practical conservation of a disused quarry: Southerham Grey Pit, site classification ED

Southerham Grey Pit is a medium-sized quarry cut in the Chalk (Figure 1.10). It exposes an important sequence which is not seen in its entirety anywhere else in Britain. Southerham Grey Pit is unusually rich in fossils. The Chalk in this pit breaks easily into small pieces, and study of the face is therefore relatively safe, particularly as it is not vertical. School parties regularly use this site for teaching geology.

The site is shielded from public view and is close to the road bypass system of the town of Lewes. The site is vacant, and is not of any commercial value in its present state. The owners of this site obviously want to realize some revenue by some form of development.

ACTIVITY 7.5

SOUTHERHAM GREY PIT FROM THE OWNER'S POINT OF VIEW

From your knowledge of the threats to sites, and any practical experience, make a list of the types of development that can be considered here.

———————————— ◆ ◆ ◆ ————————————

The quarry is well served by road communications, and is on the outskirts of the town. Lewes has little room in its town centre for large industrial or commercial developments. A scheme was originally drawn up for the development of this site for the siting of an out-of-town supermarket.

▼ Consider whether the siting of a supermarket in the quarry is compatible with conservation of this site. Remember the conservation principles.

▲ The supermarket development was denied planning permission, but in fact its development would have been compatible with the maintenance of the exposure, providing that successful solutions satisfactory to both the developers and conservation interests could have been negotiated (Figure 7.2(a), overleaf).

193

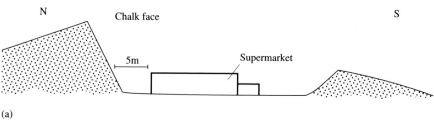

(a)

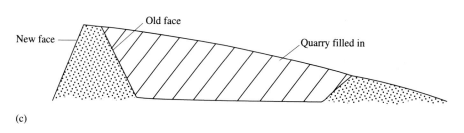

(b)

Figure 7.2 *Alternative schemes for development at Southerham Grey Pit compatible with conservation interests. (a) Quarry floor development – acceptable compromise. (b) Landfill – unworkable and dangerous. (c) Landfill with new exposure – acceptable compromise*

(c)

Clearly, for access to faces to be available, and for the safety of shoppers, the supermarket should be placed at least 5 metres away from the faces. Improved access facilities would enhance its importance, especially as a teaching site.

The next obvious development of the quarry would be as a landfill site. In most areas of south-east England, there is increasing pressure to find suitable landfill sites. Southerham Grey Pit would fulfil this role.

▼ Consider the implications of using this site as a landfill site. Remember the conservation principles. Can you think of any compromise solutions or alternatives?

▲ Using Southerham Grey Pit as a landfill site would effectively bury the exposure at this site. In many landfill sites it is possible to leave a face exposed and fill the rest of the quarry, with an impermeable barrier constructed between the two areas. At Southerham this would be impractical, as the face is too high to safely permit an inspection ditch between it and the landfill site (Figure 7.2(b)).

The developers were aware of the scientific importance of the site, and offered what they considered to be a compromise. They suggested that the scientific interest of the quarry could be maintained through the provision of boreholes, which would provide continuous rock cores, and through allowing access for a rescue dig to collect specimens prior to infill.

▼ Consider the implications of such a compromise. Would it satisfy the key conservation principles at this site? Remember, it is a research and teaching site.

▲ Boreholes would not be an acceptable substitute for the exposure. They would represent a tiny fraction of the beautifully exposed rock face. Large-scale features would not be seen, most fossils could not be observed, and with the advancement of science, boreholes would not provide sufficient information to restudy the site. Boreholes could not provide sufficient interest to replace the teaching and research importance of this site. A rescue dig would potentially provide unique fossil specimens, but it would not replace the value of the site for long-term study and re-examination.

Through negotiation, the developers accepted these arguments, and a practical compromise was sought. Remember that in exposure sites, *maintenance of exposure*, rather than *preservation of resource*, is the important principle. Therefore, it was decided that a new excavation, *behind* the present face, together with a small area of the existing exposure, in this case a smaller face, would be left uncovered by landfill, and so maintain exposure (Figure 7.2(c)). Because this new cut would be the same size as the old one, exposing the same material, the educational value would also be conserved. *This was an acceptable compromise solution that maintained exposure and educational value.*

Summary

1 Quarry floor developments are not usually damaging to the site as long as:
   ◆ the face is not directly obscured;
   ◆ the development is situated at least 5 metres away from the faces to allow access.

Often, the improved access can enhance the value of the site.

2 Landfill is usually damaging to Earth heritage sites unless:
   ◆ where appropriate, a trench can be provided between the quarry face and the landfill to allow access to the exposure. The landfill should be retained by an impermeable barrier to prevent the trench filling with noxious fluids, and the trench should be at least 5 metres wide to allow access for mechanical diggers to clean the face should it become filled by fallen material;
   ◆ where a trench is inappropriate, an alternative exposure, having the same features and geological horizons, can be cut elsewhere by the developers.

Practical conservation of an active quarry: Shap Quarry, site classification EA

Shap granite is one of Britain's most familiar rock types. It is probably not an exaggeration to say that most geology students in Britain have studied it at some time or other. Shap granite is an igneous rock found in several varieties, which are used as an ornamental and building stones. The quarry is still being worked, but eventually the granite will be worked out. The quarry provides fresh exposure of granite much superior to the naturally exposed upland outcrops, which are deeply weathered and degraded.

ACTIVITY 7.6
THREATS TO SHAP QUARRY WHEN QUARRYING FINISHES

Consider the potential threats to this site after the quarry has stopped being worked by the quarry operators. (Reread the description in Chapters 1 and 3 if you need to.)

◆ ◆ ◆

Obviously, as a disused quarry the site will be an attractive one for landfill. Conservation of the quarry after the end of its working life would entail negotiation similar to that for Southerham Grey Pit, in order for good faces of granite to be conserved. In addition, measures should be taken to prevent the faces degrading badly so that the exposure does not become obscured.

In working quarries in hard rocks such as granite, rock faces are highly shattered by blasting. Blocks freed by blasting may be cut to form facing stone for buildings, or broken into smaller blocks and crushed to produce road aggregate. The shot holes for the explosives are drilled at widely spaced intervals; this is known as production blasting, and it leaves an unstable and fractured face. Many quarries are left in this state even after their working life is finished, and often access is denied to the exposure since it is so unsafe because of blocks falling off the shattered face.

In the case of Shap, the quarry operators wished to extend their quarry operations. Negotiations with them led to their planning permission referring to the after-use of the site. In this case, the holes for the final blasting will be drilled close together with lighter explosive charges in each one; this will produce the effect known as smooth blasting. Keeping the holes close together will provide a stable face without fracturing, allowing safe access to the faces (Figure 6.3(a)).

Summary

In an active quarry, the after-use is the main conservation issue. Extensions of quarrying activities provide fresh exposure. They are not usually a threat unless the site contains an integrity deposit.

It is often possible to negotiate for a face to be conserved at the end of the active life of a quarry. In order to make this safe, the face should not be left in an unstable production-blasted state, with widely spaced shot holes, but in a smooth-blasted state, with closely spaced shot holes.

Practical conservation of an active landform: River Feshie, site classification IA

The River Feshie is situated in the Cairngorm Mountains and is one of the most important sites in Britain for understanding the development of a river system since the ice age (Figures 1.3, 5.2(c)). It is an extremely active site and this is the main source of its importance to geomorphologists trying to understand the development of natural river systems. The path of the river and its sediments are particularly important. Because the river system is entirely natural, it is prone to flooding, especially at its confluence with another river, the Spey. In the very recent past, a new channel has been cut by the river across agricultural land, and major floods have occurred because of the build-up of gravels at the confluence of the two rivers. The floods damage agricultural land.

ACTIVITY 7.7

SHOULD THE RIVER FESHIE BE LEFT TO RUN ITS COURSE?

This site is obviously of outstanding scientific interest. Look again at the description and illustrations in Chapter 1 (pages 14–16). What are the implications of the river system flowing through the farmers' land? Consider especially the pros and cons of leaving the river system to run its course, or modifying the river in some way.

The River Feshie is an integrity site. Its value to science is that it has been flowing largely unaltered by human activity since the ice age. It forms a unique natural laboratory. As we have seen, integrity sites, by their very nature, are susceptible to changes by people. *Any* changes in order to mitigate the problems of loss of agriculture would severely affect the scientific interest.

The maintenance of integrity sites in an unchanged state is of prime importance, and compromise solutions are less easy to achieve than with exposure sites. It is possible that some limited works to prevent the river from flooding could be carried out, but eventually this would lead to incremental loss of the site, leading to total loss of its natural integrity. A second alternative is one that the national conservation agencies have the power to carry out: offering compensation to landowners in order for a site to be protected, or in extreme cases, the purchase of the land by conservationists; this would provide a guarantee of protection.

This example is similar to almost all integrity sites. Two other case histories in Chapter 1 provide parallel examples. Achnasheen (site classification IS) is a static geomorphological site created during the ice age. Here plans to exploit the aggregates that make up the static landforms of this site were resisted. Once removed the site could not be recreated, as it is unique. Another example is the Rhynie Chert (site classification IM), a unique deposit of immense scientific importance, but of limited extent. This site was bought and remains buried to protect it from development.

Summary

For the most part, integrity sites are difficult to conserve. The conservation principles are usually clear: to protect the resource from interference. Two generalizations apply:

◆ compromise is often difficult, and where it is carried out, it should be limited and local, such as local flood hazard mitigation in the River Feshie;

◆ the best way of conserving these sites is through compensation or purchase; a good example is the Rhynie Chert.

7.6 Summary

We have now seen how the important principles of *integrity* or *exposure*, and *research* or *educational* guide the approach to site conservation.

For the most part Earth heritage sites are affected by relatively few major threats, the important effects of which would be to *bury the exposure, deny access* or *damage the integrity* of the site. These are the effects we are seeking to mitigate in protecting the site. Tables 7.2 and 7.3 summarize the typical operations that may affect exposure and integrity sites and their potential to cause damage.

Practical conservation of a site, once the conservation principles have been decided on, usually entails convincing the developers/planners of the site's worth and then agreeing an acceptable compromise reconciling development and conservation through the design of appropriate and less damaging alternative solutions.

Such compromises are usually appropriate to exposure sites, but much less so to integrity sites, where the best conservation approach is to do nothing to the site, which may mean paying the owner compensation, or buying it outright.

Table 7.2 Summary of typical operations and potential for damage – 'exposure' sites

Type of site	Usually highly damaging if unmodified	Damage can usually be avoided if work sensitively planned and carried out	Damaging only in exceptional circumstances
Disused quarries, pits and cuttings	Landfill Face reprofiling/stabilization Liquid storage/reservoirs	Quarry floor developments Forestry Minor restoration and landscaping Recreational developments Cleaning of faces Commercial and educational collecting	Tree and scrub clearance Fencing Drainage and buried services Research collecting
Active quarries and pits	Landfill/disposal of quarry waste	Quarry extensions	Normal quarrying operations Collecting
Coastal and river cliffs	'Hard' coast protection schemes, e.g. concrete structures Developments above eroding cliff Dumping at cliff foot	Beach replenishment 'Soft' coast protection schemes, e.g. offshore beams Chalets/beach huts Commercial and educational collecting Pipelines Small jetties Collecting	Signs, paths and fencing Tree and scrub clearance Tree and scrub clearance Research collecting
Foreshore exposures	Reclamation schemes	Small plantations Isolated developments	Small-scale sand removal
Inland outcrops and stream sections	Marinas, barrages and similar major developments Major afforestation Industrial/housing development	Roads/tracks Fencing and deer fences Quarrying Collecting	Changes in agricultural practice Drainage and buried services
Mines and tunnels	Adit or shaft closure Infilling Surface subsidence Effluent or waste disposal Commercial and educational collecting	'Show' mine developments Research collecting	Demolition above mines Normal agricultural operations

Table 7.3 Summary of typical operations and potential for damage – 'integrity' sites

Type of site	Usually high damaging if unmodified	Damage can usually be avoided if work sensitively	Damaging only in exceptional circumstancesunmodified planned and carried out
Static geomorphological sites	Major excavations/levelling Dumping and infilling Small plantations Major afforestation First-time deep ploughing Coastal reclamation and sea defence Industrial/housing development	Pits or small trenches Small plantations Fencing and deer fences	Sites generally vulnerable so no specific operations in this column
Active geomorphological sites	As for static geomorphological sites River management works Sand fencing Slope stabilization Dredging in active coastal 'cell' Introduction of vegetation	No specific operations although minor examples of operations to left may avoid damage	Sites generally vulnerable so no specific operations in this column
Caves and karst	Effluent disposal and dumping Quarrying Entrance closure	Changes in agricultural practice Water abstraction from boreholes Entrance control Recreational caving	Minor developments above cave passages
Unique mineral and fossil sites	Industrial and housing developments Stabilization of faces Waste disposal and infilling Reprofiling and excavation Removal of material Commercial and educational collecting	Research and small-scale amateur collecting	Sites generally vulnerable so no specific operations in this column
Mine dumps	Major afforestation and introduction of vegetation Major excavations Reprofiling and levelling Industrial and housing developments	Minor excavations Minor afforestation	Collecting

Chapter 8

SELECTING, PROTECTING AND ENHANCING SITES

Study comment

This chapter explains how people with different interests can work together to ensure that valuable Earth heritage sites are identified, conserved and used to good effect. The first section is concerned with the ways in which the interest groups concerned with Earth heritage sites interact, the roles each group fulfils and the organizational networks which have been established to further their ends. The subsequent three sections review the different types of site network (SSSIs, RIGS, and others).

8.1 People and networks

You have learnt in the preceding chapter something about the special features of the Earth heritage sites considered worthy of conservation. You have also been made aware of some of the threats to their survival. We will now consider the interested parties concerned with the conservation of sites.

ACTIVITY 8.1
WHO ARE THE INTERESTED PARTIES?

From your understanding of the conservation issues raised in Chapters 1, 6 and 7, list the categories of interest groups, organizations and so on which are interested in the fate of Earth heritage sites.

First we must recognize the site owners, who may own agricultural, industrial or urban amenity sites. Their concern will be primarily about the present uses of the sites or their possible development.

Associated with the site owners are the developers. This group covers interests ranging from quarry companies involved in the extraction of rock, sand and gravel, through industrial and commercial concerns looking for sites for development, to agricultural and forestry interests seeking more intensive cultivation.

The activities of site owners and developers are governed to a large degree by planners and other statutory bodies who represent 'community interests' and whose responsibility it is to reconcile the protection of the countryside with commercial interests through the exercise of their planning powers.

Finally, there are the conservationists who are essentially attempting to protect the

Earth heritage sites from developments which would destroy or seriously damage them. This group covers a wide range of interests, from the statutory bodies like the national conservation agencies, through a variety of geological and wildlife groups, to the environmental pressure groups like Friends of the Earth.

The roles of these four categories are explored in greater detail below.

Landowners and farmers

Owners and managers of Earth heritage sites form a diverse group, ranging from multinational corporations operating large quarries to private individuals whose landholdings include rock outcrops or landforms of importance. The success of Earth heritage conservation depends on their goodwill and support and very little can be achieved without their co-operation. Box 8.1 describes one example of fruitful collaboration. In the majority of cases conservation can happily coexist with current and future land use, and the protection of many features can be improved by making only slight changes to farming or land management practices. However, some landform features and unique fossil and mineral-bearing sites are irreplaceable and can be damaged, for example by excavation or levelling. Similarly, activities such as filling quarries and cuttings with waste will destroy virtually all features of interest. Various schemes for countering threats of this nature were considered in the previous chapter and these can be summarized as follows:

◆ manage sites (including entering into management agreements with conservation organizations) to maintain their interest, approaching the conservation bodies for guidance if uncertain;

◆ agree, where appropriate, a policy on access to the site by researchers and the public, and measures for enhancing sites;

◆ in extreme cases, such as some integrity sites, reach agreement to lease or sell sites to conservation agencies.

Box 8.1 The Onny Valley Trail: a collaborative venture involving a landowner

Shropshire is a mecca for visiting parties of geologists, for no other area of comparable size in the British Isles shows such a variety of geological features. Not surprisingly, the frequency of visits concerns local landowners. One area of concern is the Onny Valley, which was one of the itineraries included in the Geologists' Association's *Guide (No. 27) to South Shropshire*, published in 1958. At the suggestion of the landowner, a more organized route for geological parties was prepared, and published jointly by the Association and English Nature in 1992 as the Association's *Guide No. 45: Onny Valley, Shropshire: Geology Teaching Trail* by Peter Toghill. The new guide provides clear instructions on the route to be taken, and a description of each significant exposure.

On the ground, a clear trail was set out, stiles were erected by the South Shropshire Countryside Project, and National Trust volunteers cleaned up exposures and built steps at certain places.

Developers

The mineral extraction, waste disposal and construction industries have a very close connection with the conservation of Earth heritage sites. Success in conserving active sites depends heavily on the understanding and support of decision makers in these industries and there are many ways in which they can help. Chapter 7 discussed how constructional, industrial or commercial developments have been integrated with the conservation of important Earth heritage features. The role of developers in Earth heritage conservation may be summarized as follows:

◆ as landowners, participation in the activities summarized above;

◆ co-operation with conservation bodies in the development of solutions to reduce or mitigate potential conflicts of interest at industrial sites;

◆ involvement in the development of means to create new sites in the course of other activities, for example ensuring that smooth and safe faces are left in mineral workings and roadside cuttings when they are completed.

Planners and other statutory bodies

Local planning authorities and other statutory bodies (English Nature, Scottish Natural Heritage, the Countryside Council for Wales and the Countryside Commission (England), the National Rivers Authority, the Departments of Transport and the Environment, the National Park authorities, the Forestry Commission and Heritage Coast management services) can further Earth heritage conservation through the planning system and in the course of discharging their statutory roles. The ability of local planning authorities to protect the countryside through the exercise of their planning powers arises in several ways.

◆ *Recognition of sites in structure plans, in local and unitary development plans and in nature conservation strategies.* There are three kinds of development plans – structure plans, local plans (district-wide) and unitary plans (in metropolitan areas). Local and unitary development plans are site-specific, and should include Earth heritage site information in addition to that for wildlife sites. Structure plans are county-based and are strategic in their aims. They are not site-specific and only include general policy statements. Nevertheless, they are important in a policy sense for Earth heritage conservation. It is desirable that all notified and locally important Earth heritage sites are cited in local or unitary development plans, as they survey the present and future needs of their area as a whole to decide how best to accommodate the competing demands for residential, industrial and commercial development, for mineral extraction, and for recreation and leisure. Their importance can then be recognized in planning procedures.

◆ *Assessment of proposals for developments on Earth heritage sites under the planning system.* This procedure allows due notice to be taken of the importance of the site and for consultation with the conservation bodies when considering planning applications.

◆ *Protection of sites in Areas of Outstanding Natural Beauty (AONBs) and on Heritage Coasts* where the planning authorities have a responsibility to consult the Countryside Commission in England, Scottish Natural Heritage and the Countryside Council for Wales in development plan proposals. In addition,

Special Development Orders, with their stricter application of planning controls, can be applied to AONBs as well as the National Parks.

◆ In addition, the National Rivers Authority has a duty to further the conservation of Earth heritage features. The Forestry Commission has produced guidelines on the conservation of Earth heritage sites in forestry areas, while the National Trust is scheduling the wildlife and Earth heritage features of its properties.

Box 8.2 Success and failure with local planners

Success

Lowride Brickworks Pit in Oldham is an abandoned pit exposing Upper Carboniferous Coal Measures which contain interesting sedimentary structures, freshwater bivalve fossils, and fossil plants. Prior to its notification as an SSSI in 1989, planning permission for use of the site for landfill had been granted. In 1992, Oldham Metropolitan Borough Council announced their intention to buy the pit under a compulsory purchase order so that they could use it for landfill.

English Nature and the Oldham Geological Society objected to the landfill proposal, and the latter enlisted the support of the Geologists' Association, which, coincidentally, had just been asked by Oldham Sixth Form College to provide information about local sites suitable for fieldwork. Following a meeting at the site, a modified landfill scheme was developed by the council which will save the faces of geological interest in the pit. The schemes will now go to a public inquiry with the support of the original objectors.

The Geologists' Association has offered financial support to the Oldham Geological Society from its Curry Fund (a fund established to further conservation work and the activities of amateur geologists) to cover the costs of producing information boards for a geological trail once the site is secured.

The lesson to be drawn from Oldham (and elsewhere) is that it is crucial to register the importance for both research and education of geological sites with local planning officers so that they can be included in their planning strategies.

See Box 10.3 on page 244 for a press report of this success story.

Failure

Websters' Clay Pit in the suburbs of Coventry was another exposure in the local Coal Measures, and was an SSSI. The Nature Conservancy Council and many geological societies objected to the planning application to fill the site to create football pitches. Several site visits were made with the local authority in an effort to achieve a compromise which would retain some rock faces at the edges of the site for use by researchers, educational parties and local societies. These plans were rejected on the safety grounds, despite being supported by the local MP.

Conservation organizations

It is fortunate that today there is a flowering of interest in the Earth sciences and conservation in general. With the existence of so many national and local groups dedicated to conservation, there are the will and means to safeguard the legacy of the past for the generations to come. Statutory, professional and voluntary organizations are all concerned with the conservation of Earth heritage sites, together with teachers, researchers, local government officers and many others. Following sections of this chapter consider what progress has already been achieved and examine the various ways in which conservation is being organized.

Earth heritage conservation is a relatively new concept. Wildlife conservation groups have been in existence since the middle of the last century (notably the RSPCA and the RSPB) and such bodies have had a profound influence on the nature of conservation in Britain. However, the first practical steps in Earth heritage conservation can also be traced to the late 19th century when enlightened individuals gained protection for features like the fossil tree stumps of Carboniferous age in parks in Glasgow and Sheffield (Figure 8.1). The idea behind the protection of these sites was to preserve them as monuments, just as historical monuments are preserved today. This is different from the concept of conservation, which seeks to intervene through the active management and encouragement of natural processes at sites. Nevertheless, these early steps represent the first recognition of the value of Earth heritage sites for their own sake, and their need for some form of protection.

Figure 8.1 *Fossil tree stumps in Upper Carboniferous Coal Measures preserved under cover since Victorian times at the Fossil Grove, Victoria Park, Glasgow.*

Despite these and other early achievements, the systematic conservation of Earth heritage sites only began in the post-Second World War period. The Society for the Protection of Nature Reserves (now the Royal Society for Nature Conservation,

RSNC) was the first organization to act and its Geological Sub-Committee had produced by 1945 a list of some 400 Earth heritage sites worthy of protection for their scientific interest. This and other reports helped in shaping post-war government policy on conservation. The National Parks and Access to the Countryside Act 1949 not only created the National Parks but for the first time provided for conservation of natural features through planning controls.

The government conservation agencies have been the principal vehicle for statutory protection of sensitive environmental sites. Since 1949 the Nature Conservancy, then the NCC, and now the national conservation agencies have identified areas of land or water containing plants, animals, geological features or landforms of special interest. This *special interest* is determined by assessment of the sites in question against detailed scientific guidelines and they are only classified as *Sites of Special Scientific Interest (SSSIs)* if they meet strict criteria.

There are many other Earth heritage sites all over the country of great interest and importance which do not meet these particular criteria but which are worthy of protection from damage or loss. The first major initiative to identify such sites was the setting up of the *National Scheme for Geological Site Documentation (NSGSD)* in 1977. This scheme aimed to provide basic information on Earth heritage sites in order to encourage a wider appreciation of their importance and to provide a national 'stocktaking' of geological field sites. While this initiative marked a major advance, a significant part of Britain has not yet been surveyed and the documentation is far from complete in areas that have been covered.

A new initiative known as *Regionally Important Geological/geomorphological Sites (RIGS)* was launched in 1990 by the NCC to create a national network of locally conserved sites. The RIGS groups, as these organizations are known, are largely voluntary and combine the expertise of local wildlife trusts, museums and geological societies with the needs and experience of teachers, planners and site owners in selecting and conserving sites.

These three categories of Earth heritage sites (SSSI, RIGS and NSGSD) correspond to the site use designations given in the Earth Heritage Conservation Classification described in Chapter 6 (Table 6.3).

8.2 Sites of Special Scientific Interest (SSSIs)

SSSIs are sites of such outstanding interest and importance that they are protected by statutory controls. This section describes the manner in which these sites were, and are, selected and the nature of the protection they have been afforded.

National networks of Earth heritage and wildlife sites have been selected through the analogous processes of the Geological Conservation and the Nature Conservation Reviews.

The Geological Conservation Review (GCR) was initiated in 1977 by the NCC to provide a systematic review of the coverage of Earth heritage SSSIs. The review of sites was completed in 1988 and will be published in a series of 51 volumes, of which the first six were published by the end of 1993.

The main objective of the GCR is to demonstrate, by using the best and most characteristic sites, the current understanding of British geology and geomorphology, and so to identify sites with a considerable research value. As understanding of the geological history of Britain advances, so the coverage of sites selected will need to change.

The GCR uses three site assessment and selection guidelines:

◆ there should be a range of sites (not just the 'best' ones) that demonstrate current understanding of the geological and geomorphological history of Britain and the history of life;

◆ internationally recognized sites, if not covered by the above, should be included, as should 'spectacular, rare or remarkable' sites, including those that have value in demonstrating historical advances in the development of the Earth sciences;

◆ sites should be assessed and selected in discrete thematic geological networks or 'blocks' (there are in fact 97 of these!). This approach ensures that all sites, as well as being individually important, are part of a wider site network that demonstrates 'current understanding' defined by the first guideline.

Potential sites suitable for designation as SSSIs were selected by panels of experts, and the final sections made using the guidelines. There were additional guidelines to assist in selecting near-equivalent sites in order to avoid duplication and this exhaustive process has resulted in a very high standard of selection. Approximately 2200 Earth heritage SSSIs were identified; 440 of them were also identified as having SSSI-standard wildlife interest, and so carry notifications for both interests.

▼   In the GCR the geology of Britain was subdivided into a large number of discrete subject areas or 'blocks'. From your knowledge gained from Part 2 of this book, list your choice of the important subject areas. You may find it helpful to refer to the subdisciplines defined in Chapter 1 and the contents lists of Chapters 2 and 4 in compiling your list.

▲   Compare your list with the one that follows. Look at the items you did not list and consider what aspect of the Earth sciences you omitted.

The 51 volumes of the GCR will cover the following types of site:

Stratigraphic: 29 volumes, spanning the Precambrian to the Quaternary;

Palaeontological: 7 volumes, covering reptiles, invertebrates, mammals, palaeobotany, fish;

Structural: 2 volumes, one for the Caledonian and one for the Variscan and Alpine mountain-building periods;

Igneous: 4 volumes (Tertiary, Permian–Carboniferous, Caledonian, south-west England);

Mineralogy: 2 volumes, one on metal ores and the other on more 'aca-demic' mineral occurrences;

Geomorphology: 6 volumes (caves, two on coasts, rivers, karst and features formed by mass movement such as landslips).

How are SSSIs protected?

The protection of the SSSI system is commonly referred to as 'site safeguard'. This entails both the planning procedures and the development of management agreements between the national conservation agencies (NCAs) and the landowners.

When it has been decided that a site merits SSSI status, it is added to the SSSI network through the system of notification. This is the process by which the NCAs inform interested parties of the scientific importance of a site and its designation as an SSSI.

There are three interested parties:

◆ the owner and/or occupier of the site;

◆ the local planning authority;

◆ the appropriate Secretary of State (Environment in England; Scottish or Welsh).

Before notification can take place it has to be ratified by the appropriate councils of the NCAs. This acts as a quality control check and owners have at least three months to consider an objection to a notification; in such cases the notification is reconsidered by the NCA council in the light of the objection. The site formally becomes an SSSI when the notification is confirmed to the Secretary of State, within nine months of the original notification. The documents which form the notification include:

◆ a map of the boundaries of the SSSI;

◆ a statement of the special importance of the site;

◆ a list of potentially damaging operations (PDOs) which, if carried out by the owner or operator, could damage the special interest of the site.

Figure 8.2 illustrates the procedures for selecting and protecting SSSIs.

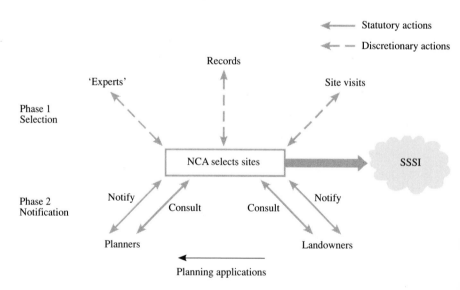

Figure 8.2 *The procedures used for selecting and protecting SSSIs.*

After notification, the NCA should be consulted over any operation that is likely to damage an SSSI. On the smaller scale, owners and occupiers are obliged to contact the NCA when they propose to undertake any of the operations listed as 'damaging' (the PDO list) in the notifying document and which generally would not require planning permission. This list is drawn up essentially to protect the site from change of use in future – it exists as a consultation mechanism. If the owners/occupiers want to carry out the operations listed then they have to consult the conservation agency and agree a course of action which would result in the safeguard of the scientific interest. However, if, for instance, the site is a working quarry, then the PDO list will either not include or provide an automatic waiver for ancillary operations such as the movement of stockpiles or the building of ephemeral structures such as site offices and so on.

The local planning authorities must consult the NCA for their opinion on any application for planning permission for development in or affecting an SSSI. The developer and the local authority officers will meet with the NCA to discuss modification of their proposals if there are aspects which endanger the scientific interest of the site. In the current climate of awareness of 'green' issues, many developers are keen to co-operate. In those instances where negotiations have failed to reach agreement, the NCA may then object to the proposal on the grounds that it will specifically damage the scientific importance of the site. The planning authority is obliged to take note of these objections, but not necessarily to accept them, for it may consider that other issues are important enough to override the conservation issues. In such circumstances the NCA may request that the appropriate Secretary of State consider the application through a Local Planning Public Inquiry. At such an inquiry an inspector is appointed to investigate the proposals by inviting evidence from both sides. The inspector then makes an impartial decision.

SSSIs and the public

You may wonder whether notification affords any public rights of access to SSSIs. The short answer is no! The designation of an SSSI is purely concerned with its protection through planning procedures and no rights of access are involved. If a member of the public wishes to visit an SSSI the permission of the landowner must be sought, unless it is on a public right of way or an open access site like a public recreation area. Even in such cases, some SSSIs are integrity sites selected for research reasons, such as a specialist palaeontological site, and general access by the public could be detrimental to the site's intrinsic value and is therefore discouraged on conservation grounds.

8.3 National Nature Reserves (NNRs)

In addition to SSSIs, there is a network of areas of outstanding importance which are managed specifically for that purpose. These are the *National Nature Reserves*, of which there are some 200 in Britain, covering nearly 150 000 hectares. Some are owned or leased by the NCAs but many are established under nature reserve agreements with owners and occupiers.

(a)

(b)

Figure 8.3

Some geological National Nature Reserves.
(a) Fyfield Down, Wiltshire: blocks of Tertiary sandstone on the down occur as remnants of younger sediments that once overlay the Chalk. They were probably transported to the valley bottom during the Pleistocene. (b) Wren's Nest, Dudley, West Midlands: underground (former limestone mines) and surface exposures, often rich in fossils, including trilobites, one species of which is termed tne 'Dudley Locust'. The photo shows a warden explaining the ripple-marked surface to visitors.

(c)

(c) The Parallel Roads of Glenroy, some 20 km north-east of Fort William, Highland Region: the parallel lines on the mountain side mark former shorelines of a glacially dammed lake.

210

Seven of these are designated reserves primarily because of their geological or geomorphological interest, namely:

◆ the unique beaches of a formerly ice-dammed lake known as the Parallel Roads of Glenroy (Figure 8.3(a));

◆ the Swanscombe Skull site in Kent (an abandoned gravel pit in which the oldest human remains from Britain were found);

◆ the active coastal landslips of Axmouth–Lyme Regis in Devon;

◆ Fyfield Down near Marlborough in Wiltshire, noted for its sarsen stone (erosional remnants of Tertiary sandstones that overly the Chalk) (Figure 8.3(b));

◆ the Silurian (Wenlock Limestone) outcrops of the Wren's Nest in the West Midlands (Figure 8.3(c));

◆ the classic exposure of the Moine Thrust at Knockan Cliff in Sutherland (Figure 4.13(a));

◆ the Ogof Ffynnon Ddu cave system in Powys.

Other reserves also have great geological and geomorphological value, for example the spectacular deeply eroded volcanic root exposed on the islands of Rhum and St Kilda in the Western Isles of Scotland; the Lewisian–Torridonian–Lower Cambrian succession of Inverpolly; the Highland Boundary Fault zone at Loch Lomond; the Lower Carboniferous succession of Moor House in the North Pennines; costal features such as Morfa Harlech in Wales (Figure 1.2) and Orford Ness in Suffolk. In general NNRs provide unique opportunities for study and research, so, like SSSIs, these areas are of prime interest for their research value.

In many cases, simply protecting an area is not enough to maintain its interest. Natural degradation of artificial excavations or other changes are detrimental to sites, and active management is required. For other types of site, the presumption is in favour of leaving natural processes to take their course.

Visitors are welcome at most NNRs so long as their activities do not conflict with conservation or research or with the interests of owners or tenants.

8.4 Other site networks

There are a number of bodies involved in the conservation of Earth heritage sites in the voluntary sector, usually at a local level. This section considers the development of a variety of informal schemes to protect sites outside the SSSI network. It suggests how you can be actively involved in practical conservation through a RIGS group.

Growth of the RIGS network

When the Geological Conservation Review (GCR) was selecting sites for SSSI status, many sites were examined which did not satisfy the strict criteria applied during the selection process.

▼ Summarize the criteria applied to the selection of Earth heritage SSSIs.

▲ Earth heritage SSSIs are selected on the basis of their *research value*, the criterion being that they are of national or international importance. From this assessment, a coherent national network of sites was selected.

The network of SSSIs conserves only a small fraction of the important Earth heritage features in Britain, and so there are many locations all over the country which are of considerable interest but do not meet the criteria for SSSI status. These sites are still worthy of active conservation and often are of more general educational value than the specialized research sites which became SSSIs. Other sites mark important developments in the early discoveries of geology or are landscape features associated with our historical and archaeological heritage. Arguments in favour of conserving important Earth heritage sites outside the SSSI network can be summarized under three headings.

◆ There is a need for a good spread of local educational sites, particularly to meet the increasing demand arising from the Earth science content of the new National Curriculum in England and Wales, and also because the sites are extensively used to train Earth science undergraduates.

◆ Many non-SSSI sites are widely used for professional and amateur studies at a local level. Such sites are part of our rich heritage of geology and geomorphology in Britain.

◆ Earth heritage sites with strong aesthetic and landscape appeal are valuable in stimulating public awareness and appreciation of geology and geomorphology and the need for their conservation.

However, such sites have little protection and year after year many are lost. In an attempt to conserve the most important of these sites, a number of local initiatives arose during the 1980s involving museums, geological societies, wildlife trusts and local authorities. They provided some degree of informal protection for sites by drawing the attention of owners and planning authorities to their value. These initiatives were analogous to the role successfully played by local wildlife groups for many years. The criteria used to select these sites – known variously as Second Tier Sites, Prime Sites, Grade 1 Sites or Sites of Geological Significance – differed from area to area. The number of sites per county also varied considerably, for example from tens in Shropshire and Staffordshire to hundreds in Somerset and Avon. The case study in Box 8.3 describes the practices followed in Shropshire which were the forerunner to the establishment of the RIGS scheme described in Chapter 9.

▼ What criteria were used to identify the geological 'prime sites' in Shropshire?

▲ The sites were of national importance and either did not have quite sufficient importance to qualify as SSSIs or duplicated listed sites. Note that the criteria used to select these geological sites are different to those subsequently used to identify RIGS, as the latter do not understudy SSSIs.

▼ How were these 'prime sites' protected?

▲ Owners and managers were encouraged to consult the Trust over changes of use affecting their importance. The locations of the sites were incorporated in official planning records and notified to statutory bodies.

Box 8.3 Geological 'prime sites' in Shropshire

The Shropshire Wildlife Trust (SWT) set up a Prime Site System in 1979 to monitor and help safeguard natural history sites within the county. Shropshire was the first county in Britain to organize this sort of systematic identification and protection, and the Trust now looks after around 600 sites. There are no legal obligations attached to Prime Sites and the SWT, through its Prime Sites Officer, operates an advisory and voluntary system of management, a process which nevertheless appears to work very well. Owners and managers are encouraged to take an interest in the natural history of their sites and consult the Trust over any change of use affecting their importance. Prime Sites are recognized by Shropshire County Council, incorporated into the County Structure Plan and feature in the Environment Record. A set of maps, which also shows SSSIs, National Nature Reserves and common land, is distributed to the Ministry of Agriculture, Fisheries and Food, the National Farmers Union, the County Landowners' Association and the Council for the Protection of Rural England.

In 1987 the author was approached by the SWT Conservation Officer to draw up a list of geological sites in Shropshire for 'Prime Site' status. A list of 21 Shropshire sites was produced which were at least nationally important but which either duplicated or just did not have quite enough importance to qualify as SSSIs. Each site was given a brief Statement of Scientific Interest and its boundary defined on a 1:10 000 map; each statement also listed a contact expert in order to provide future site advice. Working in this way, it has been possible to apply standard selection criteria and provide an even coverage of sites across the various fields of geological interest in Shropshire. Thus Shropshire's geological Prime Sites should be well protected for the foreseeable future, even though there is no legal muscle behind the system.

(Maggie Rowlands, 'Geological "Prime Sites" in Shropshire', *Earth Science Conservation*, No. 26, 1989.)

Until 1990, only six locally based Earth heritage conservation schemes existed in England. With huge projected increases in the educational use of sites with the introduction of the National Curriculum in England and Wales, and growing pressure on sites for redevelopment, constructional resources and waste disposal, it became clear that a nationwide network of locally conserved sites was needed. Detailed consultations with the groups running the existing schemes were carried out and a consensus of ideas emerged which formed the basis for the development of a new nationwide scheme.

The new RIGS (Regionally Important Geological/geomorphological Sites) initiative was launched in 1990 by the Nature Conservancy Council with the support of a wide range of national Earth heritage and conservation organizations, including the Geologists' Association, the National Scheme for Geological Site Documentation and the Royal Society for Nature Conservation. Rapid growth occurred following the launch. More than 40 counties or regions are operating RIGS schemes at the time of writing, and theyl cover all of England and most of

Wales. Initially progress was slower in Scotland, but there is every sign that a comparable network of schemes will be established.

RIGS are any geological or geomorphological sites, excluding SSSIs, that are considered worthy of protection for their educational, research, historical or aesthetic importance. They are broadly analogous to non-statutory wildlife sites and are often referred to locally by the same name. They can include important teaching sites, wildlife trust reserves, local nature reserves and a wide range of other sites. RIGS should not be regarded as 'second class' SSSIs (as were, for example, their precursors in Shropshire) but as sites of regional importance in their own right.

Chapter 9

REGIONALLY IMPORTANT GEOLOGICAL/GEOMORPOLOGICAL SITES (RIGS)

Study comment

This chapter offers practical advice on setting up and running RIGS groups, and discusses practical steps that can be made to foster relations with landowners and planners. It also comments on how groups can be funded, and offers advice on training volunteers so they can become involved in site management and the education of site users.

9.1 Introduction

As stated in the previous chapter, RIGS are any geological or geomorphological sites, excluding SSSIs, that are considered worthy of protection for their educational, research, historical or aesthetic importance.

RIGS are selected and conserved at a local level by informally constituted and voluntarily run groups, which develop locally applicable criteria for selection of sites, gather information about possible candidate sites and use the criteria to select the network of RIGS. In addition to support from the national conservation agencies, RIGS initiatives are supported by the Royal Society for Nature Conservation (RSNC), The Wildlife Trust Partnership, Shanks & McEwan (a major waste disposal company), the Clothworkers' Foundation and the Geologists' Association. This support has enabled the appointment of a full-time officer, based at the RSNC's headquarters in Lincoln, and the publication of a regular newsletter called *Exposure*. The six-stage procedure set out below summarizes the strategy for selecting and conserving RIGS, illustrated in Figure 9.1. It is put forward as a model management plan to be followed or adapted, depending upon local circumstances.

1 Set up a RIGS group.

2 Establish criteria for RIGS sites.

3 Gather local information.

4 Select the RIGS for your area.

5 Involve landowners.

6 Secure recognition by local authorities.

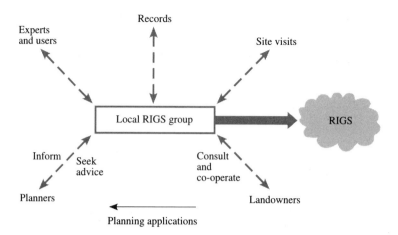

Figure 9.1 *The procedures for selecting and protecting RIGS. Note the absence of any statutory procedures, in contrast to those adopted during the selection of SSSIs (Figure 8.2).*

9.2 Setting up a RIGS group

Introduction

Establishing a site network is the prime task of any RIGS group. As indicated in the list above, this must be underpinned by collaboration between all interested parties in the region, including landowners, planners and conservationists. The first step in setting up a RIGS group is to gather support for the work to be done.

Getting started

ACTIVITY 9.1
POTENTIAL PARTNERS

Make a list of the organizations that could be interested parties for your county RIGS group. (The leaflet *Conserving our Heritage of Rocks, Fossil and Landforms* from English Nature will help you – see 'Further reading, useful information and addresses' at the end of this book.)

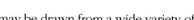

Possible interest and support may be drawn from a wide variety of local organizations.

♦ *Local geological and natural history societies* draw on the expertise of their members to provide practical input. Geologists and geomorphologists with their extensive local geological knowledge can contribute individually or through local societies.

♦ *Local wildlife trusts* are central to the nature conservation movement in Britain and many trusts are extending their work into the field of Earth heritage conservation. The existing organization of trusts for the management and

216

protection of reserves provides an obvious route for the protection of geological sites.

◆ *Museums* are likely to have information on local sites and their uses, particularly if they are local Geological Record Centres.

◆ *Schools and colleges* can play an important part in projects to interpret and clean up sites. Interested teachers, especially those teaching Earth science subjects, can link up with local initiatives.

◆ *Universities* are centres of expertise in Earth sciences and could be a potential force in the conservation of sites in their area. Staff and students could assist local initiatives with departments providing expertise and support for Earth heritage conservation.

◆ *Local authority planners and councillors* are the first line of defence for SSSIs and other nature conservation sites. It is therefore important to enrol their interest and support in local Earth heritage conservation.

◆ *Landowners* are crucial players in ensuring the success of Earth heritage conservation. Their goodwill and support is vital; very little can be achieved without their co-operation.

◆ *Quarry operators'* assistance is essential in arranging for safe study areas for properly equipped and supervised visitors (students and researchers) in active and disused quarries.

◆ *Landfill operators.* Landfill in pits and quarries can bury unique geological features. Total loss may be avoided by designing the site to leave a vital face clear, but this requires co-operation and financial support.

Meeting local needs

Local roots are the strength of RIGS schemes. The sites are selected by local people and are conserved mainly by their interest and commitment. The sites are chosen to serve generally local needs and enhance the local environment, reflecting the RIGS philosophy that 'local is best'. This emphasis contrasts sharply with the nature of the network of SSSIs, which is intended to meet national and international conservation requirements.

A fragmentary system of local schemes cannot achieve systematic nationwide coverage. Therefore there is a need for common principles of site selection and a mechanism to share ideas at a national level, and so foster a coherent national approach among existing and newly established RIGS schemes. There is a pressing need for RIGS schemes to be better publicized and for funding sources to be investigated. The national conservation agencies at present provide some of this support through advice and funding. The Geologists' Association is also active at a national level, both by encouraging its members to aid local schemes, and by providing financial support from its Curry Fund.

The composition and location of RIGS groups

General community interests suggest that RIGS schemes are best managed by county-based groups. Although this is a sound generalization for much of Britain, in some instances local interests favour a group covering adjacent county areas, as in north-east England, and in a large county such as Yorkshire more than one

RIGS group may be formed. For Scotland, a better unit might be Region-based groups, and for large, very sparsely populated areas, such as the Highlands, there may be a need to develop quite different approaches.

As demonstrated in Activity 9.1, RIGS groups should ideally include members from the local wildlife trust, the local museum and the geological, natural history or other Earth science societies, together with local authority representatives, teachers, professional Earth scientists and others with interests in geology or conservation. In addition to the core membership described above, a group should seek to attract members or support from local industry and landowners. Their knowledge will contribute considerably to the effectiveness of the group, and their presence will add to its credibility as a responsible force for conservation.

The group will need administrative support which local voluntary societies may not be able to provide. Groups centred on wildlife trusts, museums or local authorities will probably benefit from their existing infrastructures. In particular, the wildlife trusts have established record systems and channels of communications on planning issues for wildlife sites and can probably extend their systems readily to include Earth heritage sites. The inherent stability of these organizations will provide continuity during the inevitable changes in long-term voluntary membership of the group.

9.3 Establishing criteria and selecting sites

You will recall that RIGS have been defined as any geological or geomorphological sites, excluding SSSIs, that are considered worthy of protection for their *scientific, educational, historical or aesthetic importance*. This is a very broad classification; clearly, more detailed criteria are needed for specific site selection. Criteria for evaluating a site for its educational importance are set out in Box 9.1, and organizational and administrative aspects that need to be considered by a RIGS group are summarized in Box 9.2.

A General criteria

Distribution

- A local network comprising the maximum number of sites consistent with the resources available and practical conservation requirements, and which can be actively monitored and graded
- Showing locally significant phenomena
- Involving low travel costs

Accessibility

- No ownership problems and permissions easily obtained
- Open for long hours during term time
- Reasonably close parking facilities available for vehicles bringing parties of between 10 and 75 students
- Appropriate and accessible features within the site
- For all age ranges from primary to higher education

Size

- A range of sites suitable for varied party numbers

Durability

- Robust and capable of absorbing limited damage

Safety

- 'Clean' and where students up to the age of 16 can work within sight of group leaders
- For groups of up to 75 people

Conservability

- Physically conservable and to a level dicated by the resources available
- Feasible from the point of view of landowners, local schools and colleges, voluntary groups, planning authorities and industry

B Scientific criteria

1 Sites suitable for different ages and levels of ability, and where investigations and active learning are possible:

- enabling work in both structured and unstructured ways (e.g. open and closed investigations);
- where interpretations can be made in terms of modes of formation or deformation;
- where teachers can demonstrate appropriate scientific phenomena;
- where a wide range of activities, including study at close quarters (e.g. measuring and sampling), can be undertaken;
- where loose material may be removed so that hammers are not needed.

2 Sites where worthwhile materials, resources, features and relationships are apparent:

- showing straightforward relationships in terms of geology, landforms, landscape, etc.;
- where the main features are clear and simple, enabling good understanding by all ages and ability groups;
- with a wide range of features/phenomena, including those which are special or unique;
- showing a relationship with local industry, where applicable, so that local resources of economic or cultural significance can be seen and handled.

3 Sites where integrated studies are possible, both within and outside the sciences (covering for instance geology, geomorphology, biology, hydrology, agriculture, archaeology, environment, economics, human geography, social history), and which can be be related to others visited in a coherent plan.

4 Sites which permit the understanding of concepts and processes only properly understood in the field, such as:

- rock and soil types;
- unconformities, folds, faults;
- bedding, fossils, present-day processes;
- flora, fauna, ecology.

Adapted from the report on Session 2, 'Criteria for selection of sites', of 'Conservation of Earth Science Siotes for Education', a workshop held at the Geological Society on 23 October 1991.)

1 Sites chosen for educational purposes should preferably:

♦ have appropriate documentation, such as information sheets, explanatory booklets or worksheets, written in non-specialist terms to serve as guides for inexperienced group leaders as well as for students;

♦ be in directories and on maps, and be publicized locally so that schools know the opportunities available.

2 Sites should have some form of management team whose responsibility it is to carry out regular monitoring and ensure that the site is:

♦ assessed for safety;

♦ useful in educational terms on a continuing basis;

♦ regularly maintained.

3 Sites may need nearby toilet provision and picnic areas, as well as parking space situated so that any group walking to the site can do so in safety. Any such provisions and the length of walks from parking areas to sites should be made known in the documentation provided.

4 Sites should be made known to educational users, and to local planning authorities for inclusion (as a means of protection) in 'development plans'. Appropriate bodies which might help with this process are:

♦ local teachers' centres;

♦ Geological Society regional groups;

♦ Geologists' Association local groups and affiliated societies;

♦ local museums;

♦ RIGS groups;

♦ subject teacher groups: Earth Science Teachers' Association, Geographical Association, Association for Science Education;

♦ local wildlife trusts;

♦ university and college departments;

♦ local field centres.

5 All users must agree to abide by good practice and follow the appropriate codes of conduct.

(Adapted from the report on Session 2, 'Criteria for selection of sites', of 'Conservation of Earth Science Sites for Education', a workshop held at the Geological Society on 23 October 1991.)

9.4 Gathering Earth heritage information

Site records provide a starting point from which site selection can proceed. Documentation on the distribution, nature and importance of geological exposures provides the essential data to enable selection of sites to be made for conservation as RIGS. Documentation is equally necessary to justify the importance of sites to planning authorities, site owners and at public inquiries, and it is needed in order to carry out site interpretation and enhancement. *So the first task of a RIGS group will be to establish a schedule of Earth heritage sites, i.e. a geological stocktaking.*

Sources of Earth heritage information

The inadequate documentation of geological/geomorphological sites and difficulties in obtaining data about them were the original reasons for setting up the National Scheme for Geological Site Documentation (NSGSD).

The NSGSD was initiated in 1977 and over the past 16 years has grown to include 55 Record Centres covering most of England, Powys in Wales and several districts in Scotland, including Skye, Tayside, Paisley, Banff and Buchan.

The Record Centres are encouraged to record sites in a consistent manner using the same terminology. Each site is recorded as a site file and a summary kept for easy reference. The summary sheets held in the Centres were used as the input format for the computerization of the records undertaken by the British Geological Survey under contract to the Nature Conservancy Council; the work started in 1989 and was completed in Autumn 1991. The original intention was to provide a full national record which would be updated by data transfer. However, it was realized that a system must be locally based, with local updating and the possibility for updating a central register. Consequently a consultant was employed to produce a programme for Record Centres which is complementary to 'Recorder', a programme used by Biological Record Centres.

The scheme works as follows.

1   Record Centres are responsible for the collection, storage, maintenance and carefully controlled dissemination of geological locality information.
2   The information which is collected for the purpose of the scheme concerns all aspects of geological localities and is used to answer questions such as:

Where is the locality and what is it?

What is its present condition?

What are its geological features?

What is its history?

Who own and manages the locality?

Is it possible to visit the locality?

What is it used for and by whom?

How can it be used for teaching?

What published information exists?

What has been found there?

3 This information is collected according to nationally agreed methods and standards on specially designed recording forms. These forms, together with explanatory notes, are available from the National Scheme for Geological Site Documentation (see 'Further reading, useful information and addresses' at the end of this book).

The site records include data on boreholes, mines, disused and active quarries and pits, restored sites, geomorphological features and natural and temporary exposures. Each site has a site file containing information obtained initially through fieldwork and/or literature searches plus all additional material known: site maps, photographs, sections and photocopied publications. From the site file a Summary Record Sheet is is produced which gives a convenient summary of the contents of the file. The sheet is an ideal document for copying and distribution and saves considerable time and duplication of effort in the repeated searching and collating of information.

The dissemination of information is strictly controlled. No enquirer is allowed to inspect records personally or gain information from them without providing satisfactory references or acceptable reasons for their interest. Data is generally given freely to *bona fide* enquirers but may be charged for if commercial gain is possible from the data.

Clearly, there are many more potential site records than those already held and one way the scheme hopes to progress is via the great abundance of amateur and professional interest in geology. Quality information about sites needs to be attracted to the scheme. A massive store of unpublished and valuable material is locked away in the notebooks of professional geologists and the theses of final year and postgraduate students.

RIGS groups can and should use Record Centres as the basis for the search for RIGS. They may also gather additional site data which should be forwarded to the appropriate Record Centre. RIGS groups may need to become Recording Units if no Record Centre exists in their country area; indeed, they may consider setting up a Record Centre.

Despite these advances, a substantial part of Britain is not served by local Geological Record Centres. Documentation is far from complete, and is not up to date, in the areas covered. There is an urgent need to increase the number of sites documented by the NSGSD.

The local Geological Record Centre is a key operator in the development of the RIGS scheme as it provides the Earth science data upon which the selection of sites will be based. Surveys of local Earth heritage sites comprise the initial field activities on which supporters of the RIGS group can be deployed. Local groups, such as geological societies, schools, colleges and universities, could assist in this task.

ACTIVITY 9.2
RECORDING INFORMATION ABOUT POTENTIAL CONSERVATION SITES

From your knowledge of Earth science and conservation, what kinds of information do you think should be recorded about sites? Consider the geology of the site, which interest groups are likely to see it, how it fits into the Earth

Heritage Conservation Classification scheme, and the practical aspects of access and conservation. Spend a few minutes making a list of the different types of information that needs to be compiled. Do not expect to know it all – the following text gives a full review of what is needed.

———————————————————— ◆ ◆ ◆ ————————————————————

Making your own site and landscape assessment

Some of the skills of site recording were introduced in Chapter 3. The practical work of the RIGS group is centred around site and landscape assessment, and the completion of the geological record is one important part of site documentation. It is much easier to understand a practical subject like site and landscape assessment if you do it yourself rather than reading about it. Your first attempts may not be very professional, but you will learn quickly with practice.

A RIGS group undertaking a field survey will delegate groups of volunteers to study a particular district. The district could be subdivided by geological boundaries, but a more systematic method would be to split the county or district into 10 km squares, based on the National Grid, and allocate individual 10 km squares to each volunteer group.

Three distinct stages can be recognized in planning a site and landscape assessment:

◆ an initial desk study;

◆ detailed visits to the site;

◆ preparation of the site and landscape assessment and completion of the Geological Record Form.

A thorough desk study before visiting the site pays considerable benefits by enabling you to concentrate your attention in the field upon the important issues.

First look at the 10 km square selected on an Ordnance Survey map and list possible geological/geomorphological features that might merit investigation. You could draw a rough sketch map of the area, marking significant features like roads, streams, the location of SSSIs and the features that could warrant further study.

Next, study any geological survey maps that are available and mark important geological boundaries on your sketch map. You could also sketch a vertical sequence of the strata occurring in the square. Having selected the sites you wish to investigate, *set yourself modest aims – concentrate on what appear to be the most important sites and complete the assessment of one before starting another.* Find out all you can about all aspects of the sites before you visit them. This may involve a search of the relevant geological literature, including the Geological Survey Memoir accompanying the geological maps, and local geological excursion guides (such as those published by the Geologists' Association and local societies) and accounts of excursions.

Your field survey will begin the practices you learnt in Chapter 3, and continue with the evaluation of the value of the site for local conservation interests (see Box 9.3 overleaf).

Box 9.3 Site assessment

First, find out what you can about the history and geological background of the site. Check, for example, on the ownership of the site and the existence of any regulations governing its modification or development.

You will need:

◆ a notebook for recording information and drawing sketches;

◆ copies of the checklists in Box 9.1 and this box;

◆ relevant topographical and geological maps;

◆ a clipboard to hold your paper and maps together;

◆ a camera and binoculars if you have them;

◆ Ordnance Survey maps showing your site and some of the surrounding countryside. The scale of the maps is a matter of personal judgement, depending on the size of the site to be assessed. A small 'key' site like a disused quarry may need a map on a scale of 1:2500 while a 'zoned' site like an estuary will require a smaller-scale map, such as 1:10 000.

Additionally, a map on a scale of 1:50 000 or 1:25 000 may be useful for establishing viewpoints, contour lines and rights of way. If you cannot find an Ordnance Survey map at the appropriate scale of the site area, a hand-drawn sketch map would be satisfactory, but not ideal.

Select several viewpoints both inside and outside the locality from which to view the landscape and prepare a sketch map of the site. Note the viewpoints on your map and number them; note boundaries and access routes to areas of geological significance and any areas of potential danger. Describe your overall impressions in a few brief notes. If you have a camera, take photographs from each viewpoint, recording their positions on the sketch map. Make a quick sketch of the view from each viewpoint, marking significant geological and topographical boundaries.

Now undertake your assessment of the special geological/geomorphological features of the site, according to the procedures given in Chapter 3, and mark these features on your assessment map.

Your notes at this point will be fairly crude and untidy. Tidy them into a 'Site/landscape assessment summary'.

9.5 The management of Earth heritage sites

Having identified a site as a valuable local scientific or educational resource, decisions have to be made about how it will be conserved and used. This involves developing a Site Management Plan which defines objectives of conserving the site, explores the options available for managing it and proposes a formal plan of action.

As we have seen, most of the country's Earth heritage sites are in the hands of private landowners or managers, many of whom will not be aware of their importance. There is no suggestion that the existence of an Earth heritage site on a piece of land should stop development of that land – nobody wants to see a fossilized landscape. Frequently the management of land for other conservation objectives is perfectly compatible with the management of Earth heritage sites and the two may even complement each other. So the management plan and its objectives should be prepared in co-operation with the landowner and other conservation interests.

A series of stages can be recognized in the development of a Site Management Plan, as indicated in Box 9.4.

Box 9.4 Developing a Site Management Plan

Stage 1: Site and landscape assessment

This stage was described in Section 9.4 'Gathering Earth heritage information'. When assessing a site it will probably seem natural to think about how improvements might be made. However, in the context of an integrated management plan this is premature. Ideas can be noted but no decisions are made at this stage.

Stage 2: Identifying objectives and constraints

Having a clearly defined set of objectives gives stability to the process of management planning, while recognition of constraints establishes the degree of freedom that is possible.

Stage 3: Exploring and choosing options

This stage is concerned with more than the technical details and needs imagination to appreciate the possibilities.

Stage 4: Drafting a formal plan of action

This stage involves costing the alternatives in terms of available resources so that a final plan can be determined.

Stage 5: Finalizing the management plan

Use the information and draft compiled in the previous stages to produce the final plan.

Stage 2: Identifying objectives and constraints

Objectives relate to factors affecting the land use that are (or could be) under control; constraints relate to factors that cannot be controlled.

Having a clearly specified set of objectives gives stability without rigidity to the process of management planning. It can help you target action and give a benchmark against which progress can be measured. An important feature of objectives is that they are sequential – one thing leads to another, or more often, one thing leads to several others, forming what is called a hierarchy or 'tree'. An objective tree, or list of objectives and constraints, can be used to communicate a management plan to others or to keep records on a long-term basis. It is essential to include all legal and regulatory constraints, regardless of how the present manager may feel about them.

Apart from financial and legal constraints, there are also other types of constraint which are much more informal, and often much more personal. They can play havoc with the implementation of a management plan, and so it is vitally

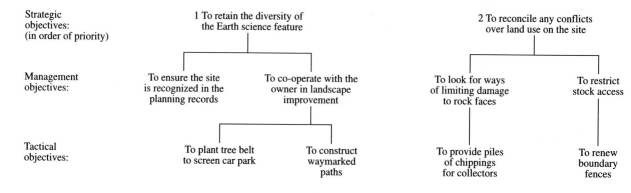

Strategic objectives: (in order of priority)

1 To retain the diversity of the Earth science feature

2 To reconcile any conflicts over land use on the site

Management objectives:

To ensure the site is recognized in the planning records

To co-operate with the owner in landscape improvement

To look for ways of limiting damage to rock faces

To restrict stock access

Tactical objectives:

To plant tree belt to screen car park

To construct waymarked paths

To provide piles of chippings for collectors

To renew boundary fences

Constraints: 1 Cash limits restrict remedial work.
2 Potential conflict of interest in protection of rare wild flower species in the quarry.
3 Site operations restricted to manual labour.

Figure 9.2 An example of an objective tree for small disused quarry situated in farmland. An objective tree is similar in structure to a family tree, but unlike a family tree objectives can be changed according to circumstances. However, this should only be done after careful thinking through the implications of the changes for other related objectives and for the site in general.

important that they are included in the list of constraints. An objective tree can usually be divided into the three distinct levels, as shown in the example in Figure 9.2. Some people prefer to construct them beginning with the strategic objectives and then to build the tree downwards. Others prefer to begin by listing all objectives that seem appropriate before trying to order them in a hierarchical fashion.

Strategic objectives are at the top of the tree and so tend to be very general, scene setting, long lasting and difficult to change. They are sometimes known as 'overall objectives'. The strategic objectives of Earth heritage conservation management are:

◆ to retain the diversity of the Earth heritage features known to exist in the landscape;

◆ to make the site satisfy the demands made upon it by society as a whole;

◆ to reconcile any conflict and competition for the use of land containing the site.

At the next level down in the objective tree there is no universal set of *management objectives* that can be applied to all Earth heritage sites. Each site should be managed within the context of its own landscape, taking account of ownership and other land uses.

Broadly, there are three groups of management objectives:

◆ curatorial management;

◆ exploitation;

◆ reserve excavation and recording.

Curatorial management: the main objective is to stop the natural and human-induced processes of degradation affecting the site. Arising from this are two *tactical objectives* of the either/or type:

◆ to conserve the site by planning day-to-day activities to avoid damaging it and to take urgent action only if it inadvertently becomes damaged, for example by fly-tipping;

226

◆ or to preserve the site by anticipating a range of specific threats and taking action to avoid them, by for example, periodic removal of vegetation and/or scree material.

Exploitation: the main objective is to permit the site to be used for public enjoyment or educational/academic interest, both of which will invariably alter its character and may contribute to its decay. Several *tactical objectives* may arise from this:

◆ to clear the site to make it visible;

◆ to improve access;

◆ to provide displays and visitor facilities;

◆ in certain cases, to excavate buried sections of significance;

◆ to undertake necessary strengthening or repair work to ensure public safety.

Rescue excavation and recording has the objective of documenting a site before it is destroyed by a development that cannot be prevented (such as landfill or construction). It may also be worth while in order to document temporary exposures, such as trenches for pipelines and foundations. Although the site is lost in such cases, it is in effect preserved on paper and on film, and perhaps by a representative collection of specimens.

The above discussion gives a general picture of the possible conservation objectives which might apply to Earth heritage sites. It is intended to show what is expected at this stage, but should not be treated as a set of rules to be slavishly copied. Particular circumstances will always be unique in some ways and this should be reflected in management plans. The three categories of strategic, management and tactical objectives overlap to some extent.

The objectives discussed so far fall into one or more simple statements: 'to maintain', to improve' and 'to create'. They are the key to good landscape and site management; choosing the right one for each situation is one of the most important skills of the manager.

Constraints block or limit the ability to achieve an objective. Financial and legal constraints often come to mind most immediately in relation to conservation. While it is possible to achieve a lot without high costs, expenditure is often a constraint on the choice of actions that can be taken.

There are many laws and regulations relevant to wildlife and landscape conservation, but these need not always be constraints.

ACTIVITY 9.3
CONSTRUCTING AN OBJECTIVE TREE

Using the model provided in Figure 9.2, draw an objective tree for Tedbury Camp Quarry (see Chapters 1 and 3 for description). First make a list of objectives and constraints and then place them in hierarchical order.

Remember to:

◆ use a large sheet of paper;

◆ incorporate general constraints as a list at the bottom of the page;

◆ add any specific constraints that would block certain paths in the tree;

◆ note any objectives of the 'both/and' or 'either/or' type.

◆ ◆ ◆

Stage 3: Exploring and choosing options

The word 'option' implies choice; in this case it involves exploring a wide range of possible means of achieving the objectives decided above. The more imaginative and knowledgeable you are, the more likely you will be to find the best possible solution to your land use requirements.

Your knowledge about the Earth heritage criteria that led to the selection of RIGS locations, together with the conservation-based classification of sites described in Chapter 6, will form the background knowledge needed to choose the best options for your site management objectives. The other ingredient you require is imagination in stimulating creative ideas for achieving those options. Some people are gifted in this direction while others find it very difficult. Here are some ways in which you might get help!

◆ *Being stimulated by your environment.* Try to think about your objectives in a completely unrelated context, such as you see from the window on a train journey. Keep a small notebook handy and write down any ideas that occur to you.

◆ *Being provoked by friends and colleagues (brainstorming).* This is best done in a relaxed atmosphere where you will not be interrupted. Four to six people is a good number; not necessarily conservationists, but preferably people who have a detached view of your problem and have not been involved in the earlier stages of management planning. Each should suggest ideas as they occur to them, no matter how crazy they seem at the time. One person writes down all the ideas on a large sheet of paper. Every now and again when ideas seem to dry up, the group should stop and review what has come up and see if any ideas suggest ways of making progress.

◆ *Inviting criticism.* Seek out people with different views to your own. Try to get them to tell you what they think and listen to what they say. You might get some ideas you would never think of alone.

Any of these techniques is likely to come up with more options than you could ever expect to put into practice. Before drafting a formal management plan, you will need to choose a final working set of options. The criteria you use to make your choice of options should be directly related to the objectives and constraints defined at Stage 2. Remember that some of these criteria should be related to your own personal likes and dislikes. If you are not very happy with the options that seem to be favoured by the criteria you are using, this is a sign that you should go back and think again about your objectives and constraints. The number of options you choose to incorporate in your final management plan will depend upon the size and complexity of the site and also on the resources available.

Stage 4: Drafting a formal plan of action

By this stage, most of the work of management planning will have been done. All that remains is to work out the costs of your chosen options in terms of money and labour, so that you can compare one with another. Deciding the balance between these factors will be a fairly crude calculation, and the outcome will depend upon your own personal attitudes and other influences, but this is an inevitable aspect of decision making in any situation.

Stage 5: Finalizing the management plan

Once incorporated into a formal plan of action the options become management prescriptions. They should be worded clearly to make it easy to check on the extent to which they have been implemented.

The management plan (Geological Site Documentation/ Management Brief in the terminology used by the national conservation agencies) should contain:

◆ *the site description* – this includes practical aspects like location, access and site conditions; scientific aspects with geological information and references, annotated site map, detailed photographic survey, together with appendices such as the original Geological Conservation Review statement if applicable;

◆ *identification of potential threats to the site*;

◆ *a statement of the conservation principles* for the site;

◆ *a statement of the limitations* (i.e. constraints) to what can be practically done to enhance the site in future;

◆ *a list of action points*, based upon the management prescriptions, to improve the scientific/educational value of the site. Some examples of activities are given in Box 9.5.

Box 9.5 Possible site management options and improvements

Site development

◆ Clear exposed faces and create safe collecting areas. This will preserve exposures and allow safe collecting.

◆ Site improvement and enhancement should take account of special geological and geomorphological features present.

◆ Access could be improved by identifying or constructing waymarked paths, or agreed paths across private land.

◆ Exposure of certain sensitive sites to overuse could be avoided by controlling access, either by visitors obtaining a pass or a key for a closed site or by booking entry through the landowner; such precautions are exceptional.

◆ Some working quarry sites may also require restricted access, possibly from a viewing platform, but it is desirable that most sites should allow 'hands-on' experience for users.

Site safety

◆ Hazard assessments are required for the site to identify any potentially dangerous features.

◆ Reduce potential hazards by fencing dangerous areas, clearing unstable material from faces,etc.

◆ Produce a list of individual site-related hazards for party leaders. This will allow intending leaders to make their assessment of site safety considerations and suitability prior to visiting the site.

◆ A code of conduct for site users should accompany any list of site hazards, detailing instructions additional to the normal code of conduct applicable to all fieldwork.

◆ Institute a system of regular site monitoring, with users reporting on the site status.

9.6 Relations with owners and planning authorities

Establishing contacts with landowners/occupiers and planners has three important benefits.

◆ *It alerts owners and planning authorities to the importance of local sites.* The group will need adequate records of the sites in its area, providing the data that will be needed to reinforce the need for conservation. Only those sites of sufficient importance to justify conservation should be selected as RIGS.

◆ *It encourages appropriate site management.* With the owner's permission, this can lead to the enhancement of sites to develop their educational or other potential.

◆ *It promotes local interest and involvement* in Earth heritage conservation and encourages good practice by site users.

Local planning authorities and other statutory bodies should be encouraged to recognize RIGS in appropriate policy documents as an aid to land use planning. *The first lines of defence are the owners and the planning processes.* Planning authorities at both district and county levels, and the National Park Authorities, play a major part in conservation. RIGS are essentially equivalent in status to wildlife 'Sites of Nature Conservation Importance' and can be protected in the same way. The key roles of planning authorities in RIGS schemes are summarized below:

◆ recognition of sites in structure plans, in local and unitary development plans and in nature conservation strategies;

◆ protection of sites in Areas of Outstanding Natural Beauty and on Heritage Coasts;

◆ assessment of proposals for developments on Earth heritage sites under the planning system.

In addition the roles of the National Rivers Authority, the Forestry Commission and the National Trust should not be forgotten, as they are hybrids – both landowners and 'planners'.

9.7 Funding, support and training
Funding

All voluntary initiatives face the need to obtain funds! RIGS groups are no exception and they are unlikely to be able to carry out all the work they would wish without external funds. However, the need for funds and the scale of this financial support can be considered in two stages:

◆ start-up funding;

◆ site work and development.

Start-up funding on a relatively modest level will be needed to launch a RIGS group. Costs at this stage include those of sending letters seeking support, supplying recording forms for site surveys and filing systems for site records, and buying computer hardware and software if records are to be computerized. Articles in local newspapers are a means of gaining free publicity for your group, while local or constituent organizations may be willing to provide limited funding for the launch.

Site work and development. When a group contemplates work for site enhancement or to develop educational materials, the financial implications are significantly larger. There are a number of possible sources of funding which may be willing to help.

◆ Education and leisure/amenity departments of local authorities and other statutory bodies such as National Park Authorities may help where sites are being enhanced to meet their interests.

◆ 'Local Nature Reserve' designation may make sites eligible for local authority funds.

◆ The national conservation agencies may contribute through grants.

◆ The Curry Fund of the Geologists' Association is a possible source of funding for specific projects within sites.

◆ Local industries may provide financial sponsorship and/or practical help by, for example, lending machinery or providing transport.

◆ Funds can be raised through the usual activities undertaken by voluntary bodies.

The group may make use of voluntary labour, when safe and appropriate to do so.

Training

Many individuals and organizations will become involved in geological conservation work, perhaps for the first time. There will be an early need for training in the procedures the group wishes to use for field visits and compiling site records. This might best be achieved by inviting volunteers to attend training days when the completion of Geology Locality Records is described and the access and safety requirements for site visits are emphasized. Such training sessions should include an accompanied visit to an Earth heritage site where supervised practice in the completion of site records can be undertaken. This book is intended to help with such training activities.

9.8 Educating and involving site users

Having seen something of the contributions that voluntary effort can provide, let us now consider how such interest and efforts can be extended.

First, it might be of interest to ascertain which sites are most visited and what types of interests are held by the visitors. The School of Geological Sciences at Kingston Polytechnic (now Kingston University) was commissioned by the NCC to run a survey of geological and geomorphological fieldwork carried out in Britain in 1987/88. The survey assessed the nature, volume and location of fieldwork undertaken by secondary schools and institutions of further and higher education.

Some key findings were:

◆ Fourteen counties were identified as being particularly popular. England leads the field with eight counties and of these Cumbria, North Yorkshire, Devon and

Dorset top the league. Wales is represented with Gwynedd as the most visited county and Dyfed next in the ranking. The two most visited Scottish regions are Strathclyde and Highland.

◆ Over half of all visits took place in the period March–May and September–October, with the three most popular months being April, March and October. 38% of visits to individual sites lasted less than two hours, 22% lasted two to four hours and 28% lasted four to eight hours.

◆ Great variations were recorded in the sizes of parties visiting individual sites; 47% comprised less than 20 students while 14% had more than 50 members.

The survey provides an interesting analysis of visiting patterns of student parties and it can be inferred that most of the visits took place away from their home areas. This fact would have a bearing upon the availability of assistance from these sources.

However, the survey does not include fieldwork visits by adults in geological and natural history societies, by university adult education classes or by Open University parties. Members of these groups are more likely to take part in local visits and more willing to be recruited as willing helpers.

Sadly, the view of many people about Earth heritage is that rocks are boring! Much effort is put into Earth heritage conservation by both official and voluntary bodies but it will be wasted if the public at large cannot appreciate its value. It is essential that Earth heritage conservation gets its message across in order to raise awareness to levels more than comparable to the high profile of wildlife conservation (see Chapter 10).

One way of increasing awareness of conservation sites is by environmental interpretation. This is concerned with changing the attitude of visitors by explaining the significance of the site and how it has developed into its present form. It was noteworthy that the Kingston survey indicated that many of the parties would welcome a wider selection of appropriate information for their visits, such as on-site display boards, information sheets or guidebooks.

The principal reason for interpreting any site must be to aid its conservation. However, there must be specific reasons why a site warrants interpretation. It could be a unique example of a geological feature or it could have great potential as a teaching site. The site might be a fragile one suffering damage from too many visitors and the interpretation can act as a management tool to direct visitors away from the more sensitive areas to other parts of the site.

Developing interpretational aids for an Earth heritage sites is discussed in Chapter 10, Section 10.4.

Chapter 10

PUBLIC AWARENESS

Geology and geomorphology underpin many of the properties that give landscape its scenic qualities – and remember, the natural beauty of the countryside is the biggest asset of the tourist industry. The rocks not only influence the kind of plants, animals, birds and insects which we find in every part of the countryside, but also shape the lives and livelihoods of the human communities that live here.

Yet Earth science tends to be, alas, the Cinderella discipline. It is perceived to be a subject apart, poorly integrated with mainstream conservation practice, too esoteric for most tastes, too specialized, almost too scholarly. To date, work in this field has been concentrated too much, perhaps, at the academic end of the spectrum, as evidenced by the preoccupation with massive learned publications like the Geological Conservation Review (GCR). That is not to say that the GCR is unimportant – far from it; as long as the system of designating SSSIs remains in place, we must have a sound academic justification for every site we notify.

It is not quite enough to say that these sites are of scientific interest – scientific interest simply means that it is of interest to scientists. If we are to gain public support for using public money to safeguard and protect documents from the past, we have to be able to articulate valid reasons for conservation which will have relevance to the layperson. We have to establish clear links between familiar landscapes and the Earth sciences; links which would provide the opportunity to explain the countryside in terms of its geological components, and the profound and cataclysmic processes which have shaped it.

The balance between strict scientific accuracy and looser lay intelligibility is not an easy balance to get right. But demystifying the subject is a problem which we can, and must, address more vigorously.

(Magnus Magnusson, Chairman of Scottish Natural Heritage, 'Making rocks talk', *Earth Science Conservation*, No. 31, 1993, p.3.)

Study comment

This chapter starts with a restatement of the need for Earth heritage conservation (EHC) and makes comparisons with the purpose and philosophy of the biological conservation movement. This sets the scene for the main purpose of the chapter, which is to consider practical methods of enhancing public awareness of geological and geomorphological sites as an integral part of our natural heritage and to encourage involvement in real activities related to them. The practical steps discussed include:

◆ using the media;

◆ putting up information boards;

◆ building on the work of field centres;

◆ seeking a higher profile for the Earth sciences and EHC in education;

◆ building on people's awareness of and attachment to landscape and regional characteristics as a form of natural heritage.

A further little-developed option is sponsorship from organizations which have strong links with the land through use of resources or through the image they wish to project.

You will get more from the suggested activities if you can work in a small group. If real action is not possible it will still be well worth choosing one of the case study sites as a focus for a simulated awareness-raising event. There is also room for further discussion of the ethics and rationale of conservation, although this is not emphasized in the activities.

An important feature of RIGS is that they are chosen by local people to reflect local needs and conditions. In tune with such a philosophy this chapter sets out to stimulate discussion and activity, rather than to be prescriptive. The idea is that proposals and action should be a product of your own evaluation of local issues and conditions, perhaps resulting in deliberation on the best short-term and long-term strategies.

10.1 EHC and biological conservation compared

Earth heritage conservation must work to establish its own place in the ethical–economic jungle of resource management or, as many would prefer to call it, environmental management. Current decisions about biological conservation and public involvement in it are underpinned by theories about its nature and purposes. These range from the purely anthropocentric to the purely ecological, with a variety of interim positions more or less influenced by religion, political dogma, economic theory and beliefs about society and science. This section very briefly sets the scene for consideration of what may lie behind the arguments for conservation of any particular site.

In the 1960s the American forester and ecologist Aldo Leopold wrote:

> Conservation … is keeping the resource in working order, as well as preventing overuse … [it] is a positive exercise of skill and insight, not merely a negative exercise of abstinence and caution. A system of conservation based solely on economic self-interest is hopelessly lop-sided. It tends to ignore, and thus eventually eliminate, many elements … that lack commercial value … but that are essential to its healthy functioning.

(Aldo Leopold, *A Sand County Almanac*, Oxford University Press, 1966.)

Although Leopold was talking about what we now call the sustainable development of biotic systems, his comments also form a useful take-off point for a discussion of Earth heritage conservation. How can we define 'working order' and 'overuse' in terms of Earth heritage sites and landscape features? Indeed, are 'overuse' and 'working order' the main criteria for Earth heritage conservation? And what is the nature of the 'positive exercise of skill and insight' which can support it?

Maintaining an ecological system in working order is clearly a different proposition to maintaining access to sites such as quarries or coastal cliffs or managing development so that the scientific and aesthetic value of landforms and geologically interesting landscapes is retained in the long term. However, the conservation of each of these two aspects of our natural heritage still has much in common. Although the geosphere is not alive in the same way as communities of plants and animals, a reductionist view of Earth heritage conservation which defines the subject matter as simply a collection of individual sites is no more satisfactory than the reductionist view of biological conservation which regards the natural world as a catalogue of individual species. In both instances the sum of the parts is less than the whole.

Geological history is about processes operating on a global scale. Therefore it is not surprising that an anti-reductionist stance is reflected in the scope and structure of the Geological Conservation Review and the designation of Earth heritage SSSIs. Likewise, the designation of RIGS on a regional basis for education, historical, scientific and aesthetic reasons must equally recognize the interrelatedness of individual sites. Each site reveals a fragment of the story of our planet and the processes which formed it. Additionally, in some cases a site may be quite literally an important landmark in our understanding of geological processes. Thus for Earth heritage conservation we arrive at a definition of 'working order' where accessibility to *Homo sapiens*, sub-species educationists, students, etc. is a crucial element of conservation. For instance, monoculture forestry plantations may not actually destroy landforms, but they may totally obscure them, prevent access, and disturb patterns of drainage and sedimentation on which their long-term survival depends.

In some respects, *overuse* is a less serious problem for Earth heritage sites than for biological ones, unless we are dealing with an integrity site. After all, one quarry face may indeed sometimes be as good as another for displaying particular features. Moreover, resource exploitation is responsible for revealing (in quarries, mines, oil wells, pits and road cuttings) features, structures and relationships crucial to our understanding of the geological past. However, overuse and thoughtless use of exposure sites can occasionally have rather the effect of mass tourism on a beautiful beach, which after a few years no longer exhibits the very features for which it was originally exploited.

The 'positive exercise of skill and insight' which constitutes conservation of our Earth heritage is thus likely to take a variety of forms which at times diverge from the requirements of biological conservation. This is not to say they have nothing in common. On the contrary, both ethically and practically there are many links. You will have a chance to form your own views of the practicalities as you work through the rest of this chapter.

10.2 In the public eye?

Consider a giant panda, or an avocet, or a sunlit patch of ancient woodland, or the song of a whale. For millions of people these and other appealing images have come to symbolize our natural heritage. Hence, enough hearts and minds have been won for biological conservation to have some influence on policy and decisions about development and conservation. Such symbols become powerful conveyors of messages by providing a publicly accessible focus for attention on conservation. EHC must surely build on its own symbols and develop new ones if it is to gain the recognition and support it needs from beyond the small community of professional Earth scientists and enthusiasts.

When it comes to winning hearts and minds, EHC in the 1990s is still in the early stages of development, albeit perhaps on the point of major expansion. Nevertheless, it will take time before millions are moved to give any value whatsoever to the Earth science equivalent of, say, a bat colony which, before the conservationists got busy, had a strong negative popular image. But is there indeed an Earth science equivalent of a bat colony? That is, are there geological and geomorphological features which are often considered a nuisance or even dangerous?

Perhaps a worked-out gravel pit, a stretch of eroding coastal cliff or a heap of rock rubble which contains a rare mineral has even less value for people in the street, including those who make decisions about land use, than the bats and bogs of the biosphere. Can we imagine 'Friends of Coastal Erosion' societies springing up in line with bat or orchid preservation societies? Perhaps in the Earth sciences we are at times dealing with natural phenomena whose relationship to human activities are different in kind and therefore require a different approach to promoting conservation.

If biological conservation has its bats and bogs, it also has its butterflies – phenomena which are aesthetically appealing, apparently beneficial and which pose no direct threat to the human species. We have suggested one or two bat equivalents from the Earth sciences; can you now think of any butterfly equivalents?

ACTIVITY 10.1
GEOLOGICAL BATS AND BUTTERFLIES

Taken a few minutes to consider what you know of the geology, geomorphology and landscape of your local area as well as the traditional architecture and land-based industries.

What features already have popular appeal?

What features could have wide appeal if they were better known?

What features are accorded value through support from public funds or protection by planners and developers?

Can you classify any local Earth science features as 'bats' or 'butterflies'? Alternatively, look back at photos of sites in previous chapters, particularly Chapter 1, and consider whether they are 'bats' or 'butterflies'. Indeed, do you think that this is a useful way to approach the problem of public awareness of EHC?

The next point is more clear cut. Fundamental to the idea of conservation of sites of geological and geomorphological value is their inclusion in the category 'natural heritage'. Broad public awareness of natural heritage, in terms not just of flora and fauna and human activities but of the land itself, can only be a long-term goal. It is not universally appreciated that geology and its expression in soils, drainage and landscape are the templates on which plants, animals and humanity have fashioned the environment. At a more specific level there is no coal miner, wetland ecologist, land surveyor or farm worker whose livelihood, history and lifestyle is not intimately linked to this wider natural heritage.

It could be argued that EHC will have to emulate the three-stage process of development in public opinion along which biological conservation has already taken some significant steps:

1 the need to conserve species has become widely understood;

2 on this foundation, an awareness of the need to conserve habitats and communities has been built;

3 the importance of an internationalist perspective has been emphasized.

In the long term, EHC will only become established if we, as a society, are educated to understand and value this aspect of our natural heritage. Education of children and their teachers as well as those who make a whole range of decisions on land use is therefore vital.

For Earth scientists, rocks, sediments, soils and landforms are an archive of the past, telling stories that are full of both the familiar and the surprising, the obscure and the exciting. They exercise our imaginations and our intellects. They tell us of events and places and processes which are the foundation of life on Earth, including our own. They are the raw material from which we fashion predictive models. Such models may concern climatic change, suggest where concentrations of valuable minerals may be found, or where waste can or cannot be safely disposed of underground, or how long our water supplies will last. This archive of landscape and geological and geomorphological sites is a glimpse of what is, quite literally, the basis of our lives. But our knowledge of the geosphere is partial and imperfect since most of it is hidden from direct observation. Thus our few thousand Earth heritage SSSIs and RIGS, as well as non-designated but locally important Earth heritage sites, are a precious and finite resource for research and education as well as simply a source of pleasure and interest to many people.

As you are well aware, geological processes operate on a large scale in space as well as time. This means that our understanding of the nature of these processes is built on the comparison and correlation of rocks across large geographical areas. Consequently we need to conserve not just individual Earth heritage sites but a network of localities which together tell a more complete story than any single one can do. Instances of every kind of field evidence on which geological and geomorphological theory is founded, and just as importantly, challenged, must be available for future research and teaching. Sites are also needed at local level to promote informal interest and pride in the natural heritage in order to foster public awareness and concern. Each success for conservation on a local level thus takes on its full significance in a wider context as part of a countrywide (indeed international) network.

It would be idle to suppose that without extensive education (in its broadest sense) large numbers of people will come to appreciate the value of EHC. Education must promote an understanding that landforms, natural and quarried exposures and mines and caves are an essential window into our past – and indeed our future – and that they illuminate the context of our livelihood and recreation. *In short, many people still need to be convinced that both landforms and geological sites are part of our common natural heritage whose destruction we permit to the detriment of us all.*

ACTIVITY 10.2

ASSESSING PUBLIC UNDERSTANDING OF EHC

Try to quantify your own experience of public awareness of EHC by answering the following questions. If you find any of them hard to answer it may well be useful to ponder further as you read through the rest of the chapter.

	Less than 10%	10–30%	30–50%	More than 50%
Among your family, friends and acquaintances, what percentage have some knowledge of EHC?				
If you work in conservation in a professional or voluntary capacity, what percentage of your co-workers are well informed about EHC?				
If you do not work in conservation, what percentage of your colleagues or peer group have any knowledge of EHC?				
What percentage of 12-year-olds do you think would include a mention of the Earth sciences if asked to write a paragraph or two on the topic of conservation?				
In what percentage of Higher Education Earth science courses do you think conservation is studied or even mentioned?				
Think of those who make important decisions about land use, for instance, landowners, planners, architects, farmers, water authorities, local councillors. What percentage of them in your judgement, take EHC into account?				

◆ ◆ ◆

10.3 Biological conservation and EHC: on the same ground?

We have already touched on this subject earlier in the chapter. Now we will examine the issue with a view to the practicalities of useful action. Biological conservation has had some notable successes (and failures). Can Earth heritage conservation simply be approached in the same way? Or should we ask whether its nature and circumstances demand different approaches? For the purpose of exploring these questions it is worth separating public awareness of our biological and Earth heritage from knowledge of conservation issues. Let's look first at awareness.

You should already have formed an opinion on current levels of awareness of EHC from your answers to the questions posed in Activity 10.2. It would be useful to know how they compare with public awareness of biological conservation and what has contributed to both the successes and failures of the latter. The following brief treatment is intended as an initial stimulus to thought and makes no claim to deal comprehensively with this complex and interesting subject.

It could be argued that biological conservation has had significant successes by presenting conservation in an essentially anthropocentric way. That is, awareness of the scientific arguments and of the need for funding have been encouraged to grow out of what is calculated to have an immediate and wide appeal. For instance, we feel good about helping our fellow primates to survive, growing plants which sustain insects and birds, or making passageways for toads and hedgehogs beneath roads. The reward is a sense of virtue and a feeling of satisfaction that natural processes are being maintained. Sheer beauty is another powerful 'argument' for biological conservation. Ancient mixed woodland and meadows of wild flowers are beautiful, and therefore, we instinctively feel, a good thing. In conserving them, we easily perceive ourselves as doing good. Thus conservation leads us to appreciate our place in the scheme of all things natural.

Are there comparable 'feel good' strategies for the Earth sciences? Let's look at the problems from the pessimistic viewpoint first and then the optimistic end of the spectrum. You may also want to debate whether this is in fact a sensible strategy for enhancing public awareness of EHC.

Let's start rather pessimistically with the argument that popular perceptions of the Earth sciences and Earth heritage are poles apart from images of whales or meadows of wild flowers. In other words, the Earth sciences are popularly associated with destructive, terrifying and essentially inhuman and life-threatening events over which we have no control: volcanic eruptions, huge and terrifying creatures whose lives have been catastrophically extinguished, earthquakes and ice ages, quarrying and mining. And what if the other side of the coin is merely 'dusty old fossils' as seen in some of our less well funded museums? All this seems to conjure up a world of natural disasters with precious little for most of us to feel good about, so that the result may be that many people just don't want to know. There is also a perception that rocks, unlike plants and animals, are indestructible and therefore are not in need of protection.

On the other hand, EHC, like biological conservation, may hold some powerful cards (see Box 10.1 overleaf) when it comes to instant appeal, although the cards (apart from the extraordinarily popular dinosaurs) may not yet have been played so often as those in the biological pack.

ACTIVITY 10.3

APPEALING ASPECTS OF EARTH SCIENCES

'Brainstorm' your ideas about appealing aspects of the Earth sciences. Rely as much on general knowledge as on what you have learned from this book. Do not sift or structure your ideas until you have as many as possible down on paper.

◆ ◆ ◆

You may have included such things as minerals which are beautiful in themselves or as the raw material of jewellery and industrial fortunes. Perhaps you thought of interesting rock formations or landscape features, or maybe a famous fossil locality. An extended range of suggestions is made later in this chapter.

But should we simply be trying to raise awareness by playing on the 'feel good' factor? Is logic and argument, concentrating on the people who actually make decisions about land use, a better way forward? Should we rather aim to educate and foster a direct understanding of the significance of geological exposures and landforms?

Box 10.1   Geology in town and country

Landscape is often geologically interesting as well as attractive to tourists or, just as importantly, characteristic of a region and local culture. Geology determines traditional building styles which give so many people a sense of belonging to and pride in their local area, or pleasure in areas they visit as tourists. Without the conditions suitable for the deposition of the London Clay tens of millions of years ago there might have been no bricks in the London area – and no London as we know it today. Without the relatively soft clay, the City's underground system would have been much more expensive to build, and so probably less extensive. At the other end of Britain, in Caithness, the thinly bedded Devonian siltstones and sandstones yield flagstone which dominates traditional architecture. In Snowdonia, the mountains, products of ancient geological upheavals, influence climate, culture and economy. And since eroded particles of rock are the basis of many soils, it could be argued that every builder and gardener has a direct line to the Earth sciences. These are surely contexts within which enhanced public awareness of the Earth sciences can be addressed.

Growing public awareness of possible climatic and environmental change provides another avenue to raise public awareness about the importance of the Earth sciences. Our still tentative attempts to explain and model changes in climate and sea level which we could be faced with in the not too distant future has many links with studies of sediments and structures formed since the last ice age.

The Earth sciences touch all our lives in other simple and obvious ways which we will explore further later in this chapter. But what of the question posed by the title of this section? Can Earth heritage conservationists simply take on wholesale the strategies for enhancing public awareness used by biological conservationists?

In attempting to answer this question it is useful to compare the starting points as far as public awareness is concerned. The importance of biological diversity has become quite widely appreciated. Equally, the human race is understood by a substantial number of people to be dependent on other forms of life. However, it cannot be said that there exists a comparable appreciation of the central tenets of the Earth sciences and their contribution to our own development or survival. What does the average person in the street know of stratigraphy or unconformities or the origins of soils, fossil fuels and construction materials, of plate tectonics or mountain building? So alongside the practical task of establishing and enhancing RIGS and designating geological and geomorphological SSSIs there will often be a basic education and PR job to be done for the Earth sciences before EHC even becomes a planning and management issue.

If starting points for biological and Earth heritage conservation are not identical, neither is the nature of what is to be conserved always comparable. Landscapes of biological and geological value are often in coastal or upland settings where the structure of the land, that is, the geology and geomorphology, determines many of their aesthetic qualities. In such cases the two interests may well merge. However, it is interesting to explore the differences between biological conservation and EHC further under the headings of those two very useful categories: integrity and exposure sites. An Earth heritage integrity site has something in common with biological habitats, which could all be considered as integrity sites. Yet, while the regeneration or renewal of some biological systems can be imagined on the timescale of one or more generations, the replacement of a static geomorphological site such as an esker or a drumlin field would have to wait until the ice-man cometh – and goeth. That might take at least another hundred thousand years! On the other hand, Earth heritage exposure sites can literally sit side by side with other types of land use which would be incompatible with biological conservation.

When it comes to exposure sites, EHC will also – at least sometimes – have the advantage over its biological cousin. There are occasions when one exposure really is as good as another, so losses in one place may be replaced by new exposures in an adjacent site. This is where the extractive and construction industries have sometimes been of immense value in revealing bedrock, structures and sediments in innumerable building foundations, road cuttings, quarries and mines, some of which make available crucial information.

The construction and extractive industries can also operate to the detriment of conservation, so an increased awareness of Earth heritage issues amongst those who work in these industries can only be helpful. Problems arise in a number of contexts, some of which were considered in previous chapters. For instance, one huge 'super-quarry' in a remote site accessible only by sea provides much less geological information than twenty small local quarries where the strata can be correlated, the details of regional geological history filled in, and access for educational purposes maintained. Then there is the danger of wholesale destruction of unique or static geomorphological sites. But, as you know, conservation can sometimes be achieved on the basis of quite straightforward engineering or land management decisions. In essence, the future for EHC is bright as long as the public, and in particular land managers of various kinds, are made aware of our unique and wonderful Earth heritage.

In summary, satisfactory conservation of Earth heritage sites will only be achieved in parallel with improved public awareness of the Earth sciences themselves. People will not manage in a positive way a resource whose value they remain unaware of. Biological conservation now proceeds on the basis that significant numbers of people in Britain are aware of the problem of endangered species and habitats which form part of a rapidly shrinking global pool of natural resources. EHC has probably not yet reached the equivalent starting point, where the irreplaceable nature of integrity sites and the need for a representative spread of both integrity and exposure sites for research and education is widely accepted and perceived to be a land management issue. Moreover, although there are many examples of sites of equal value to biological conservation and EHC, the essential differences between animate and inanimate systems sometimes demand different approaches by land users such as the construction industries and local planners.

10.4 Enhancing public awareness – practical steps

Having considered the background to enhancing the public awareness of EHC, the rest of this chapter examines a number of practical measures that can be taken to enhance public awareness.

As discussed in Chapter 5, the NCC strategy document (1990) provided a clear framework and springboard for action. Central to the action is the establishment of RIGS and other locally important conservation sites which involve many groups with a direct interest in land use. Formal education is undoubtedly a long-term strategy in which much effort will need to be invested. However, informal education of many kinds through using the media for publicity, setting up site information boards, making use of field centres, seeking sponsorship for EHC and building on the themes of landscape and local heritage also offer a great deal of scope for enhancing public awareness of the Earth sciences and the need for site conservation.

We will consider each of the options suggested above and make suggestions for real initiatives that you could undertake in your local area. If this proves impossible, select one of the case study sites in Chapter 1 and use the data provided to do a simulated exercise. The suggestions for enhancing public awareness are wide in scope but certainly not comprehensive. Use them as a springboard for your own imagination and your particular expertise and skills. Under each heading there are one or more practical exercises. Since some exercises will be more time-consuming than others, you may wish to divide up the work among your group and report back on progress after a given period of time. If you are working on your own, choose whichever exercise will give you most satisfaction to complete.

Using the media

The media include radio, television, newspaper and magazines. It is also worth considering in this context the newsletters and publications of various field societies as well as specialist journals read by groups such as ramblers, climbers, youth hostellers, civil engineers, gamekeepers, teachers, landscape architects, conservationists or farmers. If you are short of ideas for groups concerned with land use, most main public libraries have an astonishing selection of special interest periodicals, some of which are bound to be relevant. Related to the media are leaflets for museums or a variety of other tourist and educational uses. It may be useful to do a sampling exercise to see whether conservation of geological sites actually features in any of the publications you have identified.

Where you send your Earth science story will of course depend on exactly what the story is. However, there are a few principles for successful publicity, as summarized in Box 10.2.

Box 10.2 Why the media?

News is only news if it fits into the timescale of reporting for the medium concerned (shortest for radio news, TV and daily newspapers). So a court case about landfill in a quarry worthy of conservation might be local news, but the unremitting efforts of a handful of dedicated conservationists is probably, unfortunately, not (unless they do something newsworthy).

Feature stories are much more likely to find an audience if you can hit on an angle; general worthiness and well-researched studies backed up by reliable statistics are not enough. The angle might perhaps relate to a personality involved in EHC, or to EHC in the context of other stories already in the news. On the other hand, in a specialist journal or newsletter a feature might be welcome if it provided a basis for practical activities or a regular column (i.e. free copy for the editor).

You may want to consider the problem of making news which will generate favourable publicity for EHC. There are times when conservationists must simply stand up and argue the case for what they believe to be overriding interests. However, if the public only ever hear about EHC in the context of conflict with other interests with which they may be more familiar and to which they may consequently be more sympathetic, the image of EHC may not benefit.

Personal contacts with editors and journalists are well worth cultivating. If they as individuals are not aware of the Earth sciences, never mind EHC, and do not know why their readers should be interested in it, they are unlikely to give such items priority.

ACTIVITY 10.4

PLANNING A PUBLICITY EVENT

Your task is to plan and if possible achieve a real publicity event or publication. Ideally, you should work with a small group of fellow readers of this book, or interested friends or colleagues with whom you can exchange ideas and share the work. If you are on your own, choose a smaller project which you think you can manage unaided. The checklist below is not comprehensive but it should help you consider options and plan the action you mean to take.

List as many EHC issues as you can relating to your local area.

Would you categorize them as 'news' or 'features'?

Which item do you think would generate the most helpful publicity?

What 'angles' could you hang a story on?

Who exactly do you see as the audience for your publicity?

What medium of publicity would be most effective?

Box 10.3   A media success story in Oldham

BILL HOTCHKISS (left), chairman of Oldham Geological Society, with John Guthrie and his wife, Kay, the society secretary

JOHN GUTHRIE holds a fern-like fossil, possibly 300 million years old

JOHN GUTHRIE searches for more fossils among the scree

A secret world in fossil quarry

AMONG the discarded clothing, car tyres and rusting household rubbish which litter a quarry in Oldham are fossils which can be traced back 300 million years.

Evidence of plants and shellfish can be found in the scree on the steep sides of the disused quarry.

The old mine and brickworks at Glodwick Lows, off Roundthorn Road, was declared a site of special scientific interest in 1989, but few Oldhamers know of its existence, let alone of its importance.

The layered cliff face, which local geologists hope will stay on view, is considered to be one of the most important examples of the middle Carboniferous age — the time when coal was laid down in Britain and Northern Europe.

This part of Britain was then covered by an enormous delta which extended into northern France and Germany.

Ownership poser

Since the 1940s, geology students from Manchester University have studied the site, the ownership and future use of which is now being considered by a Government official, following a public inquiry.

Oldham Geological Society hopes that the quarry will be cleared up, partly filled in and landscaped, and that the all-important rock face will remain on view.

Mrs Guthrie, the group's secretary, said: "Most other places like this have already been filled in and history has been lost. But it is part of Oldham's past and should stay exposed for future generations."

French teacher Mr Bill Hotchkiss, the chairman, said: "It is important geologically that students and researchers have access to sites like this. Very few people in Oldham know about it."

(*Evening Chronicle*, Oldham, 16 February 1993, p.16.)

(See Box 8.2 on page 204 for the conservation background to this story.)

Which journal/newspaper/programme/public venue would be most suitable?

Which individual editor, producer or main speaker will you approach?

Could you just hand this person the story or do you need to do some preparatory work?

What resources of people, money, time does your project demand?

◆ ◆ ◆

Site information leaflets and trail boards

Where better to fire people's imagination and interest in Earth heritage conservation than when they visit sites? This can be done through on-site displays and leaflets available at the site, or at a nearby outlet such as a local shop (Figures 10.1 and 10.2).

Designers of on-site interpretive media have a difficult task. They are often enthusiastic geologists, and so there is always the temptation to overload the factual content – the problem of 'the balance between strict scientific accuracy and looser lay intelligibility' mentioned in the opening quotation to this section. To be successful, designers of on-site displays and leaflets need to think carefully about the different sorts of interests people have who visit the site.

Box 10.4 (page 248) provides one such perspective, and Box 10.5 (page 249) highlights the problems of getting the Earth heritage message across to the public. Designers should not expect everyone who visits the site to even notice what has been done, let alone remember the content of the board or leaflet, as the example in Box 10.5 shows.

Figure 10.1 *Trail leaflets. These two examples are sold at local outlets. The Pwll y Wrach trail was prepared by members of the Brecknock Wildlife Trust to guide visitors around a trail developed in an existing wildlife reserve. The Onny Valley Geology Teaching trail was developed for visiting educational parties in collaboration with the landowner (see Box 8.1).*

(a)

(b)

(c)

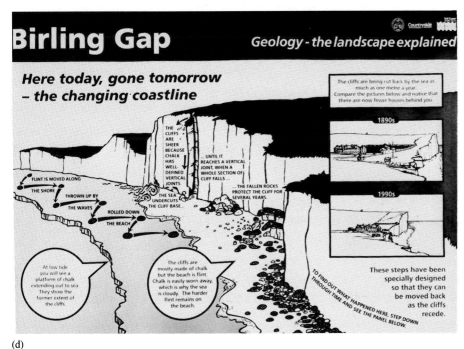

(d)

Figure 10.2 *Examples of on-site display boards with contrasting amounts of information and complexity. (a) and (b) Board at the waterfall at Pwll y Wrach, Powys, explaining the transition between marine Silurian rocks up into river deposits of Devonian age. (c) Board at Ludford Corner, Shropshire, explaining an exposure of the Ludlow Bone Bed near the top of the Silurian. (d) Board explaining view at Birling Gap, East Sussex.*

Leaflets can provide information about a site before, during and after a visit, but think about how you will distribute them. On-site dispensers are all very well but need refilling regularly and can be prone to vandalism, especially if they have a container for money. If the leaflets are to be distributed off-site, from whom will they be available?

On-site displays have the advantage of providing information to anyone visiting the site. They can range from a simple sign identifying the site and providing a contact address for more information to a purpose-built interpretive panel. Panels often cost more to produce than leaflets but can be cheaper in the long run. If you get a large number of non-specialist visitors in the summer and few in the winter, why not provide a removable, and so possibly cheaper, display that can be stored safely during the winter?

The advantage of information boards is that they catch the attention without making extravagant demands on interest or involvement; people can chance upon them and take them or leave them. Nevertheless, information boards often become a focus for tourist attention as well as adding to local people's appreciation of their environment. So they are an excellent vehicle for advancing the idea of Earth heritage sites and landscape as heritage.

Box 10.4 A spectrum of site visitors

Visitors may be regarded as being part of a continuum spanning a broad spectrum of age and interests, but for convenience they can be grouped into four potential target audiences.

A Education groups (schools, colleges, universities, adult groups)

In one sense this is a captive audience, and one which readily accepts the idea of being educated in the environment – including through the use of interactive interpretative techniques. The methodology of teaching field groups is relatively well understood, even if often not well implemented. Students are used to structured, linear learning and they match the approach adopted by most academics. They will often bring to a site a foundation knowledge which provides a tool kit with which to interpret seemingly novel environments.

B Interested information-seeking adult non-specialists

This is almost the ideal audience for the interpreter. Talking with such people is a rewarding experience. They are responsive, appreciative and interactive. Unfortunately, although their density at information points may be relatively high, they represent only a small (although influential) proportion of the adult general public. It is a group which requires little active encouragement, and satisfies the need felt by many Earth scientists to introduce others to the depth of reward that they have experienced through an understanding of rocks and landscape. This group is committed and will seek out information and education as they wish to use it.

C Thoughtful adult non-information seekers

Members of this group deliberately walk away from an information board, fretting at the imposition of official graffiti which intrudes, trespasses, violates, encroaches, stands between, and makes secondhand the experience of place.

This is the downside of interpretation. There is a feel to landscape which is beyond meaning and reason. We must be wary of encouraging the destruction of environmental experience through intrusive, inescapable interpretative control. The resistance to being processed should not be confused with a resistance to education.

The needs of this group should be addressed, not because of their numbers, which are not great, but because of their moral justification, and the powerful support they provide in creating a strong democratic lobby of conservationists.

D Mass of general public

(Only 4% of the public ever enter a bookshop.)

Sites of interest to Earth scientists often serve other valuable functions; indeed, the social role or aesthetic value of open space may be the principle reason why a site exists or is preserved. Many people visiting such sites are understandably completely unaware of the scientific value or interest of the place. Most have little interest in acquiring the sort of level of understanding of the subject implied (earlier in the article). There does seem a particular resistance in Britain to mixing leisure or recreation with education – almost a resistance to education itself. Perhaps a subconscious recognition that what was taught at school did not really serve them well?

(Peter Keene, 'Mission impossible? Educating the public on-site', *Earth Science Conservation*, No. 33, 1993.)

Box 10.5 A survey of visitors to one SSSI

For part of its length, the River Dee forms the boundary between England and Wales. Where it separates the Welsh village of Holt from the English village of Farndon, the river also slices through an excellent section of the Triassic Chester Pebble Beds formation, exposing some 162 m of the succession and some good faults. The site is an SSSI and is now managed by the Countryside Management Service of Cheshire County Council. It has a display board which was erected in 1991.

Holt and Farndon form a rural community of about 6,000 people. The two villages house both commuters to Chester and Wrexham and locally employed people but also have a significant number of retired people. With two large council housing estates and several large private housing estates, the villages contain a good mixture of all social groups. The public footpath by the river past the display board is a popular route for locals to walk with children and dogs, or just to go for an afternoon/evening stroll. It is also a popular fishing spot and a designated picnic site.

Two Open University part-time tutorial staff, Cynthia Burek and Hilary Davis, conducted a survey of visitors to the site.

On survey days everyone passing was stopped and no-one refused to answer the questions. A disappointing 51% of those questioned had not even noticed the board. 2% of those who had noticed it had not gone to read it. This left 47% to respond to further questions, 84% of whom said they found it informative. However, it was interesting to note that opinion was almost equally divided over the perception of who the board was really designed for:

◆ 26% thought it was primarily designed for the general public;

◆ 24% thought it was primarily designed for school children;

◆ 31% thought it was primarily designed for students;

◆ 19% thought it was primarily designed for professional geologists.

It was good to hear that no-one was hostile to the presence of the board and the fact that it might attract parties of students or school children to the site.

So information boards can have three related functions, both very much in tune with the overall strategy for EHC. First, they can popularize and raise awareness of the Earth sciences in a very cost-effective way. Second, they can be used to interpret sites which have already been selected for conservation for other reasons. Third, they can add an Earth science dimension to rural and urban heritage sites.

More ambitious forms of interpretation include geological trails. Here the information is usually provided by a combination of leaflets and on-site panels. Trails must be able to take a large number of visitors without giving rise to damage; by their very nature they encourage visitors to use them. Can your site cope? Are you able to provide facilities for the wheelchair visitor? 'High-tech'

Box 10.6 Leaflets – some dos and don'ts

Leaflets are a comparatively cheap method of interpretation. They provide information both on and off-site for a range of audiences. However, to be effective their content and presentation must be thought through. It is very easy to produce bad leaflets!

◆ DO plan your story before you start writing.

◆ DO remember your target audience and write to the appropriate level.

◆ DO try and keep your copy simple, avoiding jargon wherever possible.

◆ DON'T write long runs of text; break it up into short paragraphs and include illustrations where you can.

◆ DO give your text to someone else, preferably not associated with your site, to read and comment on. Be open to modifying the text.

◆ DO talk to the experts and listen to advice. It is well worth having your leaflet professionally designed. Give the designer a full brief about the site, the stories you wish to tell and your intended audience – assume he or she has no previous knowledge about the site or Earth science. Similarly, talk to a suitable printer. A good printer will be happy to advise on the best type of paper, print run, costs and so forth.

(Jonathan Wray, 'Interpreting geological sites', *Earth Science Conservation*, No. 29, 1991, pp.27–29.)

interpretation such as tape-cassettes and solar-powered listening posts are expensive to provide and maintain. Think hard before installing these: you need large numbers of fee-paying visitors to recoup your investment.

ACTIVITY 10.5

PLANNING AND INSTALLING A SITE INFORMATION BOARD

Your task is to plan and if possible get an information board put up at a site of local geological interest. Again, work in a group if possible and turn your mind to a case study site if you are stuck for a real local example. The checklist below provides some guidelines on how to go about it.

Select one or more sites you are familiar with. Which would benefit from an information board? Alternatively, choose a site from one of those described in Chapter 1.

Is your objective simply to enhance public awareness of our geological and landscape heritage or is conservation the main issue?

List the information you think the board should contain; this may involve a bit of research into the geological interest. Check your plans against the advice given in Box 10.7.

Establish who the owner of the site is.

Ascertain the situation about public access to the site.

Find out what regulations govern the siting of information boards.

Box 10.7 Producing signs – some dos and don'ts

The purpose of a sign is to provide information close to the feature being explained. To do this it must be understood, otherwise there is no point in it being there! Here are some basic tips.

Writing text

◆ DO keep the maximum number of words on a sign to 150. The reader will lose interest in longer texts so be concise.

◆ DO assume the reader is not a specialist and has no prior knowledge of the site.

◆ DON'T use jargon or write complex texts.

◆ DO ask someone not familiar with the site to read your text, together with any draft maps, to see if they can understand your message.

Maps

◆ DO keep maps simple – many people find flat plan maps hard to understand.

◆ DO include easily recognized features to which visitors can relate. Put on a scale and a north point.

◆ DO make the map big enough.

Layout of signs

◆ DO keep signs simple and clear. Break complex information into simple messages and convey each one separately within the sign.

◆ DON'T crowd signs with text. The open space on a sign is just as important as the words.

◆ DON'T use blocks of capital letters. They are difficult to read.

Siting of signs

◆ DO keep signs to a minimum. Look at your site as a whole and plan your signs accordingly.

◆ DON'T site signs where they cannot be read. The natural eyeline is slightly downwards. Children and wheelchair visitors will need signs at a lower level than adults.

(Jonathan Wray, 'Interpreting geological sites', *Earth Science Conservation*, No. 29, 1991, pp.27–29.)

If necessary, write to the owner explaining the nature and purpose of the board and asking for co-operation.

Obtain permission from the appropriate authorities to erect a board.

Establish what the job would cost and how it could be funded.

Ideally, get a board erected as soon as possible. But even if you fail, perhaps the exercise will have been worth while in itself in terms of raising awareness of Earth heritage conservation issues among key people.

Box 10.8 What one person can do

David Flaherty joined The Open University as a student in 1982. He studied the Science Foundation Course in his first year and was so enthused by the Earth science component of it that he went on to include all the Earth science courses possible in his degree, which he successfully completed in 1992. He soon became aware of the general lack of knowledge of the subject and the importance of providing opportunities for school children and students to gain some knowledge locally without the necessity for expensive field trips. He identified an abandoned local Triassic sandstone quarry as being full of useful features. He persuaded the local council, of whom he is an employee, to establish a geological trail in the quarry, which was already a woodland park.

David Flaherty at Helsby Quarry Woodland Park where he established a geological trail.

Field centres

There are hundreds of field and outdoor activity centres in Britain and their numbers are increasing with the growing popularity of environmental studies. Since the Earth sciences are an integral part of environmental studies this is a good point to jump on the bandwagon.

In some field centres, sporting activities predominate. Here there is plenty of scope for increasing the awareness of participants in sports such as hill walking, canoeing, climbing, caving, mountain biking and skiing that the settings of their activities are determined by our geological and geomorphological heritage. Involvement can begin on a very simple level if necessary. For instance, some rocks are easier to climb on than others. As you well know, this is because rocks have variable mineralogy, textures and structures and thus respond differently to the processes of weathering and erosion. This is not just interesting but useful information for a climber who can now begin to predict climbing conditions with greater confidence. Water sports too provide opportunities for appreciating the geological controls on the existence of suitable bodies of water. The lakes created after gravel extraction has ceased have provided many people with access to sailing and windsurfing that would otherwise have been beyond their means because of lack of time or finance. Sailing clubs could therefore provide opportunities for promoting greater awareness of geology and landscapes, and EHC.

Whether the field centre focuses on sport, outdoor survival skills or environmental study the task is to enlarge people's concept of the natural world and heritage to embrace the Earth sciences as well as biological sciences and human activity. There is certainly also a place for more direct teaching about the Earth sciences and site conservation in field centres.

Loosely related to field centres are some activity and special interest holidays which concentrate on for example eco-tourism, archaeology, long distance horseriding, landscape photography, ornithology, outdoor painting and sketching, cycling or local history. All of these offer opportunities for raising awareness of the Earth sciences and site conservation.

ACTIVITY 10.6
RAISING AWARENESS AT LOCAL FIELD OR OUTDOOR ACTIVITY CENTRES

The same instructions apply as before. Your task is to plan and, if possible, execute a scheme for raising awareness of our Earth heritage and site conservation in a field centre or comparable setting. The checklist is for guidance only. Try to choose a task which you have a genuine chance of completing. At the modest end of the scale (but none the less effective for that) is something like arranging a talk for a local centre or getting a leaflet printed for display at a local nature reserve to illustrate the connections between geomorphology and biological habitats. Perhaps you can persuade a field centre to include geological excursions in its programme or maybe you could offer an annual prize for a photograph of geological or geomorphological interest.

Which organization will you contact?

What group or groups of people within the organization will you target?

What aspect(s) of the Earth sciences will you emphazise?

Could your ideas be refined or improved through discussion with the staff of the organization?

What exactly is your objective? What alternatives are there for achieving it? On the basis of what criteria will you select the best alternative (publicity value, cost, time, etc.)?

What will be the costs and where will the money come from?

Could you generate some publicity for both the target organization and EHC out of this?

◆ ◆ ◆

Earth heritage conservation in education

Two general points will be clear from the preceding discussion. First, formal education goes hand in hand with informal education which could equally come under the heading of interest and information. Second, there will be limited support for EHC as long as public awareness of the Earth sciences themselves remains at a relatively low level. Yet it does not take long to think of a dozen or more ways in which the Earth sciences touch our daily lives and interests and therefore deserve a place in both general and specialized education. Some such points are listed in Box 10.9; you should be able to add to this list from your own knowledge and experience.

Here is a cornucopia of educational material suitable for everyone from five-year-olds to the University of the Third Age. If you think back to what you have read, you will undoubtedly be able to lengthen the list considerably. Within the Earth sciences are topics for everyone with interests ranging from philosophy to forestry, from physics to prehistory, from gardening to jewellery, from economics to building tunnels.

Something of the role that the Earth sciences play in our daily lives has been recognized by their inclusion in the National Curriculum in schools in England and Wales. But many teachers are unfamiliar with the subject and so need help to introduce it in a lively way, and to include field visits to local exposures. The importance of fostering the interest of young people has been recognized by the Royal Society for Nature Conservation and the Geologists' Association, as explained in Box 10.10. Yet public perception of the geological sciences as central to a balanced education is undoubtedly underdeveloped. Look no further than the science or environment sections of any bookshop. More often than not, you will find plenty of books on biology, chemistry, medical science or physics – but where are the geological sciences? All too frequently in some no-man's land between mountaineering and astronomy. Despite an increasing amount of excellent work, our Earth heritage has still to be truly popularized. Yet the above list of diverse topics (Box 10.9) is proof that it provides an ideal vehicle for teaching children and adults to hypothesize, experiment, observe, make deductions, solve problems, learn a variety of practical skills and develop a better understanding of their environment and economy. It is certainly not just career geologists who need to appreciate the relevance of the Earth sciences to daily life in all its diversity.

Thus there are many opportunities for raising the issue of EHC as a matter of course wherever the Earth sciences are taught, whether in primary schools, WEA classes or university courses. However, a measure of current awareness of the Earth sciences in education may be that while many young children now understand why wild flowers should be looked at but not picked, there are certainly still highly educated adult students of the Earth sciences who do not appreciate the damage done by uncontrolled sampling and who, more importantly, have never reflected on the need for, and often simple solutions to, active conservation of teaching and research sites.

Box 10.9 Earth science and everyday life

Some soils are originally the product of rock weathering. Soil type and distribution affect patterns of agriculture and forestry and well as natural vegetation.

Wells, springs, aquifers, the distribution of surface water and drainage patterns are all related to rock structures and landforms.

Safe waste disposal at or near the ground surface depends on good understanding of the Earth sciences.

The distribution of natural harbours, coves and beaches along our shores is geologically determined.

The formation and distribution of caves is determined by rock type and explained by processes studied by Earth scientists.

Volcanic eruptions and earthquakes frequently make the news; the latter even happen in the UK from time to time.

Our economy is heavily dependent on oil and gas, not just for transport and heating but also for feedstock for the plastics industry, without which our lives could hardly continue in their present form. Oil and gas fields are found by petroleum exploration geologists.

Gold for jewellery, mercury in thermometers, lead in church roofs, copper and nickel in coins, as well as every other mineral we use to make a host of objects from drinks cans to space shuttles, have been won from the rocks beneath our feet.

The rocks of which prehistoric monuments like Stonehenge are composed can also be traced to their source and help us understand the societies who quarried and transported them, while flints and other rocks used by ancient tool-makers provide evidence of prehistoric trading routes.

The fascinating question of where we, the human race, came from is a branch of evolutionary studies which has its basis in geological fieldwork.

Box 10.10 Rockwatching and RIGS

RockWATCH offers a unique opportunity to encourage interest and enjoyment of the Earth sciences among young people. It is a new club for all fans of fossils, rocks and dinosaurs. Sponsored by British Gas, it is run by WATCH, junior wing of Royal Society for Nature Conservation, The Wildlife Trusts Partnership, and the Geologists' Association.

Children are encouraged to investigate their local geology by participating in local surveys and events. The RockWATCH newsletter has involved thousands in the Great Shape Debate – an investigation into the texture of pebbles in Britain. The emphasis is always on local geology, and the next challenge to youngsters will be to find the 'geological collector of the year'. To win, the young person must show that they have collected and catalogued with care. It is hoped that they will look for new ways of collecting information. For example, they may photograph building stones.

RIGS involvement

Many WATCH leaders, while skilled in organizing young people's events, do not have the geological knowledge and expertise needed to lead geological outings. Geologists are needed to take local groups of children to local sites and interest them in rocks. RockWATCH offers a good opportunity to involve a young audience in geological conservation.

Benefits to RIGS

There are many benefits to RIGS. Trained WATCH leaders can deal with the organization of field trips, and offer advice on producing educational resources and on how to run activities. Events can be covered under WATCH insurance and can be advertised through the RockWATCH newsletter and the WATCH leaders' network.

More information on RockWATCH can be obtained from WATCH, RSNC (see 'Further reading, useful information and addresses' at the end of this book) or your local Wildlife Trust.

Of course, educators do not want just theory and exhortation; what they really need are resources on which to base their teaching. As a step in this direction, a short list of useful and inexpensive print material is given in 'Further reading, useful information and addresses' at the end of this book.

By now you will be aware that the problem is not so much where to start including the Earth sciences in education but where to stop. There follow three exercises related to EHC in education on which you can unleash your ideas. If you are working in a group it is probably best to share out the work then present the results to each other when you have achieved something. Once more, the ideal outcome would be a practical one so try to devise a scheme which matches your resources of time, knowledge and funding.

Your task is to introduce an Earth science topic into an educational course – at any level.

Spend some time discussing the options, but do not necessarily discard the obvious ones such as organizing an excursion to a geological site for a school physical geography class or civil engineering students at your local college. There are opportunities for students of the graphic arts and photography (and their entrepreneurial fellows) to produce calendars and greetings cards with a geological heritage theme backed up by snippets of interesting information. Provision of worksheets or information packs for hard-pressed teachers is another activity which can scarcely be overdone.

How much of your proposed activity can you do yourself and how much depends on your getting expert help? If the latter, is this readily obtainable?

Is your project just about raising awareness of the Earth sciences or does it also (or alternatively) encompass the idea of conservation? Is it capable of being repeated with different groups of students? In other words, could it readily be disseminated?

With whom will you liaise to find out if your proposal is welcome? How and when will you make contact? What will you say if you are asked, 'What's in it for me and my students?'

What resources – people, equipment, money – does your project require? Who will provide each of them?

Over what timescale will your project be completed?

You have decided to establish a small reference book collection of information on EHC, focusing on your local area. This could be extended to texts which provide a useful basis for educational fieldwork.

Which publications will you start with?

How will the work of obtaining them be shared out?

How will the collection be funded?

Who will you inform about its existence?

Where will it be kept and how will people get access to it?

How will you keep the information up to date?

ACTIVITY 10.9
RAISING AWARENESS OF EHC AMONG COLLEAGUES

You would like to initiate (or extend) awareness and knowledge of EHC among your colleagues (either at work or in your leisure pursuits) or perhaps take further your own involvement. Devise a plan for doing so.

Who will be the participants? What are their interests in land use?

Is their current awareness of conservation in general good/fair/poor?

Is their current knowledge of Earth sciences good/fair/poor?

How much time could be made available? Over what timescale?

What do you see as the outcomes of the course/training? In other words, what should participants know or be able to do at the end that they didn't know or couldn't do at the beginning?

Through what types of activity could these outcomes be achieved (e.g. talks, site visits, workshops, reading, project work)?

Name any publications you think would be useful for everyone to have.

Specify any fieldwork you would like to do.

Would it operate as a self-help group or would you get outside leaders?

What facilities or equipment would participants or leaders need?

Where and when could all this be done?

Is there someone you can sell this idea to so that it is put into practice?

Sponsorship

Talk of selling in Activity 10.9 brings us neatly to the final suggestion for raising public awareness of EHC – sponsorship. Sponsorship of EHC is a new idea and there is clearly lots of mileage in it. Companies or industries which value an environmentally friendly image might sponsor information boards and the day may yet come when contractors doing engineering works designed to conserve sites may be proud to display such information on their site signs. 'Scotch on the rocks' is only one of a host of possible slogans associated with rocks and landscape. If you think of a good one, pass it on to someone who might use it.

10.5 The international perspective

Geological processes operate on a regional or global scale which has little to do with late 20th century political boundaries. Moreover, because of the timescale involved, geographical features such as oceans or mountain ranges may intervene between sites which are crucial in unravelling aspects of the same geological story. For these reasons, international co-operation on EHC activities is vital.

Box 10.11 International declaration of the rights of the memory of the Earth

1 Just as human life is recognized as being unique, the time has come to recognize the uniqueness of the Earth.

2 Mother Earth supports us. We are each and all linked to her, she is the link between us.

3 The Earth is 4.5 billion years old and the cradle of life, of renewal and of the metamorphosis of life. Its long evolution, its slow rise to maturity, has shaped the environment in which we live.

4 Our history and the history of the Earth are closely linked. Its origins are our origins its history is our history and its future will be our future.

5 The aspect of the Earth, its very being, is our environment. This environment is different, not only from that of the past, but also from that of the future. We are but the Earth's companion with no finality, we only pass by.

6 Just as an old tree keeps all the records of its growth and life, the Earth retains memories of its past ... A record inscribed both in its depths and on the surface, in the rocks and in the landscapes, a record which can be read and translated.

7 We have always been aware of the need to preserve our memories – i.e. our cultural heritage. Now the time has come to protect our natural heritage, the environment. The past of the Earth is no less important than that of human beings. Now is the time for us to learn to protect, and by doing so, to learn about the past of the Earth, to read this book written before our advent: this is our geological heritage.

8 We and the Earth share our common heritage. We and governments are but the custodians of this heritage. Each and every human being should understand that the slightest degradation mutilates, destroys and leads to irreversible losses. Any form of development should respect the singularity of this heritage.

9 The participants of the First International Symposium on the Conservation of our Geological Heritage, including over 100 specialists from over 30 countries, urgently request all national and international authorities to take into consideration and to protect this heritage by means of all necessary legal, financial and organizational measures.

(Written on 13 June 1991 in Digne, France.)

In recent years, regional groupings such as the European Working Group on Earth Science Conservation (EWGEHC) have been formed. Even within the confines of Europe, policy and achievement on EHC very widely and we have much to learn from each other. In 1991 the international movement took a further step forward and the town of Digne in France was host to the first International Symposium on the Conservation of our Geological Heritage. The Symposium was attended by 100 delegates from 30 different countries and will, it is hoped, develop as a biennial gathering (the second meeting was held in Malvern in 1993). Guy Martini, Directeur, Réserve Géologique de Haute-Provence and General Secretary of the Symposium talked of 'the great responsibility [of geologists and geomorphologists] as translators of this memory engraved in rocks and landscapes' and of their responsibility as conservationists to 'let the Earth talk so that it recounts its history, the history of our origins, our history ...'. From the plenary session of the conference came a declaration which reflects this feeling and purpose (Box 10.11).

10.6 Conclusion

You will now be well aware of the need for EHC, the nature of EHC and a range of strategies for increasing public awareness of EHC. You will also have some measure of the extent of the task ahead and, hopefully, a range of ideas of your own about what should be done as well as some practical achievements. Through RIGS and the national framework for designating and recording sites your work can be shared and local, national and international priorities respected. The future for EHC looks promising.

We hope that this book has given you a lively interest in – or extended your existing interests in – the Earth sciences, and that you will be able to pass on to others the knowledge and expertise which you have gained through attempting the practical exercises. Earth scientists never tire of fieldwork because the diversity of natural systems means that there is always something new to see and learn. We hope you share that sense of discovery and will find satisfaction in a continuing commitment to Earth heritage conservation.

FURTHER READING, USEFUL INFORMATION AND ADDRESSES

Further reading and sources of information

The numbers in brackets included in the descriptions of publications refer to the addresses listed in the last part of this section.

General and regional geology

The magazine *Geology Today* caters for wide interests including an amateur audience and often mentions conservation issues (8).

An excellent and accessible source of information about geology is the series of well-illustrated booklets published by the Natural History Museum (12). Titles include:

Britain before Man

British Fossils

Volcanoes

Earthquakes

The Geological Map

Britain's Offshore Oil and Gas

On the Rocks.

In the same category are publications by the National Museums of Scotland (10), including *Scenery of Scotland – the structure beneath* and *Plants Invade the Land* (about the Rhynie Chert).

The former Nature Conservancy Council *(3, 4, 5)* published booklets on general geology:

The Age of Ice

Death of an Ocean.

In 1993 Scottish National Heritage (5) launched a new series of booklets on the theme 'a landscape fashioned by geology'; the first two in the series are:

Edinburgh

Skye.

Additional leaflets are published by the national conservation agencies (3, 4, 5) about many individual SSSIs. These are informative for students of geology but do not assume too much background knowledge for those seeking an introduction to the subject.

The Geologists' Association (8) has a range of interesting publications including leaflets such as *Geology in the Churchyard*, and a series of regional geology guides designed for amateurs with a good knowledge of geology.

The British Geological Survey (1, 2) sells geological maps, and publishes regional geological summaries and memoirs to accompany some map sheets.

Earth heritage conservation

The twice yearly journal *Earth Heritage* (formerly *Earth Science Conservation*) is essential reading. It is published on behalf of the three country conservation agencies by English Nature (4) and is available on personal subscription.

The former Nature Conservancy Council's publication *Earth Science Conservation in Britain – a strategy* is the blueprint for action. Its Technical Appendices give examples of engineering solutions to conservation problems. It is available from the country conservation agencies (3, 4, 5), as is a series of free leaflets:

Earth Science Conservation for Teachers and Lecturers

Regionally Important Geological/geomorphological Sites

Conserving our Heritage of Rocks, Fossils and Landforms

Conservation and the Earth Sciences

Earth Science Conservation for Wildlife Trusts

Earth Science Conservation for Farmers and Landowners.

Codes of Conduct/advice for fieldwork and collecting

A Code For Geological Fieldwork is a leaflet published by the Geologists' Association (8).

A Code of Practice for Geological Visits to Quarries, Mines and Caves is published by the Geological Society (7).

Safety in Earth Science Fieldwork – guidelines for fieldwork leadership is available from the Earth Science Teachers' Association (6).

Rocks, Fossils and Minerals – how to make the best of your collection is a guide for young enthusiasts published by the UK Geological Curators' Group (c/o 7).

Addresses

National Scheme for Geological Site Documentation

c/o Hull City Museums and Art Galleries
83 Alfred Gelder Street
Hull HU1 1EP

British Geological Survey

1   Kingsley Dunham Centre
    Keyworth
    Nottingham NG12 5GG

2   Murchison House
    West Mains Road
    Edinburgh EH9 2LF

Country conservation agencies

3   Countryside Council for Wales
    Plas Penrhos
    Ffordd Penrhos
    Bangor LL57 2LQ

4   English Nature
    Northminster House
    Peterborough PE1 1UA

5   Scottish Natural Heritage
    12 Hope Terrace
    Edinburgh EH9 2AS

Societies

6 Earth Science Teachers' Association
   c/o Geological Society
   Burlington House
   Piccadilly
   London W1V 0JU

7 Geological Society
   Burlington House
   Piccadilly
   London W1V 0JU

8 Geologists' Association
   Burlington House
   Piccadilly
   London W1V 9AG

9 Royal Society for Nature Conservation
   The Green
   Nettleham
   Lincoln LN2 2NR

National museums

10 National Museum of Scotland
    Chambers Street
    Edinburgh EH1 1JF

11 National Museum of Wales
    Cathays Park
    Cardiff CF1 3 NP

12 Natural History Museum
    Exhibition Road
    London SW7 5BD

13 Ulster Museum
    Botanic Gardens
    Belfast BT9 5AB

ACKNOWLEDGEMENTS

Grateful acknowledgement is made to the following sources for permission to reproduce material in this book:

Figure 1.1: Grayson, A. (1993) *Rock Solid*, Natural History Museum, London, © Anna Grayson; Figure 1.2b: R.E.Jones/Countryside Council for Wales; Figure 1.3a: S.Campbell; Figure 1.3b: Werritty, A. and Brazier, V. (1991) *The Geomorphology, Conservation and Management of the River Feshie SSSI*, The Nature Conservancy Council, Peterborough; Figure 1.5a: John Gordon/Scottish National Heritage Earth Science Collection; Figures 1.6a,b: Richard Wright/English Nature; Figure 1.6c: *Earth Science Conservation*, 32, p. 19, Nature Conservancy Council/English Nature; Figure 1.8a: English Nature; Figure 1.8b: *British Caenozoic Fossils* (1975), Natural History Museum; Figures 1.9, 1.10b: *Earth Science Conservation*, 30, Nature Conservancy Council/English Nature; Figure 1.10a: Colin Prosser/English Nature; Figure1.11: English Nature; Figure 1.12: R.C.L.Wilson; Figure 1.13a: Peter Wakely/English Nature; Figure 1.14a: *Earth Science Conservation*, 26, p. 12, Nature Conservancy Council/English Nature; Figure 1.14b: Goldring R. (1978), 'Devonian', in McKerrow, W.S. (ed.) *The Ecology of Fossils*, by kind permission of Gerald Duckworth & Co Ltd; Figure 2.2a: National Environment Research Council/Institute of Geological Sciences; Figures 2.2b,c, 2.35a: Aerofilms; Figure 2.2d: Peter Francis; Figures 2.7a,c, 2.13, 2.21b, 2.27, 2.37: British Geological Survey; Figures 2.7b, 2.16b: Peter Wakely/English Nature; Figure 2.10: Stewart Campbell; Figure 2.11: *New Sites For Old. A Student's Guide to the Geology of The East Mendips* (1985), Nature Conservancy Council/English Nature; Figure 2.12: Dr A.C.Waltham, Nottingham; Figure 2.16a: Peter Skelton; Figures 2.18a, 2.29: R.C.L.Wilson; Figure 2.19: Woodmansterne Publications Ltd; Figure 2.20: J.E.Brown; Figure 2.21a: Cambridge University Collection; Figure 2.22a: John Gordon/Scottish National Heritage; Figure 2.22b: McLeish, A. (1986) *Geological Science*, Thomas Nelson & Sons Ltd; Figures 2.30a, 2.31b: D.J.Edwards; Figure 2.32: British Geological Survey/HMSO; Figure 2.35b: NASA; Figure 2.36: © Chester Longwell Trust/Wells Fargo Bank Trust; Figure 2.38: Wyllie, P.J. (1976) *The Way the Earth Works*, John Wiley & Sons Ltd; Figure 2.39: Gass, I. *et al.* (1972) *Understanding the Earth*, 2nd edition, Artemis Press; Figures: 3.1a, 3.3, 3.5, 3.6a,c: R.C.L.Wilson; Figure 3.1b: Duff, K.L., McKirdy, A.P. and Harley, M.J. (1985) *New Sites For Old*, English Nature; Figure 3.8: M.Harley, English Nature; Figure 3.9: Peter Sheldon; Figure 4.1a: Peter Sheldon; Figure 4.1b: Jonathan Larwood/English Nature; Figures 4.9, 4.18: *The Geological Map* (1983), Institute of Geological Sciences, p. 269; Figure 4.11: Dietz, R.S. and Holden, J.C. (1970) *Journal of Geophysical Research*, 75; Figure 4.12: Dunning, F.W. *et al.* (1978), *Britain Before Man*, Natural History Museum; Figure 4.13a: Scottish National Heritage Earth Science Collection; Figures 4.16a, 4.17b: Anderton R. *et al.* (1979) *A Dynamic Stratigraphy of the British Isles*, Chapman and Hall; Figures 4.16b, 4.17a: Cocks, L.R. *et al.* (1982) *Journal of the Geological Society*, Vol. 139, Part 4, Blackwell Scientific Publications Ltd; Figure 4.19: Gribben, J. (1990), *Hothouse Earth*, Bantam Press; Figure 5.2a: R.C.L.Wilson; Figure 5.2b: English Nature; Figure 5.2c: S. Campbell; Figure 6.1a: Peter Wakely/English Nature; Figure: 6.1b: R.E.Jones/Countryside Council for Wales; Figure 6.2: English Nature; Figure 6.3a: Scotttish National Heritage; Figure 6.3b: Jonathan Larwood/English Nature; Figure 6.4a: Colin Prosser/English Nature; Figure 6.4b: Stewart Campbell/Countryside Council for Wales; Figures 6.4c, 6.4d: Richard Leafe/English Nature; Figure 6.5: British Geological Survey; Figure 6.6: Richard Wright/English Nature; Figure 7.1: *Earth Science Conservation*, 27, Nature Conservancy Council/English Nature; Box 8.3: *Earth Science Conservation*, 26, English Nature/Nature Conservancy Council; Figure 8.1: R.C.L.Wilson; ; Figures 8.3a,b: Peter Wakely/English Nature; Figure 8.3c: John Gordon/Scottish National HeritageBox 10.3: 'A secret world in fossil quarry', 16th February 1993, courtesy of the *Oldham Chronicle*; Box 10.4: Keane, P. (1993) 'Mission impossible? Educating the public on site', *Earth Science Conservation,* 33, Nature Conservancy Council/English Nature; Boxes 10.6 and 10.7: Wray, J. (1991) 'Interpreting geological sites', *Earth Science Conservation*, 29, Nature Conservancy Council/English Nature; Figure 10.1: Brecknock Wildlife Trust and Geologists' Association; Figures 10.2a,b: Ruth Hargest, Erwood; Figure 10.3: Cynthia Burek; Figure 10.2d: Peter Wakely/ English Nature.

INDEX